Co-ordinated SCIENCE

Physics

Stephen Pople

Oxford University Press

Oxford University Press
Walton Street
Oxford OX2 6DP

Oxford New York Toronto
Delhi Bombay Calcutta Madras Karachi
Petaling Jaya Singapore Hong Kong Tokyo
Nairobi Dar es Salaam Cape Town
Melbourne Auckland
and associated companies in
Berlin Ibadan

First Published 1989
Reprinted 1990, 1991 (twice), 1992

Oxford is a trade mark of Oxford University Press

ISBN 019 914 247 5

Typeset by MS Filmsetting Limited, Frome, Somerset
Printed in Singapore

Introduction

This book deals with physics, its practical uses and the social issues it raises. You are most likely to find the book useful if you are following a GCSE course in physics, or taking physics as part of a Co-ordinated Science Course at Key Stage 4.

To help you find things more easily, the book is written in two-page units. Each unit deals with a different topic.

● **Use the contents page** if you want to see the main headings.

● **Use the index** at the back if you want to look up information about one particular thing. The index is alphabetical.

● **Use the questions** to test yourself. The questions at the end of each unit cover the main ideas. The questions at the back of the book are from GCSE examination papers.

● **Use the reference section** near the back of the book if you need to look up the following:

    units of measurement
    electrical symbols
    how to revise
    revision checklist
    important equations
    answers to questions

Physics is an important subject in today's world. It doesn't just happen in laboratories. It's all around you, in fairgrounds, fields, farms and factories.

You'll find physics everywhere.

Stephen Pople   April 1988

Contents

1.1 Units for measuring

SI units – a common system of measuring

Which units would you use to measure:

● a length?
● or a mass?
● or a time?

There are several possibilities. But in scientific work, life is much easier if everyone uses the same system of units. Nowadays, most scientists use the **SI system** (from the French, Système International d'Unites). This starts with the metre, the kilogram and the second. Many other units are based on these.

Length

The **metre (m**, for short) is the SI unit of length.

The chart shows some of the larger and smaller length units based on the metre.

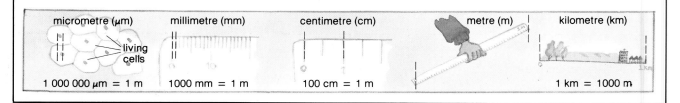

micrometre (μm)	millimetre (mm)	centimetre (cm)	metre (m)	kilometre (km)
living cells				
1 000 000 μm = 1 m	1000 mm = 1 m	100 cm = 1 m		1 km = 1000 m

Mass

Mass is the amount of matter in something. In the laboratory, it is often measured using a top pan balance. Mass is sometimes called 'weight'. This is wrong. The difference between mass and weight is explained on page 24.

The **kilogram (kg)** is the SI unit of mass.

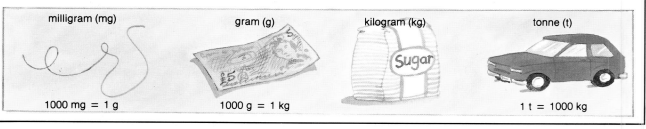

milligram (mg)	gram (g)	kilogram (kg)	tonne (t)
1000 mg = 1 g	1000 g = 1 kg		1 t = 1000 kg

Time

The **second (s)** is the SI unit of time.

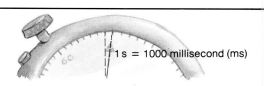

1 s = 1000 millisecond (ms)

Volume

Volume is the amount of space something takes up. It is measured in **metre cubed (m³)**. This is rather a large unit of volume for everyday use, so the litre, millilitre, or centimetre cubes are often used instead.

There are 1000 millilitres in 1 litre, and 1000 centimetre cubes in 1 litre. So 1 millilitre is the same as 1 centimetre cubed.

Measuring volume

If something has a simple shape, its volume can be calculated. For example:

volume of a
rectangular block = length × width × height

Liquid volumes of about a litre or less can be measured using a measuring cylinder. Pour in the liquid, and the reading on the scale gives the volume.

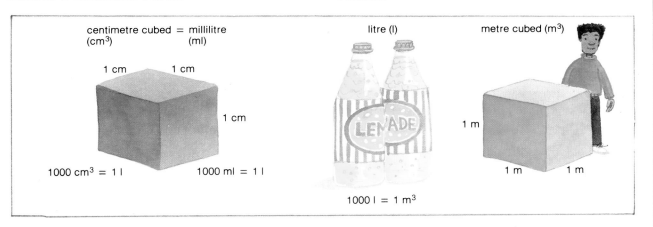

centimetre cubed = millilitre
(cm³)   (ml)

1 cm   1 cm

1 cm

1000 cm³ = 1 l   1000 ml = 1 l

litre (l)

metre cubed (m³)

1 m

1 m   1 m

1000 l = 1 m³

1 Copy and complete the table:

	Unit	Abbreviation
Length	?	m
?	kilogram	?
Time	?	?

2 What do the following stand for:
mm, t, mg, ms, l, cm?

3 Which is the greater?
1600 g or 1.5 kg?
1450 mm or 1.3 m?

4 *10, 100, 1000, 100 000, 1 000 000:*
Which of these is
a the number of mg in 1 g?
b the number of mm in 1 cm?
c the number of cm in 1 km?
d the number of cm in 1 m?
e the number of mm in 1 km?

5 Write down the value of
a 1 m in mm
b 1.5 m in mm
c 1.534 m in mm
d 1652 mm in m

6 Write down the values of
a 2.750 m in mm   **b** 1.600 km in m
c 6.500 g in mg   **d** 150 cm in m
e 1750 g in kg

7 Which is the odd one out in each of the boxes?

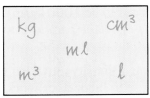

kg   cm³
    ml
m³   l

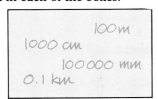

100 m
1000 cm
100 000 mm
0.1 km

8 What is the volume of the liquid in the measuring cylinder in the diagram?
What is the volume
– in cm³?
– in litres?

ml
1000

500

9 What is the volume of a metal block 3 cm long by 2 cm wide by 4 cm high?
What would be the volume of a block twice as long, wide and high?

1.2 Density

Is lead heavier than water? Not necessarily. It depends how much lead and water you are comparing. However, lead is more dense than water – it has more kilograms packed into every cubic metre.

You can calculate the density of a material if you know its mass and its volume:

$$\text{density} = \frac{\text{mass}}{\text{volume}}$$

Take the case of water:
a mass of 1000 kg has a volume of 1 m³
a mass of 2000 kg has a volume of 2 m³
a mass of 3000 kg has a volume of 3 m³
and so on.

Using any of these sets of figures in the above equation:
the density of water works out to be 1000 kg/m³. There are 1000 kilograms of water packed into every metre cubed.

The kg/m³ is the basic SI unit of density. But it isn't always the easiest unit to use in laboratory work. When masses are measured in grams and volumes in centimetre cubed, it is simpler to calculate densities in g/cm³. Changing to kg/m³ is easy: 1 g/cm³ = 1000 kg/m³.

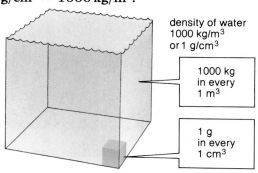

density of water
1000 kg/m³
or 1 g/cm³

1000 kg in every 1 m³

1 g in every 1 cm³

How dense?

The least dense material you are ever likely to see from Earth is the dimly glowing gas in the tail of a comet. The gas stretches for millions of miles behind the comet's head. It is so thin, that there is less than a kilogram of gas in each kilometre cubed.

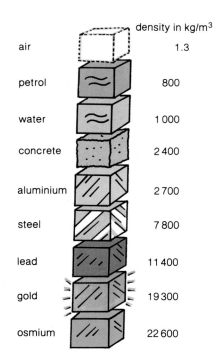

	density in kg/m³
air	1.3
petrol	800
water	1 000
concrete	2 400
aluminium	2 700
steel	7 800
lead	11 400
gold	19 300
osmium	22 600

The rare metal osmium is the densest substance found on Earth. It is about twice as dense as lead. If this book were made of osmium, it would weigh as much as a television set.

Density calculations

Start with the equation:

$$\text{density} = \frac{\text{mass}}{\text{volume}}$$

Then rearrange it:

$$\text{mass} = \text{volume} \times \text{density}$$

and:

$$\text{volume} = \frac{\text{mass}}{\text{density}}$$

These are useful if you know the density of something, but want to find its mass or volume. This triangle may help you to remember all three equations – cover 'Volume' if you want the equation for volume, and so on:

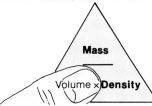

Example *A block of aluminium has a volume of 2 m³ and a density of 2700 kg/m³. What is its mass?*

Using the triangle: mass = volume × density

so, $\qquad \text{mass} = 2\,\text{m}^3 \times 2700\,\text{kg/m}^3$

$\qquad\qquad\quad = 5400\,\text{kg}$

The mass of the aluminium is 5400 kg.

Brewing with gravity

Ask brewers how strong their beer is, and they might tell you that it has a 'gravity' of 1020°. Their scale of gravity is actually a scale of density, because beers become more dense as they get stronger. Plain water is the weakest 'beer' of all. This has a gravity of 1000° on the brewer's scale.

Assume $g = 10\,\text{N/kg}$.

To answer these questions, you will need to use some of the density values in the chart on the opposite page.

1 Work out:
a the mass of water needed to fill a 4 m³ tank;
b the volume of a storage tank which will hold 1600 kg of petrol;
c the mass of air in a room measuring 5 m × 2 m × 3 m.

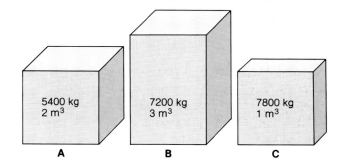

2 Which block has:
a the greatest mass;   **b** the greatest volume;
c the greatest density?
Use the chart to decide which material each block could be made from.

3 A builder wants to load a stack of 100 solid concrete blocks on his lorry.

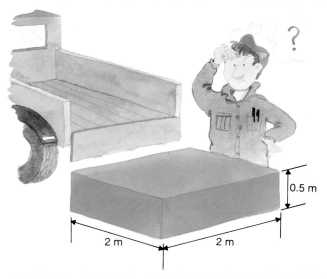

The stack measures 2 m × 2 m × 0.5 m. Work out:
a the volume of the concrete;
b the mass of the concrete;
c whether he can safely carry all the blocks on the lorry, if the maximum load is 3000 kg. And if not, how many blocks he can carry.

1.3 Measuring density

Who needs to?

Airline pilots need to know air density before they take off.

Geologists use density measurements to help identify types of rock.
This information is useful to . . .

  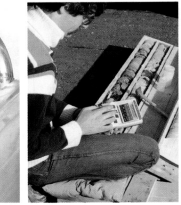 

Brewers, like milk inspectors use density checks to help maintain quality.

. . . **Civil engineers** who must calculate the mass of their building materials, and decide if the ground can support the weight.

250 BC: A Greek Scientist who Discovered how to Investigate Density

The King of Syracuse gave his goldsmith some gold. 'Make a crown', he said. So the goldsmith did. But the king was suspicious. Perhaps the goldsmith had kept some of the gold. Perhaps he had mixed in cheaper silver to takes its place. He asked Archimedes to test the crown.

Archimedes knew that the crown was the correct mass. He knew that silver was less dense than gold. So, if the crown contained any silver, it would have more volume than it should. But how could he check the volume of the crown? Stepping into his bath one day, Archimedes noticed the rise in water level. Here was the answer to the problem! Put the crown in the water and measure the rise in level. Put an equal mass of pure gold in the water. See if the rise in level was the same. 'Eureka', he shouted. Which is Greek for 'I have found it'.

Was the crown made of pure gold? Unfortunately, nobody wrote down the result. So we shall never know . . .

How to measure a density

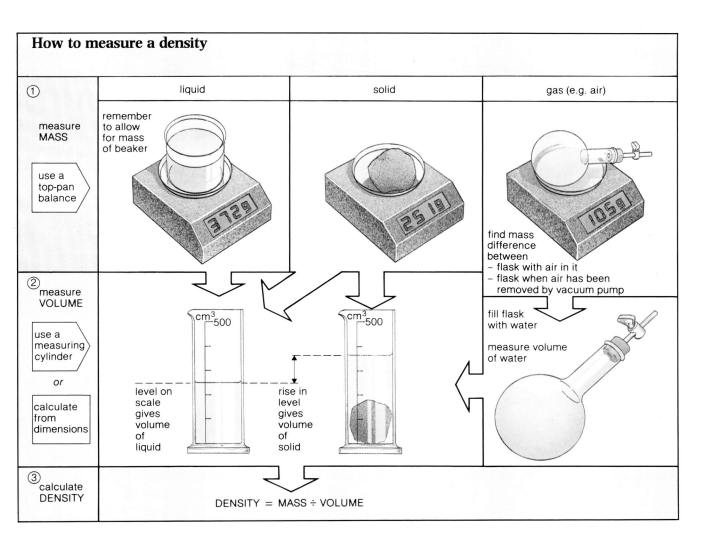

	liquid	solid	gas (e.g. air)
① measure MASS — use a top-pan balance	remember to allow for mass of beaker		find mass difference between – flask with air in it – flask when air has been removed by vacuum pump
② measure VOLUME — use a measuring cylinder *or* calculate from dimensions	level on scale gives volume of liquid	rise in level gives volume of solid	fill flask with water measure volume of water
③ calculate DENSITY	DENSITY = MASS ÷ VOLUME		

1

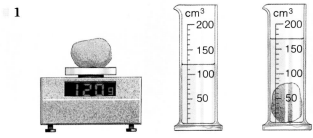

What is:
a the volume of the stone in cm³
b the density of the stone in g/cm³?

2

Volume of liquid in beaker	= 200 cm³
Mass of beaker	= 110 g
Mass of beaker, filled with liquid	= 270 g

What is:
a the mass of the liquid
b the density of the liquid in g/cm³?

3 Solve the same problem as Archimedes using the information given here – no need to take a bath!:

	A	B	C
mass in g	3800	3800	3800
volume in cm³	380	200	300

The density of gold is 19 g/cm³

The density of silver is 10 g/cm³

Decide which crown is gold, which is silver, and which is a mixture.

1.4 On the move

Speed

The police can check the speed of a car with a radar 'gun'. But there's a simpler method. Measure the distance between two points along a road – say, two lamp posts. Measure the time a car takes to travel between these points. Then calculate the speed:

$$\text{average speed} = \frac{\text{distance moved}}{\text{time taken}}$$

For example, a car which travels 50 metres in 5 seconds, has an average speed of 10 metres per second – written 10 m/s for short.

On most journeys, the speed of a car varies, so the actual speed at any moment is usually different from the average speed. To find an actual speed, you have to find the distance travelled in the shortest time you could measure.

Velocity

Like speed, velocity is measured in metres per second (m/s). Velocity tells you the speed at which an object is travelling. But it also tells you the direction of travel:

$$\text{average velocity} = \frac{\text{distance moved in a particular direction}}{\text{time taken}}$$

In diagrams, you can show a velocity using an arrow:

$$\xrightarrow{\quad 10\,\text{m/s} \quad}$$

Or you can use a + or − can to give the direction. For example:

$$+10\,\text{m/s} \quad (10\,\text{m/s to the right})$$
$$-10\,\text{m/s} \quad (10\,\text{m/s to the left})$$

Quantities like velocity which have a direction as well as a value are called **vectors**.

What they mean		
A steady speed of 10 m/s	A distance of 10 metres is travelled every second	
A steady velocity of + 10 m/s	A distance of 10 metres is travelled every second (to the right)	
A steady acceleration of 5 m/s²	Speed goes up by 5 metres/second every second	
A steady retardation of 5 m/s²	Speed goes down by 5 metres/second every second	

Acceleration

From a standing start, a rally car can reach a velocity of 50 m/s in 10 s or less. It gains velocity very rapidly. It has a high **acceleration**.

Like velocity, acceleration is a vector. It is calculated as follows:

$$\text{acceleration} = \frac{\text{gain in velocity}}{\text{time taken}}$$

For example, if a car gains an extra 50 m/s of velocity in 10 seconds:

$$\text{acceleration} = \frac{50}{10} \text{ m/s per second}$$

$$= 5 \text{ m/s per second}$$

which is written as 5 m/s² for short.

Retardation is the opposite of acceleration. If a car has a retardation of 5 m/s², it is *losing* 5 m/s of speed every second.

1 A car travels 500 m in 20 s, what is its average speed?
Why is the actual speed of a car not usually the same as its average speed?

2 How far does the car travel in 1 s? 5 s? 10 s?

10 m/s

How long does it take to travel 90 m?

3 Copy and complete:
A motor cycle has a steady _____ of 3 m/s². This means that every __ its _____ increases by _____.

4 A car has steady acceleration. The chart shows how its speed increases. Copy and complete the chart.

After	1 s	2 s	3 s	4 s	5 s	?
Speed	4 m/s	8 m/s	?	16 m/s	?	28 m/s
Steady acceleration = ? m/s²						

5 An aircraft on its take-off run has a steady acceleration of 3 m/s².
How much velocity does it gain in 10 s?
If the aircraft has a velocity of 20 m/s as it passes a post, what is its velocity 10 s later?

6 A motor cycle takes 8 s to increase its velocity from 10 m/s to 30 m/s. What is its average acceleration?

7 A rally driver has 5 s to stop her car, which is travelling at 20 m/s. What is her average retardation?

How to do calculations

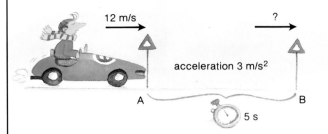
12 m/s   ?
acceleration 3 m/s²
A   B
5 s

The car in the diagram passes point A with a velocity of 12 m/s.
The car has an acceleration of 3 m/s².
What is the velocity of the car as it passes point B 5 s later?

The car is gaining an extra 3 m/s of velocity every second.

So, in 5 s, it gains an extra 15 m/s of velocity on top of its original velocity of 12 m/s.

Its final speed on passing B is therefore 12 m/s + 15 m/s, which equals 27 m/s.

This could be written in another way:
Final velocity = original velocity + extra velocity
or

Final velocity
= original velocity + (acceleration × time)

It sometimes helps to remember the above equation in symbols:

$v = u + at$
where
v is the final velocity, a is the acceleration,
u is the original velocity,
t is the time taken.

In the case of the car,

$$v = 12 + (5 \times 3) \quad \text{m/s}$$
$$= 12 + 15 \qquad \text{m/s}$$
$$= 27 \text{ m/s}$$

The equation works for retardation as well. Just call the retardation a negative acceleration. For example, a retardation of 5 m/s² is an acceleration of − 5 m/s².

1.5 Motion graphs

You can learn a lot from motion graphs. They can tell you how far something has travelled, how fast it is moving, and all the speed changes there have been.

Distance–time graphs

Imagine a car travelling along a road. There is a post on the road. Every second, the distance of the car from the post is measured. Distance and time readings are recorded in a chart, and used to plot a graph.

Here are the results from just four possible journeys. One is hardly a journey at all.

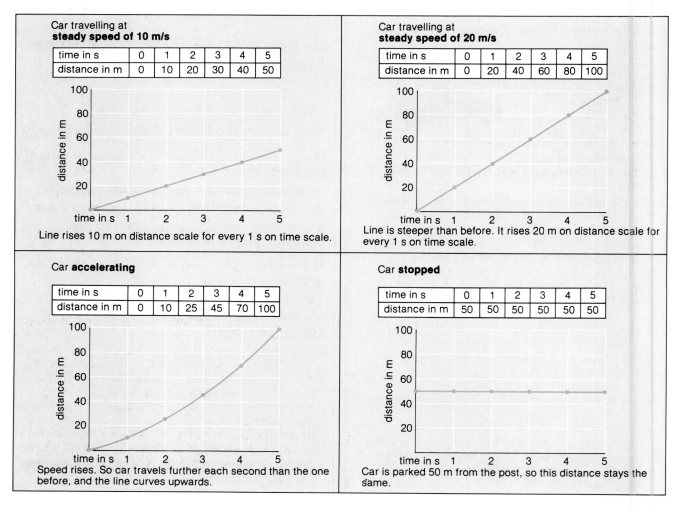

Car travelling at **steady speed of 10 m/s**

time in s	0	1	2	3	4	5
distance in m	0	10	20	30	40	50

Line rises 10 m on distance scale for every 1 s on time scale.

Car travelling at **steady speed of 20 m/s**

time in s	0	1	2	3	4	5
distance in m	0	20	40	60	80	100

Line is steeper than before. It rises 20 m on distance scale for every 1 s on time scale.

Car **accelerating**

time in s	0	1	2	3	4	5
distance in m	0	10	25	45	70	100

Speed rises. So car travels further each second than the one before, and the line curves upwards.

Car **stopped**

time in s	0	1	2	3	4	5
distance in m	50	50	50	50	50	50

Car is parked 50 m from the post, so this distance stays the same.

Speed–time graphs

Don't confuse these with distance–time graphs. The shapes may look the same, but their meaning is very different.

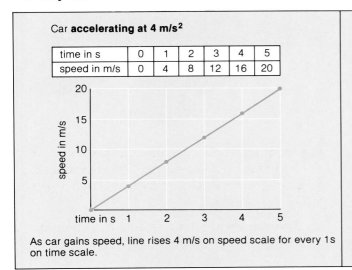

Car **accelerating at 4 m/s²**

time in s	0	1	2	3	4	5
speed in m/s	0	4	8	12	16	20

As car gains speed, line rises 4 m/s on speed scale for every 1 s on time scale.

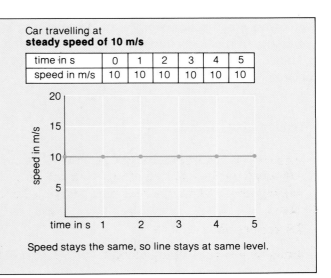

Car travelling at **steady speed of 10 m/s**

time in s	0	1	2	3	4	5
speed in m/s	10	10	10	10	10	10

Speed stays the same, so line stays at same level.

1 A motor cycle passes a lamp post. Every second, its distance from the post is measured:

time/s	0	1	2	3	4	5	6	7	8	9
distance/m	0	3	10	22	34	46	54	56	56	56

a Plot a distance–time graph
b Mark on your graph the sections where the motor cycle:
has acceleration; is travelling at a steady speed; has retardation; is stopped.
c How far does the motor cycle travel in the first 7 seconds?
What is its average speed over this period?
d How long does it take the motor cycle to travel from 10 m to 46 m? What distance does it cover?
What is its average speed over this distance?

2 The graph shows a speed–time graph for another motor cycle.

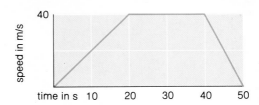

a What is the maximum speed of the motor cycle?
b For how many seconds does the motor cycle stay at its maximum speed?
c For how many seconds is the motor cycle actually moving?
d How much speed does the motor cycle gain in the first 20 seconds?
How much speed does it gain every second?
What is its acceleration?
e What is the retardation of the motor cycle during the last 10 seconds?

3 It takes a driver 10 minutes to get to work. She stops to buy a paper on the way, has a set of traffic lights on her route, and a short section of motorway. Sketch a typical speed–time graph for her journey, and don't let her break any speed limits.
(1 m/s is about 2 mph)

4 An ice skater skates once round an oval rink. He accelerates down the length of the rink, but takes the ends more slowly. He falls over once. Sketch a speed-time graph for him.

1.6 Timing with tape

A piece of paper tape is rather like a graph. It can give you a complete record of how something is moving. In this case, however, it isn't a car being studied, but a trolley moving on a laboratory bench.

Trolley experiments

A 'black box' flight recorder records the motion of an aircraft on magnetic wire.

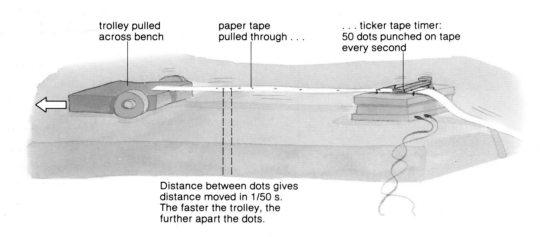

trolley pulled across bench

paper tape pulled through . . .

. . . ticker tape timer: 50 dots punched on tape every second

Distance between dots gives distance moved in 1/50 s. The faster the trolley, the further apart the dots.

Examples of tapes

start

steady speed: distance between dots stays the same

higher steady speed: distance between dots greater than before

acceleration: distance between dots increases

acceleration — — — — — — — then — — — — — — — retardation

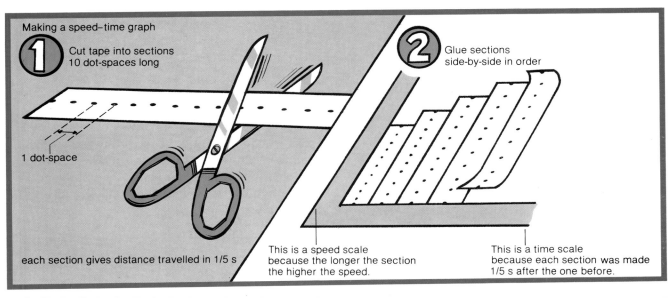

Making a speed–time graph

1 Cut tape into sections 10 dot-spaces long

1 dot-space

each section gives distance travelled in 1/5 s

2 Glue sections side-by-side in order

This is a speed scale because the longer the section the higher the speed.

This is a time scale because each section was made 1/5 s after the one before.

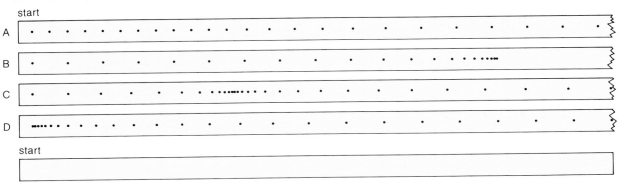

start

A

B

C

D

start

1 Which of the tapes above shows
a acceleration, then a steady speed?
b retardation until stopped, then acceleration?
c a steady speed, then acceleration, then a higher steady speed?

2 A trolley travelling at a steady speed, loses speed, stops, then accelerates. Copy the blank tape above. Mark in the pattern of dots you might expect to see.

3 In the questions which follow, you have to make measurements on the paper tape shown below. The ticker-tape timer made 50 dots on paper tape every second. The distance from one dot to the next is called a *dot-space*.

a How long did it take the timer to make 5 dot-spaces?
b How many dot-spaces are there between A and B?
c How long did it take the tape to move from A to B?
d Use a mm ruler to measure the distance from A to B.
e What was the average speed (in mm/s) of the trolley between A and B?
f Measure the distance from C to D, then work out the average speed of the trolley between C and D.
g Section CD was completed exactly one second after section AB.
By how much did the speed of the trolley increase in this time?
h An acceleration of 1 mm/s² means that the speed increases by 1 mm/s every second.
What was the acceleration of the trolley in mm/s²?

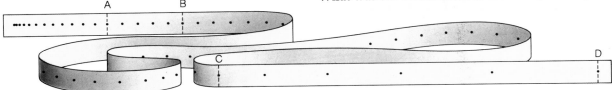

1.7 Falling freely

When Flight Lieutenant Alkemade first left his aircraft, he fell towards the ground with an acceleration of $10\,\text{m/s}^2$. Rushing air quickly reduced this acceleration. Otherwise, he would have hit the ground at over 700 mph (about 300 m/s).

Air resistance slows down some things more than others. It doesn't slow a falling rock very much. But it slows a feather a lot. Without air resistance, all things falling near the Earth would have the same acceleration of $10\,\text{m/s}^2$. This is the **acceleration of free fall**, g.

So, without air resistance, anything dropped would speed up like this:

0 s	no speed
after 1 s	10 m/s
after 2 s	20 m/s
after 3 s	30 m/s

and so on

acceleration of free fall
g
is $10\,\text{m/s}^2$
for all objects

Calculating how far

With the value of g, and the time something takes to fall, you can work out the height fallen. Here is a problem about a falling stone. The problem is done in two ways – with actual values, and with letter symbols.

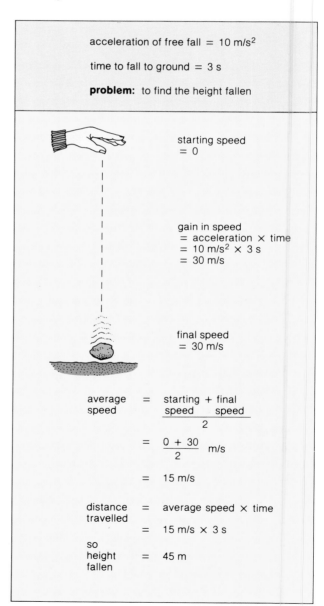

acceleration of free fall = $10\,\text{m/s}^2$

time to fall to ground = 3 s

problem: to find the height fallen

starting speed
= 0

gain in speed
= acceleration × time
= $10\,\text{m/s}^2$ × 3 s
= 30 m/s

final speed
= 30 m/s

$$\text{average speed} = \frac{\text{starting speed} + \text{final speed}}{2}$$

$$= \frac{0 + 30}{2}\ \text{m/s}$$

$$= 15\ \text{m/s}$$

distance travelled = average speed × time

= 15 m/s × 3 s

so height fallen = 45 m

Measuring g

First rearrange the equation for h below to give an equation for g:

$$g = \frac{2h}{t^2}$$

Drop a metal ball. Measure the height (h) it falls in metres. Measure the time (t) it takes to fall in seconds. Then use the new equation to work out g.

Careful measurements show that g has a value of 9.8 m/s². However, the value of 10 m/s² is simpler to use, and accurate enough for most calculations.

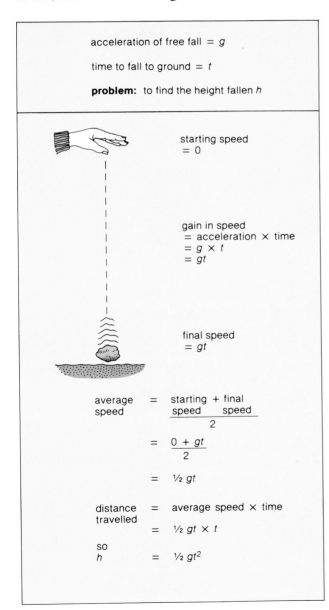

acceleration of free fall = g

time to fall to ground = t

problem: to find the height fallen h

starting speed = 0

gain in speed
= acceleration × time
= $g \times t$
= gt

final speed
= gt

average speed = $\dfrac{\text{starting speed} + \text{final speed}}{2}$

= $\dfrac{0 + gt}{2}$

= ½ gt

distance travelled = average speed × time

= ½ $gt \times t$

so
h = ½ gt^2

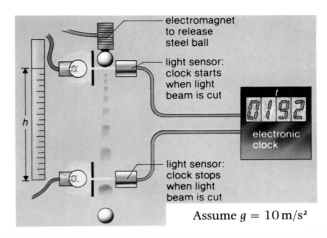

electromagnet to release steel ball

light sensor: clock starts when light beam is cut

electronic clock

light sensor: clock stops when light beam is cut

Assume $g = 10$ m/s²

1 Is each of the following TRUE or FALSE?
Without air resistance:
a a heavy stone falls more quickly than a light stone.
b near the earth falling things all accelerate at the same rate.
c dropped from the same height a heavy stone takes exactly the same time to reach the ground as a light stone.

2 Copy the chart, filling in the missing information about the falling stone:

time in s	0	1s	2s		?	?
speed in m/s	0	10	?		40	50
speed gained every second = ?						
acceleration = ?						

3 The metal ball below has been falling for 5 seconds.
What is its acceleration?
What is its speed?
What is its average speed?
What height has it fallen?
How far will the ball have fallen in the first 10 seconds?

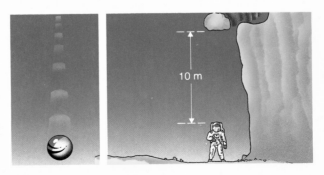

10 m

4 The astronaut is on a planet where the acceleration of free fall is only 1 m/s². It takes him 4 seconds to move sideways. Will he escape the falling rock?

1.8 Thrills and spills

This car can reach 60 mph in just three seconds. That's an acceleration of $10 \, m/s^2$, the same as the acceleration of free fall, g.

If you were in the driving seat, you would feel the acceleration as a push in the back – a push as strong as your own weight.

These rides give you the effects of high acceleration by making you travel round tight bends very fast.

This roller coaster ride lasts just over a minute. You experience speeds up to 25 m/s (50 mph), and accelerations up to $3 \, g$.

High acceleration can drain blood from your head to your feet and make you 'black out'. But not during this ride. Sitting with your knees up stops the rush of blood to your feet.

A $3 \, g$ ride. You may feel most scared at the high point of the swing. But it's near the low point that you are most firmly pushed into your seat.

For this $5 \, g$ ride, you need skill and a million pounds worth of training. And a special suit which squeezes your limbs tightly to reduce the flow of blood from your head.

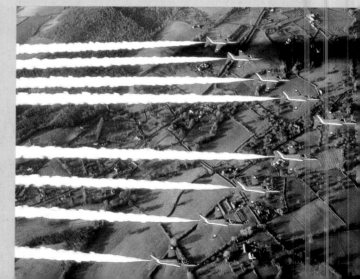

If another car crashes into the back of yours, a headrest can save you from serious neck injury. It makes sure that your head accelerates forward at the same rate as the rest of your body.

Why not build them stronger?
In a crash, it's safer for the passengers if the front of the car *does* collapse. It means lower deceleration and less risk of injury. But the metal body must form a strong 'cage' round the passengers to stop them being crushed.

Most thrill machine rides have plenty of built-in safety. If one metal part breaks, there are still others left to support you. But how many fairground rides can you think of where your safety depends on the strength of just one metal part?

If rear-facing seats are safer, why has no airline decided to 'go it alone' and fit them? Can you suggest reasons?

In thrill machine rides, you can experience accelerations of 3 g or more. But without headrests, accelerations like this wouldn't be safe. Why not?

The safest way to travel – backwards.
If a plane makes a crash landing, the deceleration can be very high. Rear-facing seats give the best chance of survival. Which is why the RAF fit them to their transport aircraft. But airlines haven't taken up the idea.

1.9 Force
– the secret of acceleration

A force is a push or a pull. It is a vector because it has a direction.

Rolls Royce engines use a test rig to measure one rather large force – the forward thrust from a jet engine.

Like all forces, the force from a jet engine is measured in **newtons (N)**. Some typical force values are:

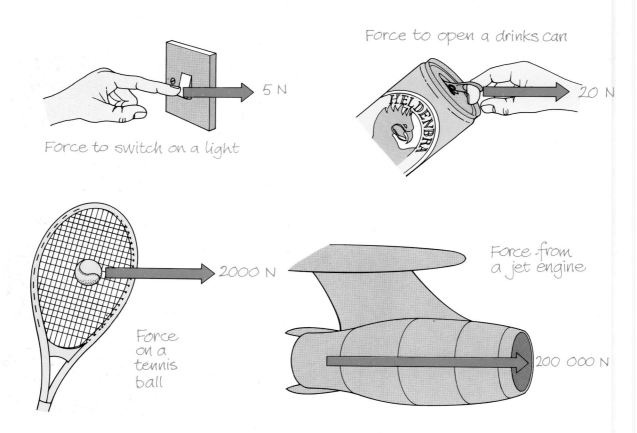

Force to switch on a light — 5 N

Force to open a drinks can — 20 N

Force on a tennis ball — 2000 N

Force from a jet engine — 200 000 N

Small forces can be measured with a **spring balance**. The greater the force, the more the spring is stretched, and the higher the reading on the scale.

Resisting acceleration

It takes over an hour for an ocean-going tanker to reach full speed – and over an hour for it to be stopped when the engines are put in reverse. Like all masses, the tanker resists any change in velocity. The effect is called **inertia**. The more mass something has, the greater its inertia, and the more it resists acceleration.

Making mass accelerate

It takes a force to make a mass accelerate.
The greater the mass, and the greater the acceleration, the more force is needed.

There is a simple link between force, mass and acceleration:

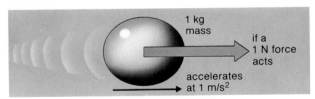

A 1 N force is needed to accelerate 1 kg at 1 m/s².
A 2 N force is needed to accelerate 1 kg at 2 m/s².
A 2 N force is needed to accelerate 2 kg at 1 m/s².
A 8 N force is needed to accelerate 4 kg at 2 m/s².

In all cases,

Force = mass × acceleration

In symbols,

$F = ma$

This equation can be rearranged in two forms,

$$a = \frac{F}{m} \qquad m = \frac{F}{a}$$

You would use the left hand equation, for example, if you knew the mass and the force, but needed to calculate the acceleration.

1 Copy and complete:
A __ is a push or pull. It is measured in __, or __ for short. Small forces can be measured with a __ __. All things resist acceleration. The effect is called __. The greater the __, the greater the resistance to acceleration. To give a __ of 2 kilograms an __ of 3 m/s², a force of __ is needed. Twice the __ pushing on the same __ would produce __ the acceleration.

2

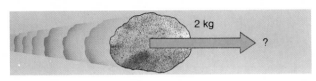

What force is needed to make the rock accelerate at
a 2 m/s²   **b** 0.5 m/s²   **c** 4 m/s²?

3 In an experiment with a 0.5 kg trolley, someone measures the pulling force, calculates the acceleration, writes down the values '10' and '5', but forgets to note which is which.
Can you decide, and add the correct units?

4

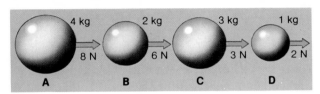

a Which masses have the same acceleration?
b Which mass has most acceleration?
c Which mass has least acceleration?

5 The three vehicles below are among the most powerful of their type.
Which wins the contest for the best acceleration? Which is the loser?

Boeing 747:
mass 400 000 kg
force from engines 800 000 N

Porsche 911:
mass 1300 kg
force from engine 7800 N

Honda 1000
mass 300 kg
force from engine 3000N

1.10 Weight: the pull of gravity

Does gravity always pull things downwards? Not according to cartoonists. They often use 'plausible impossibles' – things which seem reasonable, but aren't possible because they break the laws of physics. Walking off a cliff is probably the most well known. The character doesn't fall until he realises that he isn't standing on anything.

Gravitational force

Hang something from the end of a spring balance and you can measure the downward pull from the Earth. The pull is called a **gravitational force**.

No one knows what causes gravitational force. But several things are known about it:
All masses attract each other.
The greater the masses, the stronger the pull.
The closer the masses, the stronger the pull.

The pull between small masses is far too weak to measure – less than one millionth of a newton between you and the person next to you for example. But the Earth has such a huge mass that the gravitational pull is strong enough to hold most things firmly on the ground.

Weight

Weight is another name for the gravitational force from the Earth.
As weight is a force, it is measured in newtons:
On Earth, each kilogram of matter weighs 10 newtons.

People often use the word 'weight' when they really mean 'mass'. The person in the diagram doesn't 'weigh' 50 kilograms. They have a *mass* of 50 kilograms and a *weight* of 500 newtons.

Is there a link?

On Earth, the acceleration of free fall is $10\,\text{m/s}^2$.

On Earth, there is a gravitational force of 10 newtons on every kilogram.

These two facts are connected.
Try using the equation $F = m \times a$ to work out the acceleration of the two masses below.

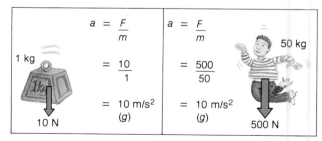

$$a = \frac{F}{m}$$

$$= \frac{10}{1}$$

$$= 10\ \text{m/s}^2\ (g)$$

$$a = \frac{F}{m}$$

$$= \frac{500}{50}$$

$$= 10\ \text{m/s}^2\ (g)$$

In each case, the acceleration is the same; *g*.
So you can think of *g*
– as an acceleration of $10\,\text{m/s}^2$.
– as a **gravitational field strength** of $10\,\text{N/kg}$.

How to lose weight quickly

Go to the Moon. Even better, go deep into space, far away from all planets.

As different planets have different masses and sizes, your weight would vary from one place in the Universe to another. Take the case of a person with a mass of 50 kg:

	mass	weight
deep in space	50 kg	zero
near surface of the Moon	50 kg	80 N
near surface of Jupiter	50 kg	2700 N
near a black hole – a collapsed star whose gravitational pull is so great that even light cannot escape	50 kg	100 million million N

Travelling around space isn't going to get rid of the kilograms. Weight may vary, but mass stays the same. On the Moon for example, the gravitational pull is much less than on Earth. But the amount of matter in something is just the same. And it is just as difficult to speed up or slow down.

1 Copy the following, and fill in the blanks:
a __ is another name for the gravitational __ on something.
b Weight is measured in __.
c All masses __ each other. The closer the masses, the __ the pull between them.

2 Write down the weights of the following masses on Earth:

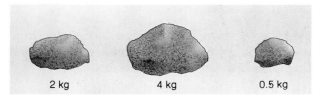

2 kg   4 kg   0.5 kg

3 'A bag of sugar weighs one kilogram'.
People might say this in everyday language. But the statement is wrong.
Why is it wrong?
What should it say?

4

A	B
$g = 10 \text{ m/s}^2$	$g = 10 \text{ N/kg}$

Describe in words what A and B tell you about a mass of one kilogram.

5 Aliens land on several planets, including Earth. Here is some information about the aliens:

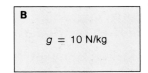

alien	mass in kg	weight in N
A	40	80
B	20	200
C	10	200
D	20	40

a Which alien landed on Earth?
b Which two aliens landed on the same planet?
c The aliens have to jump from their spacecraft when they land.
Which alien will fall with the greatest acceleration?
d If all the aliens came to Earth, which would weigh least?

6 A 16 kilogram lump of rock weighs 10 N on the Moon.
a What is the acceleration of free fall on the Moon?
b What is the gravitational field strength on the Moon?
c How much would the rock weigh on Earth?

1.11 Balanced forces

The spacecraft Pioneer 10 was launched more than ten years ago. Now deep in space, it doesn't need engines to keep it moving. With no forces to slow it, it will keep moving for ever.

Sir Isaac Newton was the first to describe how things would move if no forces were acting on them. His **first law of motion** states:

If something has no force on it, it will

if still, stay still

if moving, keep moving at a steady speed in a straight line.

Slowed by friction

On Earth, unpowered vehicles quickly come to rest – slowed by the force of friction. Friction is the force that tries to stop materials sliding across each other. There is friction between your hands when you rub them together, and friction between your shoes and the ground when anything slides over it. Friction is partly due to tiny bumps on the surfaces, and partly due to atoms in the two materials which tend to stick to each other.

Fluid friction

Liquids and gases are called fluids. They can also cause friction. When a car is travelling fast on a motorway, air resistance is by far the largest frictional force pulling against it.

Using friction

Friction is needed to give your shoes grip on the ground.

Reducing friction

Car bodies are designed so that the air flow is as smooth as possible. Less air resistance means less wasted fuel.

Forces in balance

Most things have several forces acting on them. For example, everything feels the pull of gravity, and moving things have friction trying to slow them down. Sometimes, the forces on something all cancel each other out. Then it behaves as if it has no force on it at all, and obeys Newton's first law.

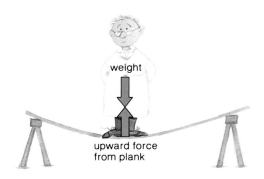

weight

upward force from plank

When the man stands on the plank, it sags, until the springiness of the wood produces enough upward force to oppose his weight. Then the forces cancel, so the man stays still. The ground isn't as springy as the plank, but it too produces an upward force to equal your weight when you stand on it.

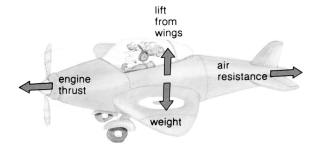

lift from wings

engine thrust

air resistance

weight

The aircraft is moving through the air at high speed. The weight of the aircraft is balanced by the lift from the wings. And air resistance is balanced by the thrust from the engine. The forces all cancel, so the aircraft keeps moving at a steady speed in a straight line.

If the thrust were *greater* than the air resistance, the aircraft would *gain* speed, and not keep a steady speed.

Terminal speed

As a skydiver falls, the air resistance increases as her speed rises. Eventually, air resistance is enough to balance her weight. If she weighs 500 newtons, then the air resistance rises to 500 newtons. She stops accelerating and falls with a maximum speed called her **terminal speed**. This is usually about 60 metres/second, though the actual value depends on air conditions, as well as her size, shape and weight.

If air resistance balances the skydiver's weight, why doesn't she stay still? There wouldn't be any air resistance unless she was moving.

Surely her weight is greater than air resistance if she is travelling downwards? No, if it were, she would gain speed, instead of keeping a steady speed.

Assume $g = 10\,\text{N/kg}$

1 If something has no forces acting on it at all, what happens to it if it is
a still   b moving?

2 Say whether friction is USEFUL or a NUISANCE in each of the following cases:
a a car tyre on the road
b sledge runners on snow
c a ship moving through water
d brake blocks on a cycle wheel
e shoes on a pavement
f a skydiver falling through air
g someone's hand holding a screwdriver
h a wheel spinning on an axle
Which of these are examples of fluid friction?

3 A skydiver weighing 600 N falls through the air at a steady speed of 50 m/s.
a Draw the diver, showing the forces acting on him.
b What name is given to his steady speed?
c What is the air resistance on him, in newtons?
d What is his mass?
e Why does he lose speed if he opens his parachute?

1.12 Action and reaction

Here are some pairs of forces:

backward force
on boat

forward force
on shoe

backward force
on rifle

forward force
on bullet

In fact, no force can exist by itself.
All forces are pushes or pulls between *two* things.
So they *always* occur in pairs.
One force acts on one thing. Its equal but opposite partner acts on the other.

Sir Isaac Newton was the first to realise that forces occur in pairs. His **third law of motion** states:

For every action there is an equal and opposite reaction.

or

When A pushes on B, B pushes with an equal but opposite force on A.

If forces always occur in pairs, why don't they cancel each other out?
The forces in each pair are acting on two *different* things, *not* the same thing.

Why doesn't the ground move backwards when someone runs forward?
It does. But Earth is so massive, that the force has too small an effect to be noticed.

Rocks, rockets, and jets –
Pairs of forces at work

Moving about in space is no problem if you have a rock handy.

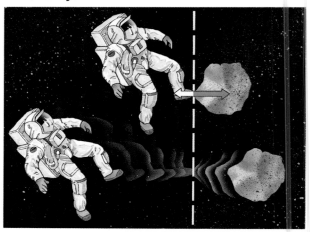

A pair of forces is produced when the astronaut pushes on the rock with her foot.
One force pushes the astronaut to the left.
An equal force pushes the rock to the right.
The astronaut has less mass than the rock. So the force has a greater effect on her.
She accelerates more than the rock.

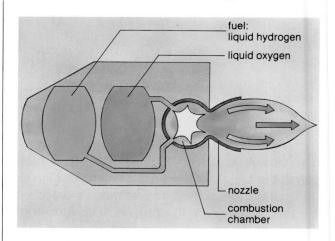

fuel:
liquid hydrogen

liquid oxygen

nozzle

combustion
chamber

Rocket engines use a similar idea. But they push out large masses of gas, rather than rocks.
In a rocket engine, fuel and liquid oxygen are mixed together in the combustion chamber. The

fuel burns fiercely in the oxygen, turns to gas, and expands.

Huge forces are produced, which push engine and burning fuel apart.

One force pushes the burning fuel backwards. An equal but opposite force pushes the rocket forward.

How can a rocket accelerate through space if it has nothing to push against?

It does have something to push against – a huge mass of burning fuel. Fuel and liquid oxygen make up over 90% of the mass of a rocket.

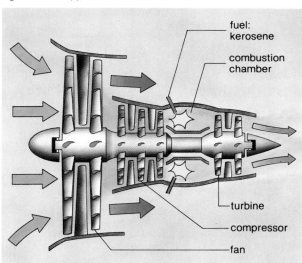

A jet engine doesn't need a supply of liquid oxygen.

Instead, it uses a series of fans, called a compressor, to draw in large masses of air from the atmosphere.

The compressor is driven by the turbine.

The turbine is rather like a windmill. It is blown round by the fast moving gases leaving the engine.

Most of the air drawn in by the jet engine doesn't go through the combustion chambers. It is pushed straight out by the huge fan at the front. This means less noise and better fuel consumption.

A large fan can push out over a quarter of a tonne of air every second.

1 One force in each pair is missing in the diagrams below. Copy the diagrams. Draw in and label the missing forces.

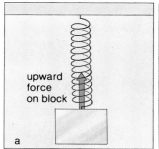
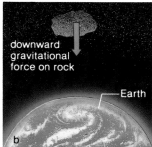

2 Use the first letters of the answers below to make a word. You'll find this whenever there is any action.

a	?	Engine using fuel and liquid oxygen
b	?	Every force has its __
c	?	If there is a reaction, it has to be there
d	?	It pushes air into the combustion chambers
e	?	This double-page is about the __ law of motion
f	?	First name of answer **h**
g	?	Forces in every pair are equal but __
h	?	He put forward the laws of motion

3 Jet engines and rocket engines both push out large masses of gas.
Why can't a jet engine work in space?
Why aren't airliners powered by rocket engines?

4 Look at the diagram of the astronaut pushing on the rock. If the astronaut had more mass than the rock, what effect would this have?

5

A woman stands on a plank. Her weight is exactly balanced by an upward force for the plank.
Dave says that this is an example of Newton's third law of motion.
Sue says that it isn't.
Who is right? And why?

1.13 Speedy delivery

Out of the way!

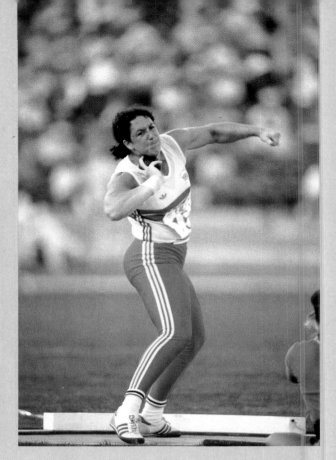

William 'The Refrigerator' Perry, lead blocker for the Chicago Bears. His job is to charge through the defence lines, clearing gaps for the running backs to pass through. Mass is the secret of his success. At 145 kilograms, he has more than twice the mass of the average male. And once he starts running he is extremely difficult to stop.

Someone else who needs mass as well as strength. When she pushes the shot forward, there's a backward push on her body which slows her down and reduces the speed of the shot. The more mass she has, the less effect this backward push has.

Who wins over 1500 metres?

1.5 m/s   7 m/s   12 m/s   15 m/s

30 mph

Swimmers lose out because water resistance is much higher than air resistance. Cyclists are fastest of all. And even faster if there's another vehicle in front to reduce the air resistance. The

highest speed ever reached on a bicycle was 63 metres/second (140 mph) – behind a car with a windshield on the back.

Fast service

Nice style. Shame about the action.
Could you work out the speed of the racket from this photograph? If not, why not?

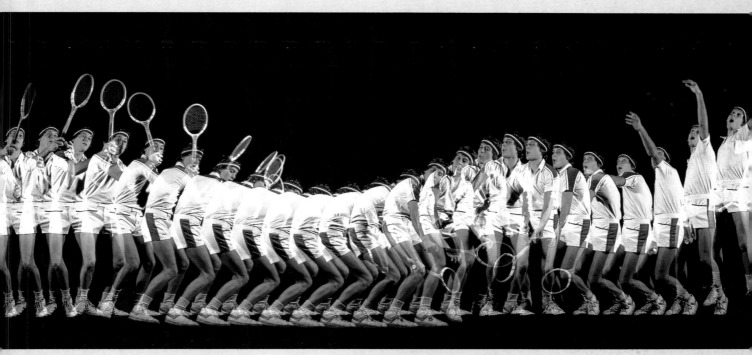

Getting the elbow

A top player uses a racket with tight strings to help her serve the ball really fast. She tries to hit the ball near the centre of the racket. Otherwise, the forces can injure her elbow.
An ordinary player uses racket strings that are less tight. The strings stretch more when the ball is hit, which cuts the speed down. But, if the player hits the ball off-centre, the forces on the elbow are small and not so damaging.

Explain why:
- runners can travel faster than swimmers;
- cyclists can travel faster than runners.

In Olympic speed events, competitors need to keep their air resistance as low as possible. Try to find out how the following reduce their air resistance:
- sprint cyclists;
- speed skaters;
- swimmers.

Describe what happens to the speed of a tennis racket from the beginning of a serve to the end.

Make a list of the games players or athletes for whom plenty of mass is:
- an advantage:
- a disadvantage.

1.14 Turning effects

What's needed to turn these?

Something which increases the turning effect of your hand.

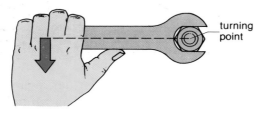

The nut is easy to turn with a spanner.

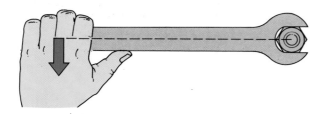

It is easier still if the spanner has a long handle. You can increase the turning effect in two ways;
1 increase the force
2 move the force further away from the turning point.

Moments

The turning effect of a force is called a **moment**. It can be calculated as follows:

Moment = force × distance from turning point

Moments are **clockwise** or **anticlockwise** depending on which way they turn. For example:

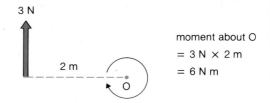

moment about O
= 3 N × 2 m
= 6 N m

This force has a clockwise moment of 6 N m about point O.

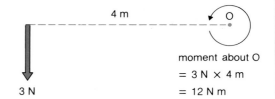

moment about O
= 3 N × 4 m
= 12 N m

This force has an anticlockwise moment of 12 Nm about point O. It has twice the turning effect, but in the opposite direction.

Torque

In engines and motors, several forces act together to produce a turning effect. The turning effect is called a **couple** or **torque**. Typical torque values are:

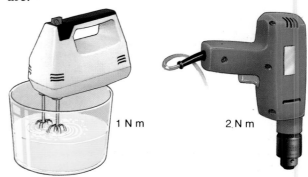

1 N m   2 N m

Moments in balance

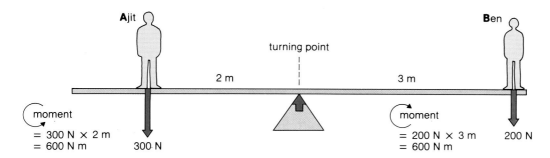

There are two turning effects at work on the see-saw; Ajit has an **anticlockwise** turning effect; Ben has a **clockwise** turning effect. The two moments are equal. So their turning effects cancel, and the see-saw balances. This is an example of the **principle of moments**:

If something is in balance, about the turning point the total clockwise moment is equal to the total anticlockwise moment.

The principle works in more complicated cases as well. In the diagram below, there is one anticlockwise moment about the turning point, but two clockwise moments. Add up the two clockwise moments.

The total is the same as the anticlockwise moment. So the see-saw balances.

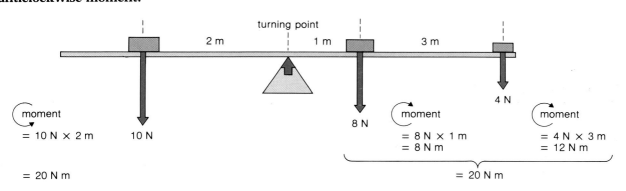

1

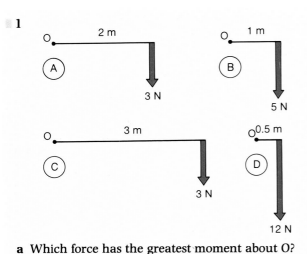

a Which force has the greatest moment about O?
b Which forces have the same moment about O?
c Which force has the least moment about O?

2

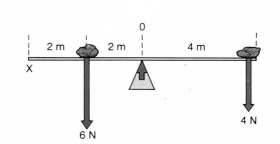

Someone is trying to balance a plank with stones.
a Calculate the moment of the 4 N force about O.
b Calculate the moment of the 6 N force about O.
c Will the plank balance?
If not, which way will it tip?
d What extra force would be needed at X to balance the plank?

1.15 Centre of gravity

Balancing for Gold

Most people would find it impossible to walk along such a narrow beam, let alone perform handstands and somersaults on it.

The secret lies in how you position your weight. Every particle in your body has a small gravitational force acting on it. Together, these forces act like a single force pulling at just one point. This single force is your **weight**.

The point is called your **centre of gravity** or **centre of mass**.

Keep your centre of gravity over the beam and you stay on. Allow it to move to one side, and your weight produces a turning effect which tips you off.

Simple shapes, like a metre rule, often have a centre of gravity exactly in the middle. Vehicles usually have a low centre of gravity because most of their heavy mechanical parts are low down.

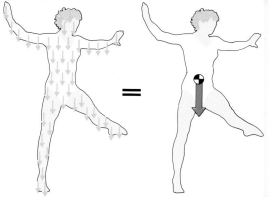

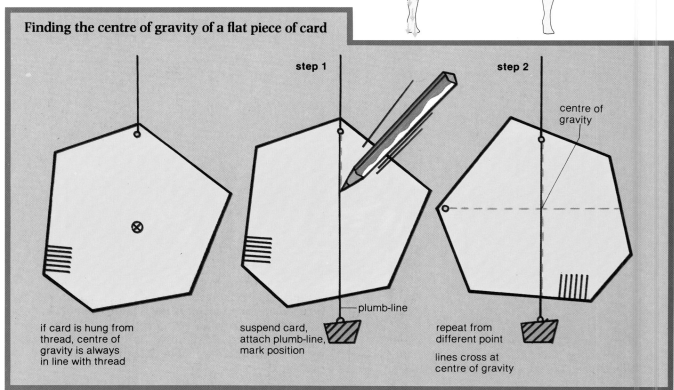

Finding the centre of gravity of a flat piece of card

step 1

step 2

centre of gravity

plumb-line

if card is hung from thread, centre of gravity is always in line with thread

suspend card, attach plumb-line, mark position

repeat from different point

lines cross at centre of gravity

How stable?

base

base

base

If something won't topple over, its position is stable:

This truck is in a stable position. If it starts to tip, its weight will pull it back again. As long as its centre of gravity stays above its base, it won't topple over.

This racing car is even more stable than the truck. It has a lower centre of gravity and a wider base. It could be tipped much further before it started to topple.

Clever stunt driving – but it has put the truck in an unstable position. If the truck tips any further, its centre of gravity will pass over the edge of its base. Then its weight will pull it right over.

Equilibrium

Like the vehicles above, the shapes below are all in a state of balance or **equilibrium**.

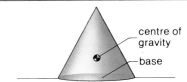

stable equilibrium
Even if you tip the cone a little, the centre of gravity stays over the base.

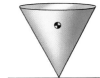

unstable equilibrium
The cone is balanced, but not for long. Its pointed 'base' is so small that the centre of gravity immediately passes beyond it.

neutral equilibrium
Left alone, the ball stays where it is. Moved, it stays in its new position. Wherever the ball lies, the centre of gravity is always exactly over the point where it touches the bench.

1 In the diagram, the kitchen stool is about to topple over. Copy the diagram and mark on the position of the centre of gravity.

Would the stool be MORE stable, or LESS stable, if it had
a a higher centre of gravity
b a wider base?
Explain why three-legged stools aren't as stable as stools with four legs.

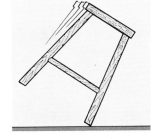

2 a Redraw the diagram, showing the weight as a force arrow.

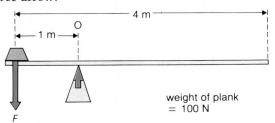

weight of plank = 100 N

b How far is this force from the point O?
c What is the moment of this force about O?
d If the plank balances, what must be the moment of the force F about O?
e What is the value of F?

1.16 Stretching and compressing

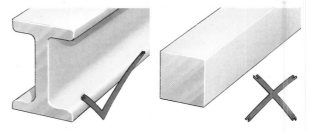

In every case, the more cross-sectional ('end-on') area the bar has, the more it resists being put out of shape.

At 555 metres, the CN tower in Toronto is the tallest building in the world. However, its steel and concrete structure isn't quite as rigid as it looks. In high winds, the top can sway up to half a metre. And the tower is actually shortened by several centimetres because the structure is compressed by its own weight.

Whenever several forces act on something, its shape changes – though sometimes only by a small amount.

Some things are designed to bend and twist. Some springs for example. However, the steel frames used in most modern buildings are designed to change shape as little as possible. The frames are made using I-section beams. An I-section beam has a much greater resistance to bending than a solid square section beam made from the same amount of metal.

Acting together, forces can have the following effects:

Elastic and plastic

To engineers, these don't have quite the same meaning as in everyday language.
Bend a ruler a little. Then release it.
It goes back to its original shape.
Materials which behave in this way are **elastic**.

Press a piece of Plasticine, then release it. It doesn't return to its original shape.
Materials which behave in this way are **plastic**.

A bumper on a car is elastic – provided it isn't bent too far. Given too much force, it passes its **elastic limit** and stays out of shape.

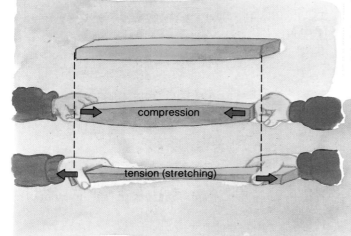

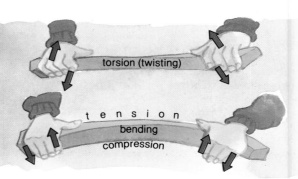

Hooke's law

Many materials obey a simple law when compressed or stretched. Take the case of a spring:

The spring is stretched in stages by hanging masses from one end. The stretching force is called the **load**.

As $g = 10 \, \text{N/kg}$, there is a 1 N load for every 100 g hung from the spring.

Each time the load is changed, the **extension** of the spring is measured. The extension is the difference between the stretched length of the spring and its original unstretched length.

Typical readings are shown in the chart.

The readings can be used to plot a graph of extension against load.

Up to the point E,

1 the graph is a straight line through O.

2 every extra 1 N of load produces the same extra extension (10 mm in this case).

3 if the load is doubled, the extension is doubled, and so on.

Mathematically, these all mean that **the extension is directly proportional to the load**. This is sometimes called **Hooke's law**.

E is the **elastic limit** of the spring. If this point is passed, the spring doesn't go back to its original length when the load is removed. It ends up longer than before.

Steel bars don't stretch as much as springs. But they obey the same law. So do glass, wood, and many other materials.

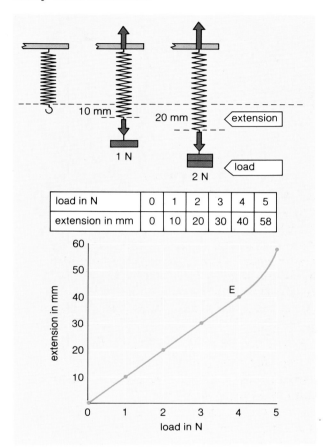

load in N	0	1	2	3	4	5
extension in mm	0	10	20	30	40	58

1 a Write down the parts of the ridge tent which are under TENSION; in COMPRESSION; BENDING

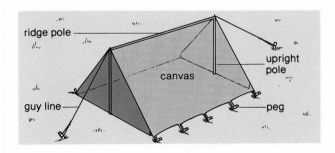

b What would happen to the ridge pole if its ELASTIC LIMIT were exceeded?

c The force on the guy line is increased. The guy line doesn't break. What does happen to it?

How would the result be different if a thicker guy line, made from the same material, were used?

2 The table shows the readings taken in a spring-stretching experiment:

Load in N	0	1	2	3	4	5	6
Length in mm	40	49	58	67	76	88	110
Extension in mm							

a Copy and complete the table.

b What is the unstretched length of the spring?

c Plot a graph of EXTENSION against LOAD.

d Mark the ELASTIC LIMIT on your graph. What happens to the spring beyond this point?

e What load is needed to produce an extension of 35 mm?

f What load is needed to make the spring 65 mm long?

1.17 Pressure

Which causes most damage?
Believe it or not, the stiletto heel.
It can ruin carpets and punch holes in floors. Not just because of the high downward force. But because the force is concentrated on such a small area. It produces a high **pressure**.

Pressure tells you how concentrated a force is. It is calculated using the equation:

$$\text{pressure} = \frac{\text{force}}{\text{area}}$$

and measured in **newton/metre² (N/m²)** or **pascal (Pa)**

For example:

What the figures mean

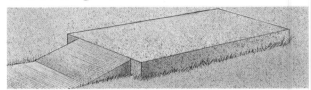

Pressure under concrete garage base: 8000 N/m².
There is a force of 8000 newtons on every square metre of ground.

Pressure under stiletto heel: 2 000 000 N/m².
Much less than a square metre here of course. But the heel has the same squashing effect on the floor as a 2 000 000 newton force spread over a full square metre.

Pressure problems

Rearrange the pressure equation, and you get:

force = pressure × area

This equation is useful if you know the pressure, and the area over which it is acting, but you need to find the force.

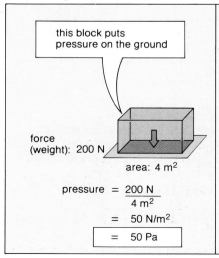

this block puts pressure on the ground

force (weight): 200 N
area: 4 m²

$$\text{pressure} = \frac{200 \text{ N}}{4 \text{ m}^2}$$
$$= 50 \text{ N/m}^2$$
$$\boxed{= 50 \text{ Pa}}$$

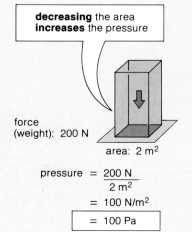

decreasing the area **increases** the pressure

force (weight): 200 N
area: 2 m²

$$\text{pressure} = \frac{200 \text{ N}}{2 \text{ m}^2}$$
$$= 100 \text{ N/m}^2$$
$$\boxed{= 100 \text{ Pa}}$$

increasing the force **increases** the pressure

force (weight): 400 N
area: 2 m²

$$\text{pressure} = \frac{400 \text{ N}}{2 \text{ m}^2}$$
$$= 200 \text{ N/m}^2$$
$$\boxed{= 200 \text{ Pa}}$$

keeping the **area** high
and the **pressure** low

walking on sand hurts less
than walking on pebbles:
less pressure means
less pain!

load-spreading washer
ensures that the head
of the bolt isn't pulled
through the woodwork

heavy animals need thick legs,
or their bones wouldn't cope
with the pressure

keeping the **area** low
and the **pressure** high

studs on hockey or football boots:
enough pressure here for
them to sink into the ground

blade on knife:
the sharper it is,
the higher the pressure

point on drawing pin:
far more pressure
than wood can stand

Assume $g = 10\,\text{N/kg}$.

1 Copy out, and fill in the blanks:
Pressure tells you how concentrated a __ is. It is measured in __ or __, and is calculated using the equation: pressure = __ __. A force of $12\,\text{N}$ acting over an area of $2\,\text{m}^2$ causes a pressure of __.
If the area were less, the pressure would be __.

2 The suitcase, the hover mower and the paving stone are all resting on the ground.

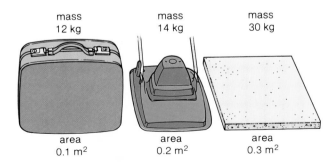

mass
12 kg

mass
14 kg

mass
30 kg

area
$0.1\,\text{m}^2$

area
$0.2\,\text{m}^2$

area
$0.3\,\text{m}^2$

Calculate
a the weight of each
b the pressure on the ground from each.

3 Sid is heavy. He weighs $720\,\text{N}$.
He also has big feet. They cover an area of $0.12\,\text{m}^2$.

720 N

$0.12\,\text{m}^2$

The ice can stand a pressure of $5000\,\text{Pa}$ before it cracks. Sid thinks he is safe. Is he right?

4 Sid can't iron the creases out of his jeans unless the pressure on them is at least $1500\,\text{Pa}$.
a If Sid's iron has an area of $0.02\,\text{m}^2$, what downward force is needed to produce this pressure?
b If the iron weighs $10\,\text{N}$, what downward force must Sid use on the iron to get rid of the creases?

1.18 Pressure in liquids

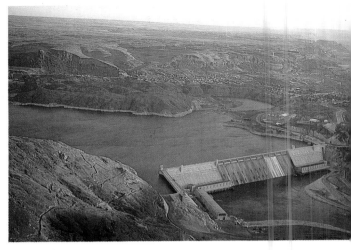

It took nearly nine years and 20 million tonnes of concrete to build the Grand Coulee Dam in Washington State, USA. If special air channels hadn't been left through the structure, the concrete would still be drying today, over forty years later. At its base, the dam is more than 60 metres thick. It has to be. Otherwise it would never withstand the pressure from the 150 metre deep lake of water on the other side.

Gravity pulls any liquid downwards in its container. This puts pressure on the container. And it puts pressure on anything put into the liquid.

The pressure pushes in all directions A liquid under pressure pushes on every surface it touches, whether the surface is facing upwards, downwards or sideways.

The pressure increases with depth Dams are thicker at the base than the top because they have to withstand a greater pressure at the bottom of the lake. The deeper into a liquid you go, the greater the weight of liquid above.

The pressure is affected by the density of the liquid Put petrol in the lake instead of water, and the pressure everywhere would be less. Petrol is less dense than water, so there is less weight to produce the pressure.

The width or shape of the container doesn't affect the pressure In the diagram, the pressure at the bottom of each 'lake' is the same. The bottom of

A submarine is built to withstand water pressure in all directions.

the wider lake does have a greater weight of water to support. But that weight is spread over a larger area.

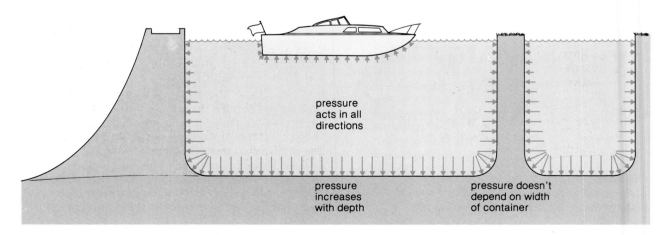

pressure acts in all directions

pressure increases with depth

pressure doesn't depend on width of container

Working out the pressure

You can calculate the pressure at any point in a liquid provided you know the depth and the density of the liquid:

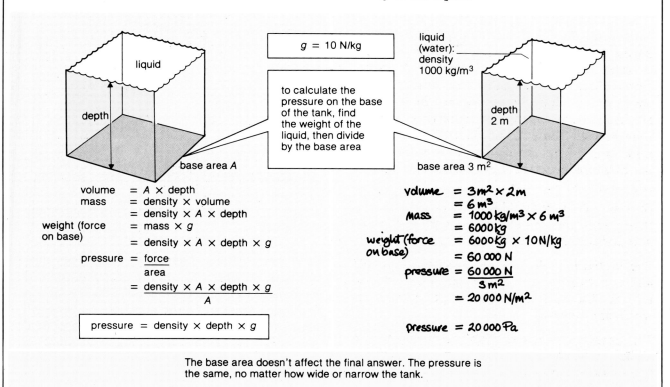

$g = 10$ N/kg

to calculate the pressure on the base of the tank, find the weight of the liquid, then divide by the base area

liquid (water): density 1000 kg/m³

depth 2 m

base area A

base area 3 m²

volume = $A \times$ depth
mass = density $\times$ volume
= density $\times A \times$ depth
weight (force on base) = mass $\times g$
= density $\times A \times$ depth $\times g$
pressure = $\dfrac{\text{force}}{\text{area}}$
= $\dfrac{\text{density} \times A \times \text{depth} \times g}{A}$

pressure = density $\times$ depth $\times g$

volume = $3\,m^2 \times 2\,m$
= $6\,m^3$
mass = $1000\,kg/m^3 \times 6\,m^3$
= $6000\,kg$
weight (force on base) = $6000\,kg \times 10\,N/kg$
= $60\,000\,N$
pressure = $\dfrac{60\,000\,N}{3\,m^2}$
= $20\,000\,N/m^2$

pressure = $20\,000\,Pa$

The base area doesn't affect the final answer. The pressure is the same, no matter how wide or narrow the tank.

$g = 10$ N/kg; the density of water = 1000 kg/m³

1

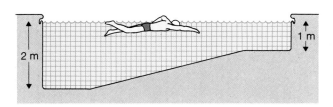

2 m

1 m

Calculate the water pressure at the bottom of this swimming pool
a at the shallow end   **b** at the deep end.

2 Calculate the water pressure on a scuba diver as she descends into a freshwater lake at
a 10 m below the surface
b 20 m
c 30 m?
d What effects do you think that this pressure will have on her?

3 Sian's shower won't work properly because the pressure at the spray end is too low. She decides to solve the problem by lengthening the pipe and raising the tank.

0.75 m

What is the water pressure at the spray?
How high must she raise the tank so that the pressure at the spray is 15 000 Pa?
4 What is the water pressure on the submarine in the photograph opposite if it dives to a depth of 50 m in fresh water?
How deep can the submarine safely dive in fresh water if its hull can withstand a pressure of 1 000 000 Pa?
Sea water is more dense than fresh water. Is the safe diving depth in sea water MORE or LESS than in fresh water?

1.19 Pressure from the atmosphere

The atmosphere is a deep ocean of air which surrounds the Earth. In some ways, it is like a liquid
– its pressure acts in all directions
– its pressure gets less as you rise up through it.
However, unlike a liquid, air can be squashed. This makes the atmosphere much more dense at lower levels. The atmosphere stretches hundreds of kilometres into space. Yet most of the air lies within ten kilometres of the Earth's surface:

The evidence

Atmospheric pressure can be quite crushing – literally. Take an 'empty' oil can. Pump out all the air, using a vacuum pump. And watch the dramatic result.

Most 'empty' things have air in them. They don't normally collapse because the air pressure inside balances the air pressure outside. This is why your body isn't crushed by the atmosphere. However, your ears are very sensitive to small *changes* in air pressure. They give you a popping sensation when you rise quickly through the atmosphere – in a car travelling uphill, for example.

How much?

Down at sea level, atmospheric pressure is about 100 000 Pa.
That's equivalent to the weight of ten cars pressing on every square metre. Or the pressure from a column of water 10 metres deep:

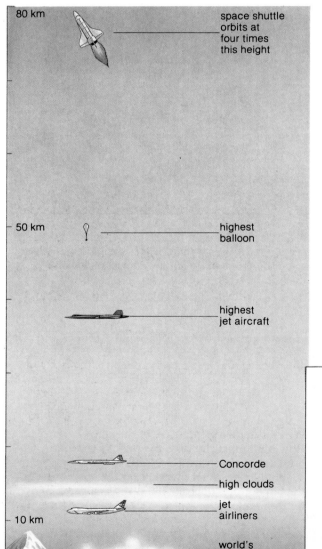

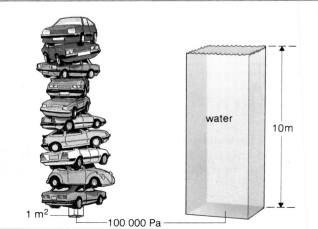

Using atmospheric pressure

Sucking through a straw

You use your lungs to lower the air pressure in the straw. Atmospheric pressure does the rest. It *pushes* the liquid up the straw.

air removed

Vacuum cleaner

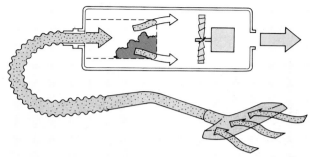

The fan lowers the air pressure just beyond the bag. The atmosphere rushes in, carrying dust and dirt with it. The bag stops the dust, but not the air.

Power-assisted car brakes

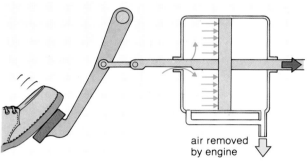

air removed by engine

Extra help from the atmosphere when you push on the pedal. Outside air enters the empty cylinder and pushes the piston to the right.

Vacuum forming

Remove the air under a sheet of warm, soft plastic, and the atmosphere will push the plastic into any shape you like.

Assume atmospheric pressure is 100 000 Pa – the same as the pressure due to a column of water 10 m deep.

Jeff works as a diver on an oil rig. He regularly dives to the sea bed, 50 m beneath the surface, to inspect and maintain the rig.

Jeff's breathing equipment supplies him with a special air mixture. To prevent him being crushed, the air pressure is automatically adjusted so that it exactly balances the outside pressure.

What is the pressure of the air he breathes when he is working

a at sea level

b 10 m beneath the surface

c on the sea bed?

Jeff's breathing equipment can't function safely at pressures above 800 000 Pa. Jeff's boss wants him to take on a salvage operation at a depth of 100 m. Should he refuse? How deep can he safely go?

2 Is it possible to 'suck' the water out of the bottle in the diagram? If not, why not?

1.20 Measuring air pressure

Who needs to?

Weather forecasters know that atmospheric pressure changes slightly from hour to hour, depending on the weather. Rainclouds form in areas of lower pressure called depressions. So a fall in pressure often means that bad weather is on the way.

Skin divers need to know the pressure of the air in their cylinders. The lower the pressure, the less air they have left to breathe.

Pressure measurers

Instruments which measure atmospheric pressure are called barometers.

Mercury barometer This is a long glass tube, sealed at one end, with the other end dipped in a dish of liquid mercury. The atmosphere presses on the mercury in the dish and this keeps a column of mercury up the tube. The greater the pressure, the higher the column. The space in the top of the tube is completely empty – it is a **vacuum**. If air were trapped in the tube, its pressure would stop the mercury rising so far.

Atmospheric pressure is sometimes measured in 'millimetres of mercury', rather than pascal. At sea level, its average value is about 760 millimetres of mercury.

Mercury is used in a barometer, rather than any other liquid, because it is so dense. If the barometer contained water, the tube would have to be over 10 metres long.

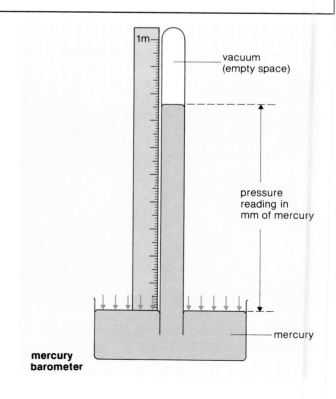

mercury barometer

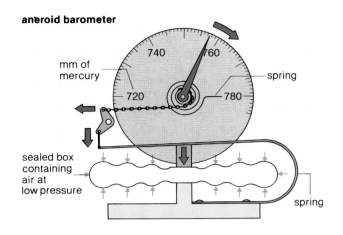

aneroid barometer

mm of mercury

spring

720   780

sealed box containing air at low pressure

spring

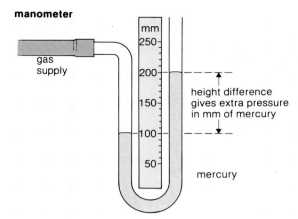

manometer

gas supply

height difference gives extra pressure in mm of mercury

mercury

Aneroid barometers These are the barometers which people hang in the hall to forecast the weather. They aren't as accurate as a mercury barometers. But they are more robust, simpler to read, and easier to move about.

In the middle of the barometer is a sealed metal box with flexible sides. Most of the air has been removed from the box, so it is squashed by the atmosphere. The greater the pressure, the more the sides are pushed in, and the further the pointer moves round the scale.

Pilots and mountaineers use a special type of aneroid barometer called an **altimeter**. Its reading tells them their height above sea level.

Manometers are used to measure gas and liquid pressures. The one in the diagram is filled with mercury. The height difference tells you the *extra* pressure that the gas supply has on top of atmospheric pressure – 100 mm of mercury in this case. If you want to know the actual pressure of the gas, you need to add on the value of atmospheric pressure.

Bourdon gauges are the pressure gauges you see on the top of gas cylinders. They aren't as accurate as manometers, but they are tougher and more portable. They contain a bent hollow metal tube which partly unbends when the pressure inside rises. This moves a pointer across a scale.

Assume $g = 10$ N/kg

1

mm 1000

500

mercury

mm 1000

500

gas supply

Study the diagram, then write down:
a the name of instrument on the left;
b the name of instrument on the right;

c the value of atmospheric pressure, in mm of mercury;
d the reading on instrument on the right;
e the pressure of the gas supply.
2 BOURDON GAUGE, MERCURY BAROMETER, ANEROID BAROMETER, MANOMETER
Say which of these instruments you would use to measure:
a atmospheric pressure, as accurately as possible;
b atmospheric pressure half way up a mountain;
c the pressure of gas in a cylinder;
d the pressure of a laboratory gas supply, as accurately as possible.

3

Mercury barometer:
Height of mercury column = 760 mm of mercury
density of mercury = 13 600 kg/m³

Use this information, and the equation on page 41, to calculate a value for atmospheric pressure in pascal.

2.1 Work and energy

Who is doing most work?

In everyday language, 'work' can mean anything from writing an essay to digging the garden.
To scientists and engineers, work has an exact meaning:
Work is done whenever a force moves.

The unit of work is the **joule (J)**.
1 joule of work is done when a force of 1 newton moves a distance of 1 metre (in the direction of the force).

There is an equation for calculating work:

Work done = force × distance moved (in the direction of the force)

For example:

6 J of work is done when a force of 2 N moves 3 m
12 J of work is done when a force of 4 N moves 3 m
24 J of work is done when a force of 4 N moves 6 m
and so on.

Larger units of work are the **kilojoule** and the **megajoule**:
1 kilojoule (kJ) = 1000 J
1 megajoule (MJ) = 1 000 000 J

Work done . . .	
in shutting a door	5 J
in throwing a ball	20 J
in climbing the stairs	1 kJ
in loading a lorry	1 MJ

Energy

Things have energy if they can do work.
A tankful of petrol has energy, so does a stretched spring. Each can be used to make something move. In each case, you can think of the energy as a promise of work to be done in the future. There are several different types of energy.

Potential energy

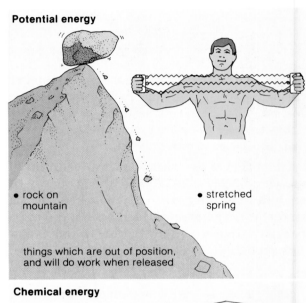

- rock on mountain
- stretched spring

things which are out of position, and will do work when released

Chemical energy

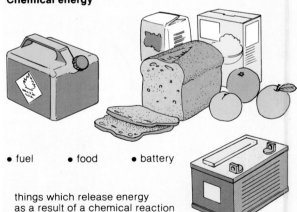

- fuel
- food
- battery

things which release energy as a result of a chemical reaction e.g. burning of fuel, combustion of food in the body

Nuclear energy

- radioactive materials

things which release energy as a result of changes in the nuclei (centres) of their atoms

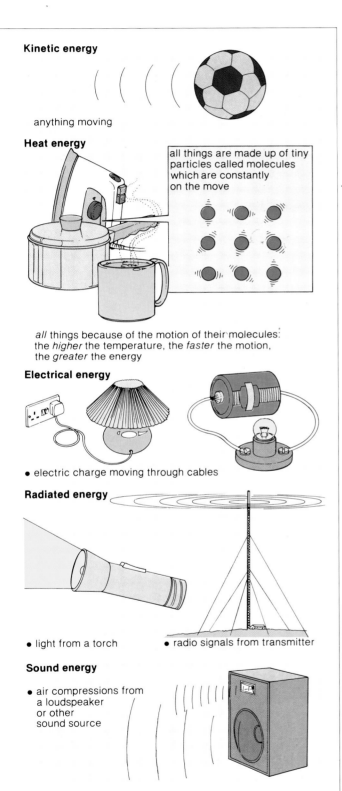

Kinetic energy

anything moving

Heat energy

all things are made up of tiny particles called molecules which are constantly on the move

all things because of the motion of their molecules: the *higher* the temperature, the *faster* the motion, the *greater* the energy

Electrical energy

• electric charge moving through cables

Radiated energy

• light from a torch   • radio signals from transmitter

Sound energy

• air compressions from a loudspeaker or other sound source

How much energy?

Like work, energy is measured in joules (J).
100 000 joules is the energy you could get from....

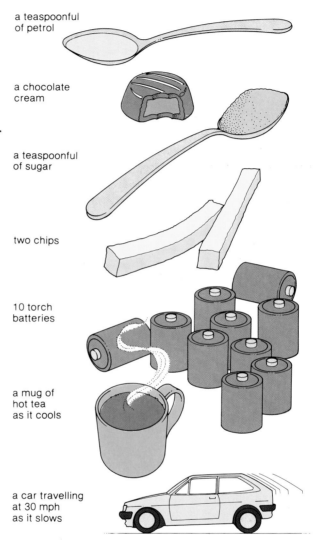

a teaspoonful of petrol

a chocolate cream

a teaspoonful of sugar

two chips

10 torch batteries

a mug of hot tea as it cools

a car travelling at 30 mph as it slows

1 How much work is done when:
a a 6 N force moves 3 m?
b a 12 N force moves 0.5 m?
c a 10 N force moves 10 mm?

2 In the 'How much energy?' chart above, which of the items have
a CHEMICAL energy?
b POTENTIAL energy?
c KINETIC energy?

3 Which is likely to release most energy
a burning a canful of petrol? – or dropping it?
b catching a falling apple? – or eating it?

2.2 Energy changes

A super-heavyweight and his daily menu:

1 grapefruit	1 bowl of cornflakes
7 pints of milk	12 eggs
8 steaks	1 kg cheese
30 slices of bread	1 kg butter
4 tins of pilchards	2 tins of baked beans
1 rice pudding	1 pot of honey

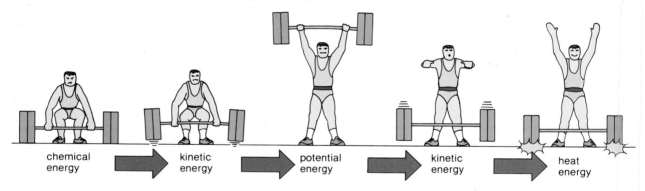

chemical energy → kinetic energy → potential energy → kinetic energy → heat energy

The weightlifter's menu is not a healthy diet for most people but what you might be eating if you were breaking Olympic weightlifting records. Much of the food is used for muscle building. But some provides energy for the lift.

The weightlifter has to supply about 4000 J to lift the weights above his head. The energy is stored in the body as chemical energy. However, during the lift, it is changed into other forms.

When the weights hit the ground, the impact makes the molecules move faster. This means that ground, air and weights are all a little warmer than before. The 4000 J of energy has become heat energy.

From the first stage to the last, the *type* of energy changes, but the total *amount* of energy stays the same.

This is an example of the **law of conservation of energy**:

Energy can change from one type to another, but it cannot be made or destroyed.

Energy change and work

Work is done whenever energy changes from one form to another. For example:

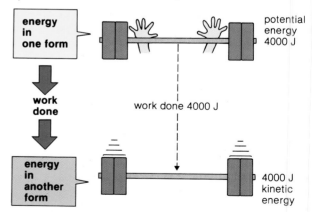

energy in one form

work done

energy in another form

potential energy 4000 J

work done 4000 J

4000 J kinetic energy

After the weights are dropped, 4000 J of potential energy is changed into 4000 J of kinetic energy: 4000 J of work is done in speeding up the weights during the fall:

work done = energy changed

Energy converters

An energy converter changes energy from one type into another.

The weightlifter is an energy converter. So are you.

So is each of the following:

an iron changes **electrical** energy into **heat** energy

brakes change **kinetic** energy into **heat** energy

telephones change **sound** energy into **electrical** energy

. . . into **sound** energy

a swing changes **kinetic** energy into **potential** energy into **kinetic** energy into **potential** energy into . . .

Most energy converters lose some of their energy as heat.

For example, to do 4000 J of work, the weightlifter has to release about 25 000 J of stored energy by 'burning' food he has eaten. The spare 21 000 J makes him hot – which is why he sweats.

When things move, they often lose energy because of air resistance of friction. The swing slowly loses its energy as heat.

As it pushes through the air, it slows down and the air molecules speed up.

1 Which of the above:

a changes CHEMICAL energy into KINETIC energy?

b changes ELECTRICAL energy into HEAT energy?

c changes CHEMICAL energy into ELECTRICAL energy?

d changes ELECTRICAL energy into RADIATED energy?

e changes ELECTRICAL energy into SOUND energy?

2 A pole-vaulter has 3500 J of energy when he crosses a bar 7 metres high.

How much kinetic energy will he have just before he reaches the ground?

3 This is an unusual way of describing the first half hour of someone's day:

  gets up at 7:00 a.m.
  gains chemical energy
  gains heat energy
  leaves house
  kinetic energy rises
  jumps on vehicle
  potential energy rises
  kinetic energy rises
  kinetic energy fall to zero
  potential energy falls to zero

Rewrite, to show what could actually be happening to the person.

2.3 Potential and kinetic energy

Moving fast, high above the earth, travelling at around 8 kilometres per second, the space shuttle has a great deal of both potential and kinetic energy.

When the shuttle re-enters the atmosphere, that energy is changed into heat energy. But how much energy?

If you were designing the thousands of heat resistant tiles that protect the surface of the shuttle, you would need to know.

Potential and kinetic energies can be calculated, but it is easier to start with something lighter and slower than the shuttle.

Like a stone lifted above the ground, or thrown.

The same by any route

When calculating potential energy, it is the height lifted against gravity that matters, not the actual distance moved.

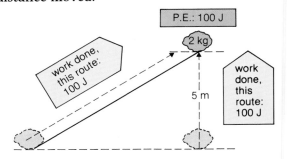

When the stone is lifted above the ground it gets the same potential energy whether it is lifted straight up or pulled up the slope. It takes less force to pull the stone up the slope. But the distance is further.

Result: the work done is the same by either route.

Calculating potential energy (P.E.)

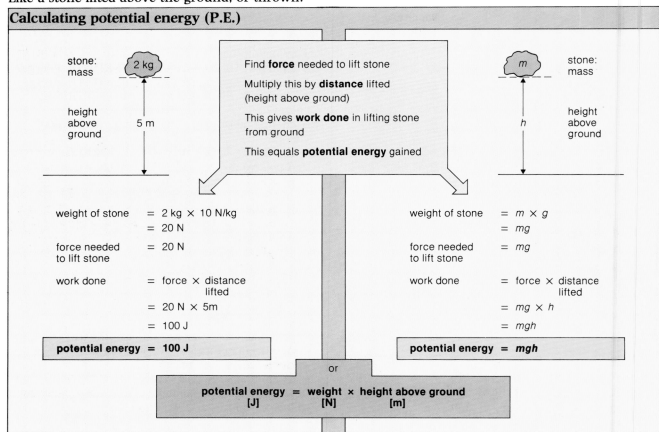

Find **force** needed to lift stone	
Multiply this by **distance** lifted (height above ground)	
This gives **work done** in lifting stone from ground	
This equals **potential energy** gained	

weight of stone	= 2 kg × 10 N/kg
	= 20 N
force needed to lift stone	= 20 N
work done	= force × distance lifted
	= 20 N × 5m
	= 100 J

potential energy = 100 J

weight of stone	= $m \times g$
	= mg
force needed to lift stone	= mg
work done	= force × distance lifted
	= $mg \times h$
	= mgh

potential energy = mgh

or

potential energy = weight × height above ground
[J]   [N]   [m]

Calculating kinetic energy (K.E.)

To calculate the kinetic energy of a stone, mass m and velocity v, use the equation:

kinetic energy $= \frac{1}{2}m v^2$

Look at the box if you want to find out why.

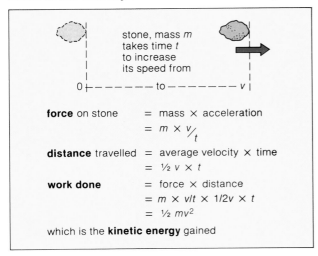

force on stone $=$ mass $\times$ acceleration
$= m \times v/t$

distance travelled $=$ average velocity $\times$ time
$= \frac{1}{2} v \times t$

work done $=$ force $\times$ distance
$= m \times v/t \times 1/2v \times t$
$= \frac{1}{2} mv^2$

which is the **kinetic energy** gained

For example, take a stone of mass 2 kg travelling at a velocity of 6 m/s:

$$\text{kinetic energy} = \frac{1}{2} \times 2 \times 6^2 \quad J = 36\,J$$

Adding energies

What happens if you lift the 2 kg stone 5 m above the ground, *and* throw it at 6 m/s?
The stone has 100 J of potential energy and 36 J of potential energy.
This gives it a total of 136 J. The energies add together easily because energy is not a vector and you don't have to allow for direction.

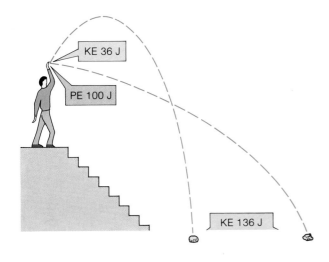

KE 36 J
PE 100 J
KE 136 J

Just before the stone hits the ground, all this energy will be kinetic energy (assuming the stone doesn't lose energy because of air resistance). The stone ends up with the same kinetic energy – and the same speed – whether it is thrown upwards, downwards, or sideways. The direction of throw makes no difference.

Assume $g = 10\,\text{N/kg}$

1

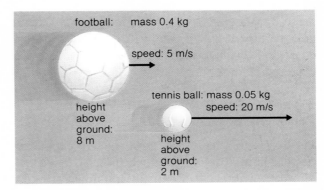

football: mass 0.4 kg
speed: 5 m/s
tennis ball: mass 0.05 kg
speed: 20 m/s
height above ground: 8 m
height above ground: 2 m

Use the information in the diagram to work out:
a the potential energy of each ball
b the kinetic energy of each ball
c the kinetic energy of each ball just before it reaches the ground.

2 Here is some information about a space shuttle in orbit:

mass: 100 tonnes
speed: 8 km/s
height above ground: 100 km

a What is the mass in kg?
b What is the speed in m/s?
c What is the height above the ground in metres?
d What is the potential energy the shuttle?
e What is its kinetic energy?
f How much energy must it lose before coming to a halt on the ground?
g What happens to this energy?

2.4 Engines

For smooth running, there's nothing quite like a steam engine under the bonnet. And this 1920 Stanley Steamer was the last production car to have one. You lit the fuel, waited 20 minutes for the water to boil, and were off – at anything up to 80 mph.

The job of all engines is to make things move. They do so by turning energy in their fuel into kinetic energy. Steam is still used in the world's largest engines. But for modern road vehicles, there are other possibilities:

Petrol engines

Petrol engines use the force of an exploding petrol/air mixture to produce motion. Most engines follow a cycle of four up and down strokes. During one of the strokes, the mixture is exploded, and the force used to move a piston in a cylinder. During the other three strokes, burnt gases are removed and a fresh mixture prepared for explosion.

Diesel engines

Diesel engines also follow a four stroke cycle. But they use fuel oil instead of petrol.

Air entering the engine is compressed so much that it becomes very hot. Fuel oil is squirted straight into the cylinders. The oil ignites as soon as it meets the hot air. So diesel engines don't need spark plugs.

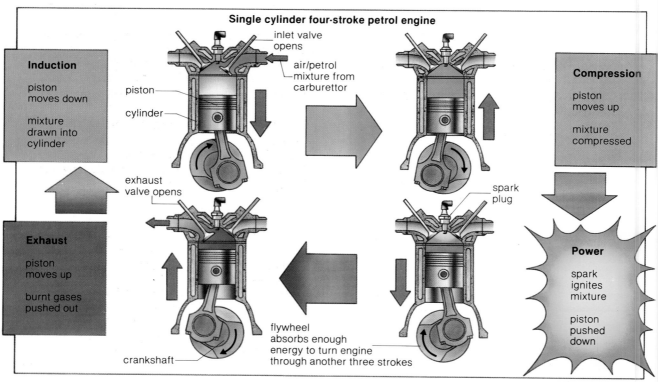

Single cylinder four-stroke petrol engine

Induction

piston moves down

mixture drawn into cylinder

inlet valve opens

air/petrol mixture from carburettor

piston

cylinder

Compression

piston moves up

mixture compressed

spark plug

exhaust valve opens

Exhaust

piston moves up

burnt gases pushed out

crankshaft

flywheel absorbs enough energy to turn engine through another three strokes

Power

spark ignites mixture

piston pushed down

How engines compare

The fuel for petrol and diesel engines comes from crude oil – and the Earth's stocks of that are slowly running out. Electric motors don't use fuel directly. But they need an electric current, and that may well come from a fuel-burning power station. However, there is one type of engine that doesn't have these problems. . . .

	petrol	diesel	electric	human
engine				
energy source	petrol	fuel oil	battery	food
advantages	• good performance for low cost and weight	• uses less fuel than petrol engine	• quiet • no air pollution from motor • works well at low speeds	• quiet • little air pollution • works well at low speeds • fuel can be regrown
disadvantages	• work poorly at low speeds, need clutch and gearbox • pollute atmosphere fuels cannot be replaced	• heavier, more expensive than petrol engine	• batteries very heavy and can't store much energy	• poor at moving heavy loads quickly

1 Vans with diesel engines cost more to buy than vans with petrol engines. But they use less fuel. Electric-powered vans are slower than either, and very expensive. The table below gives some information about the cost of hiring each type of van.
a Which van has the lowest fuel or energy bill for a 100 kilometre journey?
b How long does each van take to travel 100 km?
c What is the total cost of a 100 km journey in each van? Remember to include hire charges as well as fuel or energy costs.
d What is the total cost of a 300 km journey in each van?

e If you wanted to use as little energy as possible, which van would you select?
f If you were interested in keeping your costs down, which van would you select for a short journey? Which would you select for a long journey?

2 Petrol and diesel engines take in fuel and produce movement.
a What type of energy do they take in?
b What happens to this energy inside the engine?
c What type of energy do they give out?

	hire charge van and driver	energy cost per 100 km	average speed
Van A: petrol	£20 (+£5 per hour)	£6 (fuel)	50 km/hour
Van B: diesel	£24 (+£5 per hour)	£4 (fuel)	50 km/hour
Van C: electric	£30 (+£5 per hour)	£2 (recharging)	25 km/hour

2.5 Efficiency and power

Like most other engines, the human engine is a wasteful user of fuel.
If you are pedalling hard on a bike;
for every 100 joules of energy released from your food, only about 15 joules is used to work;
the rest is turned into heat – you sweat to get rid of it.

The efficiency of an engine is calculated as follows:

$$\text{efficiency} = \frac{\text{work output}}{\text{energy input}}$$

So the efficiency of a cyclist = 15/100.
This can be written as a percentage; 15%.
Here's how other engines compare:

For every 100 J of energy put into a . . .		the work done is . . .	the efficiency is . . .
petrol engine		25 J	25%
diesel engine		35 J	35%
electric motor		80 J	80%
human engine		15 J	15%

Only the electric motor seems to have a high efficiency. But that value is deceiving. Electricity for the motor has to be generated, and the efficiency of that process is only about 30%.

Why are engines such poor energy converters? It isn't the fault of the manufacturers. They constantly seek new ways of reducing engine friction and improving fuel burning. The problem lies with the laws which govern how molecules behave. Once molecules absorb heat, it is impossible to use some of that energy for work.

Power

A Metro engine can do just as much work as a Land Rover engine. But it takes longer to do it. The Land Rover engine has more power than the Metro engine; it can do more joules of work *every second*.

Power is measured in **watts (W)**.
An engine with a power output of 1000 watts can do 1000 joules of work every second.
An engine with a power output of 2000 watts can do 2000 joules of work every second. And so on.

Power is calculated using the equation:

$$\text{power} = \frac{\text{work done}}{\text{time taken}} \quad \text{or} \quad \frac{\text{energy changed}}{\text{time taken}}$$

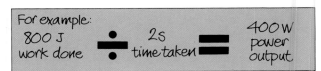

For example:
800 J work done ÷ 2s time taken = 400 W power output

Powers are sometimes given in **kilowatts** or **megawatts**:
1 kilowatt (kW) = 1000 watts
1 megawatt (MW) = 1 000 000 watts

Typical power outputs

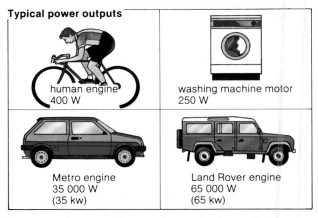

human engine 400 W

washing machine motor 250 W

Metro engine 35 000 W (35 kW)

Land Rover engine 65 000 W (65 kW)

Power values can be used to calculate efficiency:

$$\text{efficiency} = \frac{\text{power output}}{\text{power input}}$$

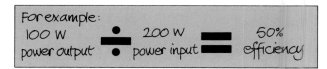

For example:
100 W power output ÷ 200 W power input = 50% efficiency

How to measure your power output:

Assume $g = 10\,\text{N/kg}$.

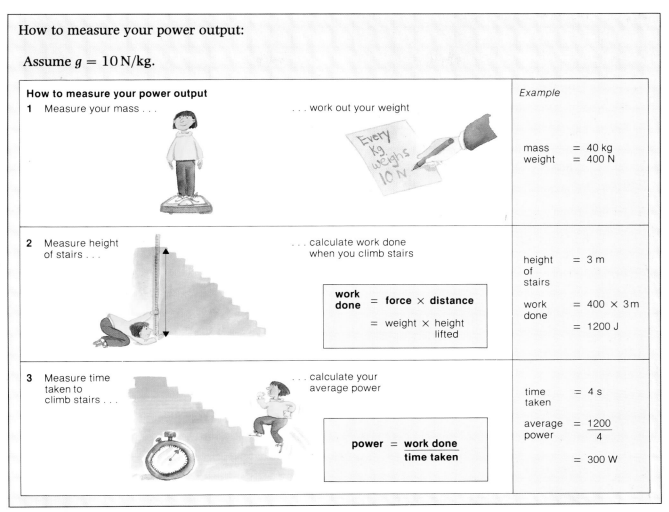

How to measure your power output		Example
1 Measure your mass . . . . . . work out your weight		mass = 40 kg weight = 400 N
2 Measure height of stairs . . . . . . calculate work done when you climb stairs **work done = force × distance** = weight × height lifted		height of stairs = 3 m work done = 400 × 3 m = 1200 J
3 Measure time taken to climb stairs . . . . . . calculate your average power **power = $\dfrac{\text{work done}}{\text{time taken}}$**		time taken = 4 s average power = $\dfrac{1200}{4}$ = 300 W

Assume $g = 10\,\text{N/kg}$.

1 The cheetah is the fastest creature on land. A typical cheetah, at full speed, has a power output of 1000 W, and an efficiency of 15%.

Mike is possibly the slowest creature on land. When he works in the garden (which isn't very often), his power output is 100 W, and his efficiency 5%.
Calculate
a the work done by the cheetah in 1 second.
b how long it takes Mike to do the same amount of work.
In unfolding his garden chair, Mike gets 2000 J of energy from the food he has eaten.
Calculate
c how much work he does.
Write down what happens to the rest of the energy released.

2 A skier has a mass of 50 kg.
It takes her 40 seconds to climb 20 m (vertically) to the top of a slope.
Calculate
a her weight.
b the work done when she climbs the slope.
c her average power output.
Why, in reality, will she have to do more work than you have calculated?

2.6 Machines

Anything which makes forces more convenient to use is called a **machine**. It may be as complicated as a gearbox or as simple as a pair of scissors.

Some machines are **force magnifiers**.
A pair of pliers for example. These give you a greater force at the jaws than you put in at the handles.

Some machines are **movement magnifiers**.
A bicycle for example. One downward push on the pedals takes you forward over 3 metres – much further than one step would take you if you were walking.

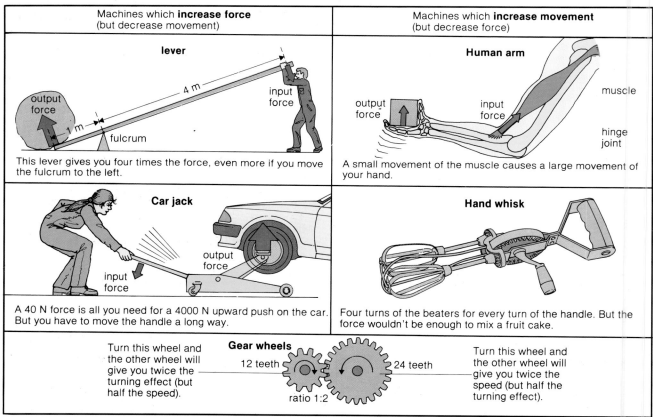

Machines which **increase force** (but decrease movement)	Machines which **increase movement** (but decrease force)
lever 4 m / output force / 1 m / input force / fulcrum This lever gives you four times the force, even more if you move the fulcrum to the left.	**Human arm** muscle / output force / input force / hinge joint A small movement of the muscle causes a large movement of your hand.
Car jack input force / output force A 40 N force is all you need for a 4000 N upward push on the car. But you have to move the handle a long way.	**Hand whisk** Four turns of the beaters for every turn of the handle. But the force wouldn't be enough to mix a fruit cake.
Turn this wheel and the other wheel will give you twice the turning effect (but half the speed).	**Gear wheels** 12 teeth / 24 teeth / ratio 1:2	Turn this wheel and the other wheel will give you twice the speed (but half the turning effect).

No machine magnifies both force *and* movement. If it did, you would get more work out of the machine than you put into it:

work = force × distance moved

so, if a machine *increases* force, it must *decrease* distance moved. And vice versa.

Most machines have friction between their moving parts. This means that some energy is lost as heat. And you get less useable energy out of the machine than you put in.
In other words:
the work output is less than the work input; the efficiency is less than 100%.

Measuring the efficiency of a machine

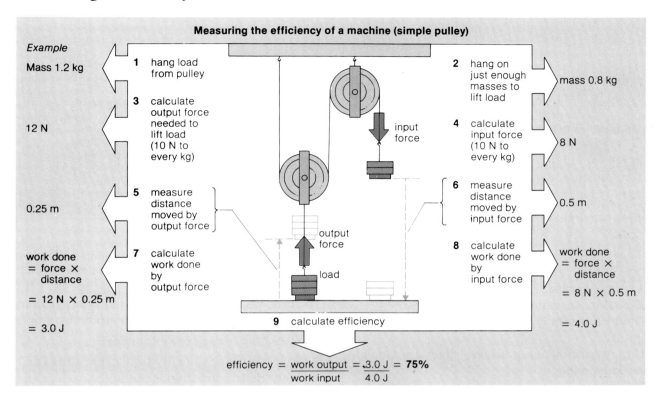

Measuring the efficiency of a machine (simple pulley)

Example

Mass 1.2 kg

1 hang load from pulley

2 hang on just enough masses to lift load — mass 0.8 kg

12 N

3 calculate output force needed to lift load (10 N to every kg)

4 calculate input force (10 N to every kg) — 8 N

0.25 m

5 measure distance moved by output force

6 measure distance moved by input force — 0.5 m

output force

load

input force

work done = force × distance

7 calculate work done by output force

8 calculate work done by input force

= 12 N × 0.25 m

= 3.0 J

work done = force × distance

= 8 N × 0.5 m

= 4.0 J

9 calculate efficiency

efficiency = $\dfrac{\text{work output}}{\text{work input}}$ = $\dfrac{3.0\ \text{J}}{4.0\ \text{J}}$ = **75%**

---

1 Make two lists to show which of these are FORCE magnifiers and which are MOVEMENT magnifiers:

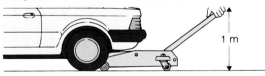

Nail clippers   Kitchen scales
Bottle opener   Hole punch
Pincers   Hand drill
Door handle   Tin opener

2 Dave and Sue are about to use a car jack to lift their car. Here is some information about the car and the jack:

car	car jack
force needed to lift rear of car = 2000 N	distance moved by handle during one stroke = 1 m
	input force to lift rear end of car = 20 N

How much work must be done to lift the rear of the car 1 metre?
Sue says that it will take at least 100 strokes to lift the rear of the car 1 metre. Dave says it won't. Who is right? And why?

3 A mechanic uses a pulley to lift an engine out of a car.
The engine weighs 500 N, and is lifted 2 m.
The mechanic uses a force of 200 N on the rope, which is pulled downwards a distance of 10 m.
Calculate
a the work done on the engine in lifting it.
b the work done by the mechanic.
c the efficiency of the pulley.

4 A, B, and C are three gear wheels.

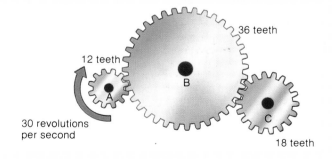

36 teeth
12 teeth
B
A
C
18 teeth
30 revolutions per second

A is rotated 30 times per second.
Copy the diagram.
Show which direction each wheel is turning.
Write down the number of times per second each wheel is turning.

2.7 Liquid machines

In the digger in the photograph the shovels are moved by high pressure oil in flexible pipes.

The basic idea is simple:

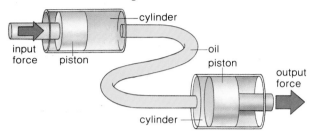

A pump or piston pushes on the oil at one end. The oil moves a piston at the other end.

The idea works because liquids have two special features:

1 they cannot be squashed – they are virtually incompressible.

2 if a trapped liquid is put under pressure, the pressure is transmitted to all parts of the liquid.

Machines which use trapped liquids in this way are called **hydraulic** machines.

Force magnifiers

Most hydraulic machines are force magnifiers. They give out more force than is put in. This happens because the output piston is larger than the input piston. To find out why, study the simple hydraulic jack on the opposite page.

Like all other machines, hydraulic machines can't give out more *work* than is put in:

work = force × distance moved

so, if a machine *increases* force, it *decreases* the distance moved. In other words, the output force doesn't move as far as the input force.

Hydraulics in action

Caterpillar tracks: driven by hydraulic motors fed with high pressure oil from a pump.

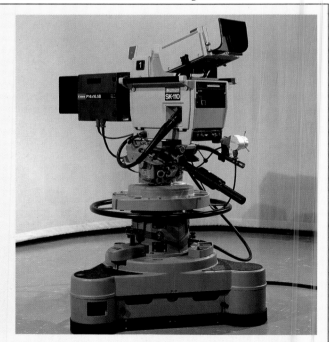

TV camera: hydraulic action raises and lowers the camera on its mount.

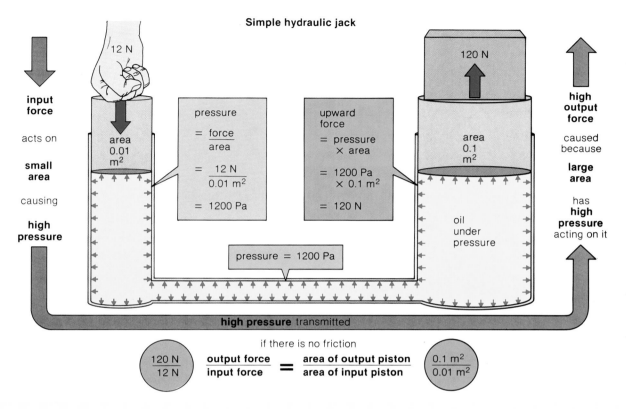

Simple hydraulic jack

12 N

input force

acts on

small area

causing

high pressure

area 0.01 m²

pressure = force / area = 12 N / 0.01 m² = 1200 Pa

upward force = pressure × area = 1200 Pa × 0.1 m² = 120 N

120 N

high output force

caused because

large area

has high pressure acting on it

area 0.1 m²

oil under pressure

pressure = 1200 Pa

high pressure transmitted

if there is no friction

120 N / 12 N   **output force / input force** = **area of output piston / area of input piston**   0.1 m² / 0.01 m²

1 Decide whether each of the following statements is TRUE or FALSE.
a Liquids are virtually impossible to compress
b If a trapped liquid is under pressure, the pressure is transmitted throughout the liquid
c A machine can give out more force than is put into it
d A machine can give out more work than is put into it.
2 The diagram shows the basic layout of a car's hydraulic brake system.
The brake pedal is a simple lever which magnifies the force from the foot.
The disc is attached to a road wheel. It slows down when the brake pad is pushed against it.

(In an actual car, the disc would be squeezed between two pads. And the fluid would be piped to brakes on all four wheels.)
Using the information in the diagram, calculate
a the force on the piston A
b the pressure on the fluid at B
c the pressure on the fluid at C
d the force on the brake pad
Say whether the force on the pad would be MORE or LESS
e if the connecting point O was nearer the pivot
f if the area of piston A was less
Can you think of any reasons why water isn't used in the brake system?

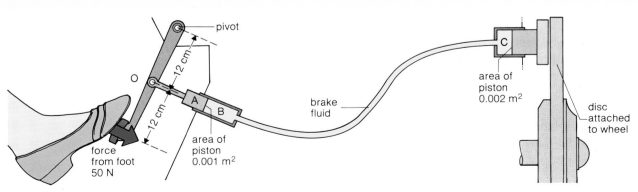

pivot

O

12 cm

12 cm

A
B

force from foot 50 N

area of piston 0.001 m²

brake fluid

C

area of piston 0.002 m²

disc attached to wheel

2.8 Energy resources

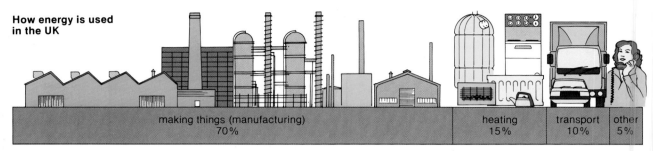

How energy is used in the UK

| making things (manufacturing) 70% | heating 15% | transport 10% | other 5% |

Industrial societies need huge amounts of energy. Most comes from fuels which are burnt in power stations, factories, homes, and vehicles.

The energy in fuels originally came from the Sun. So did the energy in the foods we eat.

Energy from the Sun...

...in fuels

...in foods

natural gas

oil

coal

plants take in radiant energy from the Sun as they grow

fossil fuels formed from decayed plants and animals which lived over 200 million years ago

animals eat plants

When food is eaten, more can be grown. It is a **renewable** energy source. But coal, oil and natural gas can't be renewed. And the Earth's supply of them is gradually running out. At present rates of use,
– there is probably enough oil and natural gas left to last for 50–100 years;
– there is enough coal left to last for 200–300 years.

Oil is an especially useful material:
– it contains fuels like petrol and diesel. These aren't very bulky, so they can be carried and used in vehicles.
– it is the raw material from which most plastics are made.
With oil supplies running out, it makes sense to save what is left for transport and plastics.

Alternative energy sources

Here are some alternatives to coal, oil and natural gas. Most are renewable. Once used, the energy is replaced naturally.

Wind energy Giant windmills are used to turn electrical generators.	*For:* renewable energy source *Against:* windmills large and costly, with relatively low power output. Not enough wind in many areas.
Hydroelectric energy Rivers fill a lake behind a dam. Fast-flowing water from the lake turns generators.	*For:* renewable energy source *Against:* few areas of the world suitable.
Tidal energy A dam is built across an estuary. A lake behind the dam fills up at high tide, and empties at low tide. Fast flowing water turns generators. The Earth's movement is the source of tidal energy. The Moon's gravitational pull causes 'bulges' of sea water on the Earth's surface. As the Earth rotates, each part passes in and out of a bulge – the tide rises and falls.	*For:* renewable energy source. *Against:* very expensive to set up; few areas suitable.
Solar energy Mirrors and panels are used to capture the Sun's radiant energy – usually as heat.	*For:* renewable energy source *Against:* continuous sunshine needed.
Nuclear energy Radioactive materials naturally release heat. A nuclear reactor speeds up the process. The heat is used to generate electricity (see page 184).	*For:* Small amounts of nuclear fuel give large amounts of energy. *Against:* Nuclear radiation extremely dangerous. High safety standards needed. Waste materials from power stations stay radioactive for thousands of years.
Geothermal energy Water is heated by the hot rocks which lie many miles beneath the Earth's surface. The heat in the rocks comes from radio-active materials naturally present in the Earth.	*For:* renewable energy source. Huge quantities of energy available. *Against:* Deep drilling very difficult and expensive.
Biomass energy Fast growing plants, or *biomass*, used to make alcohol. Alcohol used as a fuel, like petrol.	*For:* renewable energy source *Against:* Huge land areas needed to grow plants; this may upset the balance of nature.

1 What is the difference between a renewable and a non-renewable source of energy?

2 COAL OIL BIOMASS WIND TIDES NATURAL GAS
Which of these are renewable energy sources, and which are not?

3 When you eat a cheese sandwich, you take in energy which came from the Sun. How does the energy pass from
a the Sun to the bread
b the Sun to the cheese?

2.9 Saving energy

Escaping heat

Lost heat can cost a family well over £500 a year in fuel bills. This is how the heat escapes from a house:

New air for old

Stopping draughts and air changes saves most on the fuel bills. But it can put your health – and even your life – at risk. If rooms are tightly sealed, the oxygen used by people and fires isn't replaced. And dangerous chemicals collect in the air:

For safety's sake, there should be at least one complete change of air in a room every hour. In a draughty house, there may be 15 more. This is good for clearing the air, but it makes the house very expensive to heat.

Low-energy families

The Birkebaeks live in Denmark. They had this low-energy house specially designed and built for them. In winter, the power of a one-bar electric heater is enough to heat the whole house.

The house cost them over £250 000, including the land and architect's fees.

10% roof

30% walls

15% windows

35% draughts and air changes

10% floor

radioactive radon gas seeping from bricks and ground

methanal fumes from chipboard furniture

cigarette smoke

nitrogen dioxide from gas cooker

carbon monoxide from gas fire

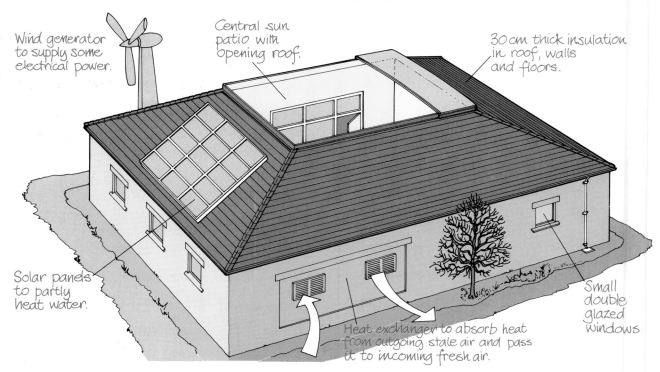

Wind generator to supply some electrical power.

Central sun patio with opening roof.

30 cm thick insulation in roof, walls and floors.

Solar panels to partly heat water.

Heat exchanger to absorb heat from outgoing stale air and pass it to incoming fresh air.

Small double glazed windows

The Cottrells live in Newcastle. Their house is sandwiched between two others. This helps stop some heat loss. But the house is still cold and draughty. They would like to replace the doors and windows with modern ones that fit properly. But they can't afford to. They save energy by heating only one room. It means that their bedroom is very cold in winter, but they can pay the fuel bills.

When power stations generate electricity, much of the energy from their fuels is lost as heat. The heat warms up the cooling water that flows through the power station. Usually, the energy is

wasted. But one idea is to use the warmed water to heat buildings nearby.

But there is a problem. Power station water isn't quite hot enough for room heating. To produce hotter water, each power station would have to lose some of its power output. And that would make it more difficult for the Electricity Board to stay in profit.

Going to waste

What causes the greatest loss of heat in most houses?
Why can it be dangerous to stop this loss completely?

Design a laboratory experiment to find out which loses most heat – a terraced house, a semi-detached house, or a detached house.

How would you set up the experiment and what measurements would you make?

When comparing houses, how would you make sure that your results were 'fair'?

How would you modify your experiment to test whether:
● big houses lose more heat than small houses;
● houses with big windows lose more heat than houses with small windows?

terraced

semi-detached

detached

2.10 Moving molecules

Like the land, sea and air in the photograph, everything around you is either a solid, a liquid or a gas. The **kinetic theory of matter** tries to explain how solids, liquids and gases behave. Read the evidence, then judge for yourself.

The kinetic theory

According to this theory, solids, liquids, and gases are made up of tiny particles called **molecules**. These are far too small to see. They are constantly on the move. When close, they attract each other strongly, and may even stick together.

A **solid**, such as rock, has a fixed shape and volume. Its molecules are held close together by strong forces of attraction. They vibrate to and fro, but can't change positions.

A **liquid**, such as water, has a fixed volume, but can flow to fill any shape. Its molecules are still close together. But they vibrate so vigorously that the forces of attraction can't hold them in fixed positions.

A **gas**, such as air, has no fixed shape or volume. It quickly fills any space available. Its molecules move about at high speed – colliding with each other and the walls of their container. They attract each other hardly at all, and are too spread out to stick together.

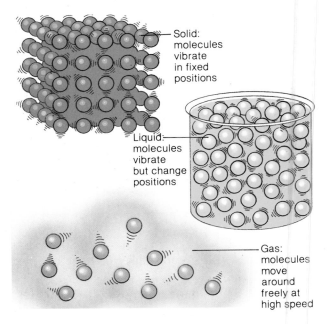

Solid: molecules vibrate in fixed positions

Liquid: molecules vibrate but change positions

Gas: molecules move around freely at high speed

Moving molecules – the evidence

Look at smoke through a microscope, and you see a very interesting effect. Glinting in the light, thousands of tiny 'bits' of smoke wobble about in zig-zag paths as they drift through the air. This is called Brownian motion, after the scientist Robert Brown, who first noticed it.

The kinetic theory explains the effect as follows: The smoke particles are just big enough to be seen, but small and light enough to be bumped and jostled by the invisible air molecules around them. They make their jerky movements because air molecules keep crashing into them.

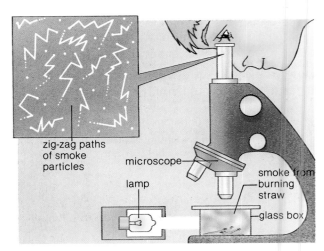

zig-zag paths of smoke particles

microscope

lamp

smoke from burning straw

glass box

Wandering molecules

Sit and watch the sugary bits on top of a trifle for a day or two, and you may notice that the colours run. According to the kinetic theory, loose molecules from the colouring material slowly wander through the surrounding material as they are bumped and jostled by its molecules. The process is called **diffusion**.

Smells spread by diffusion. Smells are wandering gas molecules which come from whatever it is that happens to be smelling.

Molecules – how big?

The diagram shows an experiment you can carry out to estimate the size of a molecule of olive oil. The idea is to place a small drop of the oil onto the surface of some water, so that it spreads to form a thin circular layer. When the oil has spread as far as it can, it will be just one molecule thick.

First, sprinkle some lycopodium powder over the surface of some clean water in a tray. The powder makes it easier to see the edge of the oil layer.

Next, pick up a small drop of olive oil on the end of a wire. Use a millimetre scale to measure the diameter of the drop, so that you can calculate its volume.

Then, put the oil drop onto the water surface, and see how far it spreads. Measure the diameter of the circular layer and calculate its area.

The volume of the oil drop is exactly the same as the volume of the circular layer, so:

volume of drop = area of layer × thickness

rearranging

$$\frac{\text{thickness}}{\text{(size of molecule)}} = \frac{\text{volume of drop}}{\text{area of layer}}$$

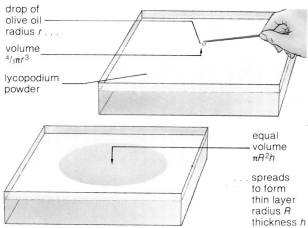

drop of olive oil
radius r . . .

volume
$^4/_3\pi r^3$

lycopodium powder

equal volume
$\pi R^2 h$

. . . spreads to form thin layer
radius R
thickness h

Experiments show that molecules vary enormously in size. Molecules of proteins from living tissue, for example, are many thousands of times larger than the smallest molecules. In the case of a medium-sized molecule like olive oil, there are around a million to each millimetre. You can use the readings in question 4 to estimate the size for yourself.

1 Say whether each of the following describes a SOLID, a LIQUID or a GAS:
a molecules moving about at high speed;
b molecules vibrate but can't change positions;
c fixed shape and volume;
d molecules vibrate but can change positions;
e no fixed shape or volume;
f fixed volume, but no fixed shape;
g forces of attraction very weak.
2 What do you see if you look at smoke through a microscope?
How does the kinetic theory explain the behaviour of the smoke?
3 Which of the following are examples of *diffusion*?
a water flowing and changing shape;
b ink spreading when dropped in water;
c a smell travelling across a room;
d the molecules in a solid vibrating.
4 A drop of olive oil has a volume of $0.3 \, \text{mm}^3$.
Placed on water, it spreads to form a circular layer of area $200\,000 \, \text{mm}^2$. What is the size of a molecule of olive oil?

2.11 Temperature

Death Valley, California. The hottest place on Earth. Certainly hotter than ice. But not as hot as boiling water. You can tell that from its **temperature**.

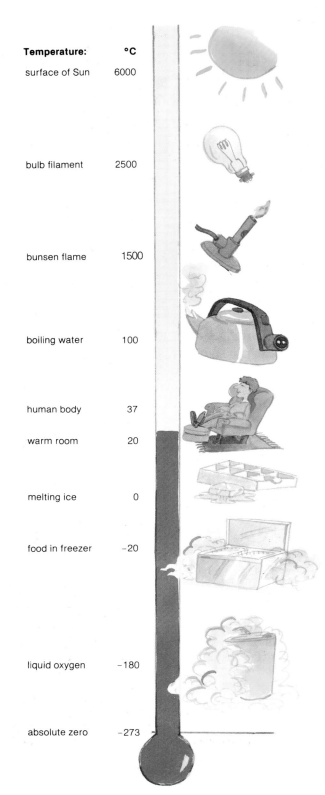

Temperature:	°C
surface of Sun	6000
bulb filament	2500
bunsen flame	1500
boiling water	100
human body	37
warm room	20
melting ice	0
food in freezer	−20
liquid oxygen	−180
absolute zero	−273

The Celsius scale

The **Celsius** or centigrade scale is the most widely used temperature scale.

On this scale:
The numbers are called **degrees Celsius**, and written °C;
Pure ice melts at 0°C;
Pure water boils at 100°C
(provided atmospheric pressure is exactly 760 mm of mercury)

Many things are colder than melting ice. These are given minus temperatures on the scale.

What is temperature?

If your soup is too hot to eat, you don't have to do anything about it. Just wait. As time passes, the molecules of the soup lose heat energy to the air. They slow down, and the temperature falls. Eventually, the soup cools to the same temperature as the air. Heat energy no longer flows from soup to air because each soup molecule has exactly the same kinetic energy, on average, as each air molecule.

When the temperature falls, molecules move more slowly.

Two things have the same temperature if their molecules each have the same average kinetic energy.

Same temperature, different heat energy

Don't confuse temperature with heat. The soup in the spoon is at the same temperature as the soup in the bowl. But you would get much less heat energy from it if you accidentally spilled it over yourself.

Absolute zero

Nothing can be cooled below −273°C. This is the coldest possible temperature. It is called **absolute zero**.

As something cools, its molecules move more slowly. They can never stop moving altogether. But at absolute zero, their movement is the minimum possible. They can't go any slower, so the temperature can't fall any more.

The Kelvin scale

Scientists often measure temperatures using the **Kelvin** temperature scale. Its 'degree' is called a **kelvin**, and written **K**. Each kelvin on the scale is the same size as a degree Celsius. But the zero on the scale is at absolute zero.
Converting from one scale to another is easy:

$$\text{Kelvin temperature} = \text{Celsius temperature} + 273$$

Temperature:	Celsius	Kelvin
	200 °C	473 K
boiling water	100 °C	373 K
melting ice	0 °C	273 K
	−100 °C	173 K
absolute zero	−273 °C	0 K

1

−273	0	100	273	373

Say which of these is the temperature of
a boiling water in °C   **b** boiling water in K
c absolute zero in °C   **d** absolute zero in K
e melting ice in °C   **f** melting ice in K

2 One day in August, these were the temperatures at midday in four holiday resorts:

IBIZA	33°C
TORREMOLINOS	300 K
PALMA	38°C
BENIDORM	309 K

Rewrite the list in order of temperature, with the warmest resort at the top.

3
Nick grows tomato plants in a small greenhouse. One summer's day, this is how the temperature in his greenhouse varied, from 9 o'clock in the morning onward:

time in hours	0	1	2	3	4	5	6	7	8
temperature in °C	24	28	32	36	39	40	38	36	33

a Plot a graph of temperature against time. Mark the side axis in °C and the bottom axis in hours.
b What was the maximum temperature in the greenhouse in kelvin?
c For how long was the temperature above 36°C?
d Nick meant to open a window when the temperature reached 30°C, to stop his plants getting too hot. But he forgot. At what time should he have opened the window?

2.12 Thermometers

To measure a temperature, you need a thermometer. The problem is deciding which type.

Mercury thermometers

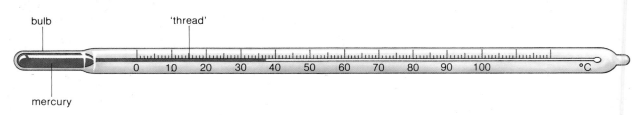

These are made of glass. They have a bulb at one end containing mercury. When the temperature rises, the mercury expands and moves further along the narrow tube.

Mercury thermometers can't measure temperatures below $-39°C$ because the mercury goes solid. Most just cover the range from $0°C$ to $100°C$.

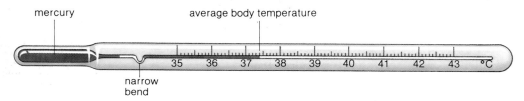

The clinical thermometer Doctors and nurses uses a special type of mercury thermometer to measure the temperature of the human body:
– it only covers a few degrees either side of the average body temperature of $37°C$. But it measures these temperatures very accurately.

– the tube has a narrow bend at the bottom to stop the mercury running back into the bulb. This means that you can take the reading after the thermometer has been taken out of the patient's mouth. You then have to shake the mercury back into the bulb.

Alcohol thermometers

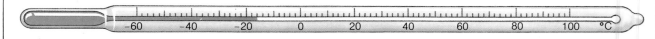

These work in just the same way as mercury thermometers. But they are cheaper, easier to read, and they can measure lower temperatures. Alcohol doesn't turn solid until $-115°C$.
If you have a thermometer in your 'fridge or freezer, it's probably an alcohol thermometer.

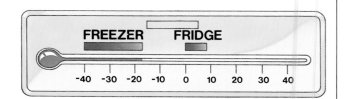

Electrical thermometers

ANSWER:

GO ELECTRICAL!

● **EASY TO READ**
Choice of pointer reading or digital display

● **READINGS IN COMFORT**
Scale can be placed well away from the temperature detector

● **CAN BE READ BY COMPUTER**
For automatic temperature readings, feed the electrical signal straight to a computer.

● **WIDE TEMPERATURE RANGE**
−200°C to 1600°C or more

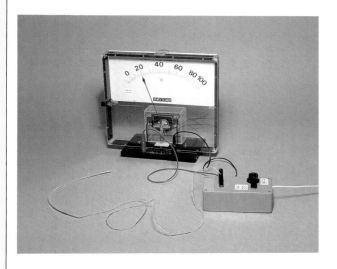

A thermocouple thermometer. If one junction is hotter than the other, a current flows. This moves the pointer along the scale.

1 Explain why you probably wouldn't use the following:
a an ordinary mercury thermometer to measure your body temperature.
b a clinical thermometer to measure the temperature of some water as it cooled rapidly.
c a mercury thermometer to measure the temperature of 'dry ice' (about −80°C).
d a clinical thermometer to measure the temperature at which salted water boils.

2 Say what type of thermometer you would use to measure:
a the temperature of 'dry ice'.
b the temperature of a furnace at around 2000°C.
c the temperature of a kiln around 1000°C.
d the temperature in a freezer.
3 Look at the diagrams on the opposite page. Then write down the temperature reading on:
a the ordinary MERCURY THERMOMETER
b the CLINICAL THERMOMETER
c the ALCOHOL THERMOMETER

2.13 Expansion

The plane that grows

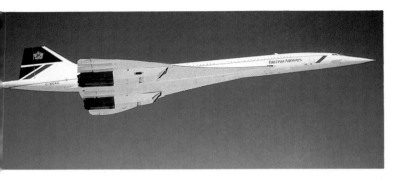

How long is Concorde?

It depends on the temperature.

Like most other materials, the metal body of Concorde expands when heated. At supersonic speeds, when friction from the air heats Concorde's outer skin to around 1000°C, the plane is nearly half a metre longer than it is on the ground.

Expansion problems

Materials which **expand** when **heated, contract** when **cooled**. Usually the change in size is too small to notice. But it can cause problems. The force produced by an expansion or contraction can be enough to break concrete blocks or buckle steel girders.

Why things expand

Heat a solid, and its molecules vibrate more rapidly. The vibrations take up more space. The molecules push each other further apart.

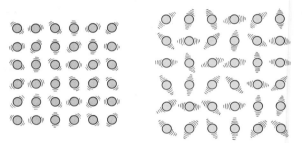

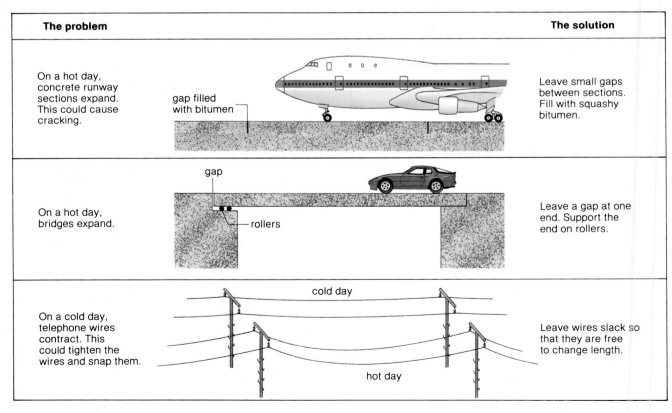

The problem		The solution
On a hot day, concrete runway sections expand. This could cause cracking.	gap filled with bitumen	Leave small gaps between sections. Fill with squashy bitumen.
On a hot day, bridges expand.	gap — rollers	Leave a gap at one end. Support the end on rollers.
On a cold day, telephone wires contract. This could tighten the wires and snap them.	cold day · hot day	Leave wires slack so that they are free to change length.

Expansions compared

Some things expand more than others when heated. The chart shows how much 1 metre lengths of different materials expand when heated by just 100°C:

Steel rods can be used to reinforce concrete because steel and concrete have the same expansion. If the expansions were different, the steel might crack the concrete on a hot day.

Put an ordinary glass dish straight into a hot oven, and the dish is likely to break. The outside of the glass expands before the inside, and the strain cracks the glass. This shouldn't happen with a Pyrex dish, because Pyrex glass expands much less than ordinary glass.

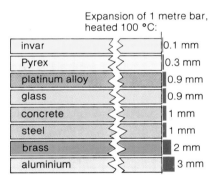

Expansion of 1 metre bar, heated 100 °C:

invar	0.1 mm
Pyrex	0.3 mm
platinum alloy	0.9 mm
glass	0.9 mm
concrete	1 mm
steel	1 mm
brass	2 mm
aluminium	3 mm

Calculating expansion

A **1 metre** bar of steel heated **1°C** expands **0.000 01 metres**:
steel has a **linear expansivity of 0.000 01/°C**

If you know the linear expansivity of a material you can work out the expansion of any length for any temperature rise:

**expansion = linear × original × temperature
(increase   expansivity   length   rise
in length)**

For example if the temperature of a 100 m bridge rises by 20°C on a hot sunny day:

increase = 0.000 01 × 100 × 20 m
in length

= 0.02 m (20 mm)

1 Copy, and fill in the blanks:
Most materials __ when heated and __ when cooled. They do so because their __ vibrate more __ and push each other apart. If expansion is resisted in can produce a very high __. To allow for expansion in bridges a __ has to be left at one end.

To answer the following questions, you will need information from the expansion chart on this page.
2 In a light bulb, platinum alloy wires, sealed in glass, are used to carry the electric current to the filament.

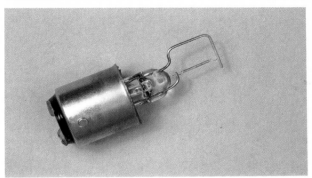

Explain why the wires don't crack the glass when the bulb heats up.
3 Expansion can be resisted. Railway lines are fixed to heavy concrete sleepers embedded in chippings, so that they hardly expand at all.
Calculate how much a 1000 metre length of steel railway line would expand, if it were free to, if the temperature rose by 10°C.
4 An engineer is designing a concrete footbridge over a motorway.
She has to allow for a maximum temperature rise of 40°C. Has she left enough room for expansion?
40°C. The linear expansivity of concrete is 0.000 01/°C. Has she left enough room for expansion?

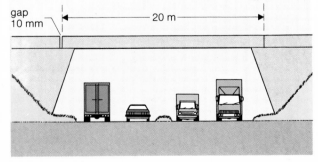

gap 10 mm   ← 20 m →

5 Explain why
a telephone wires are left slack when hung between poles
b concrete roads have bitumen-filled gaps across them
c steel can be used to reinforce concrete.

2.14 Using expansion

In home...

Can't get the top off a bottle? Try putting it in hot water. The top expands before the heat reaches the bottle. This makes it a looser fit.

The bimetal strip

This is made by bonding together two thin strips of metal. The one in the diagram is made of brass and invar.

When the strip is heated, the brass expands more than the invar. This makes the strip bend. The brass is on the outside of the bend, because the distance round the outside of the curve is greater than round the inside.

If the strip were cooled, instead of heated, it would bend the opposite way.

Making a bimetal fire alarm

... and factory

Fitting an axle into a wheel.
Liquid nitrogen cools the axle to around −200°C. This makes it contract, so that it fits easily into the wheel. When the axle warms up again, it expands to give a tight fit.

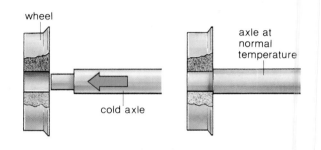

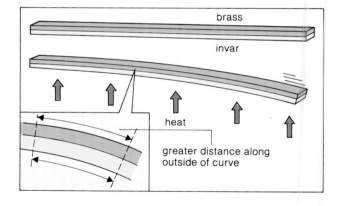

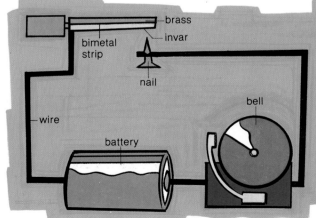

The bell can't work because there is a break in the circuit.

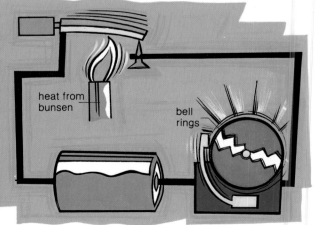

Heat bends the bimetal strip and closes the gap.

Thermostats

There is a **thermostat** fitted to each of these. Its job is to keep the temperature steady:

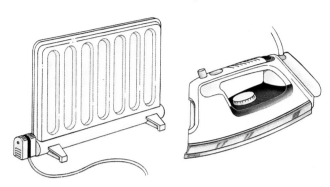

Take the thermostat in the electric room heater. If the room is too hot, it has to cut off the power to the heater. When the room cools down, it has to switch the power back on again. This is done using a small bimetal strip.

When the temperature rises, the bimetal strip starts to bend. Eventually, the contacts separate, and the flow of electricity to the heater is cut. When the temperature falls, the bimetal strip straightens. The contacts touch, and electricity again flows to the heater.

You select the temperature by turning the control knob. Answer question 3 to find out why.

1 Copy and complete:
When heated, brass __ more than invar.
When cooled, brass __ more than invar.
If strips of brass and invar are bonded together, they form a __ __. This __ when it is heated.
2 What has happened to each strip to make it bend the way it has?

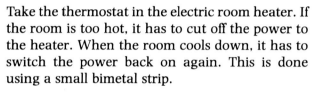

3 Study the diagram of the bimetal thermostat.
a Explain what happens when the temperature in the room rises.
b If the control knob is screwed inwards, the contacts are pushed more firmly together. Will the contacts now separate at a HIGHER or LOWER temperature than before?

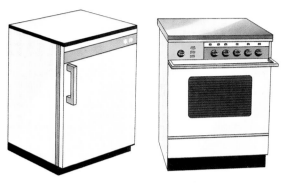

c How would you adjust the control knob to LOWER the temperature in the room?
4 The fire alarm on the opposite page is set off by a bunsen flame. What adjustment could you make so that it was set off by a much smaller rise in temperature?
5 Over 10 million bimetal strips at work every day – and that's just in the UK.

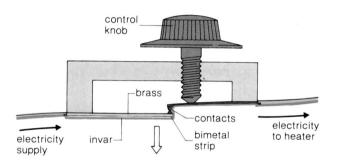

When the light is ON, so is the heating coil.
What effect does this have on the bimetal strip?
What effect does this have on the light and the coil?
What happens to the bimetal strip as a result?
What effect does this have on the light and the coil?
Can you think of a use for this process?

2.15 Expanding liquids

They don't leave space at the tops of lemonade bottles to cheat you. The space is to allow for expansion. Most liquids expand when heated. And they expand much more than solids.

Look under the bonnet of a car to see how much a liquid can expand. A bottle holds the overflow when liquid is pushed out of the cooling system by expansion. The bottle is almost empty when the engine is cold, but nearly full when it is hot.

Using liquid expansion

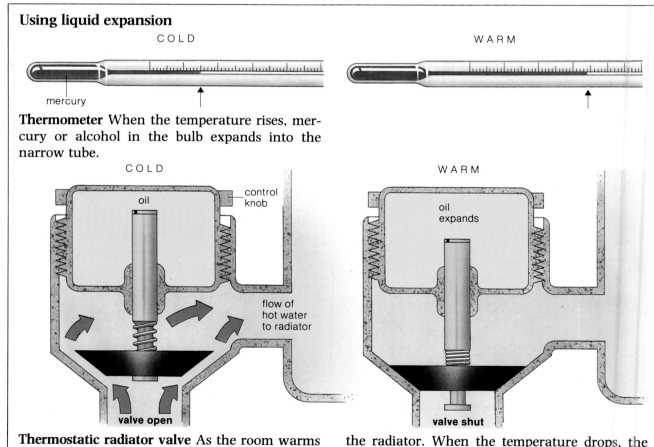

Thermometer When the temperature rises, mercury or alcohol in the bulb expands into the narrow tube.

Thermostatic radiator valve As the room warms up, the oil in the valve expands and pushes the piston down. This shuts off the flow of hot water to the radiator. When the temperature drops, the valve opens again.

Water – the liquid that's different

Water behaves in a very unusual way when heated from 0°C. As its temperature rises from 0°C to 4°C, it actually *contracts*. However, from 4°C upwards, it expands like any other liquid. This means that water takes up *least space* at 4°C. It has its *greatest density* at this temperature, and will sink through warmer or colder water around it.

A bitterly cold day.
The puddle freezes but not the lake:

However cold the weather, it takes a very long time for a lake to reach freezing point. As soon as water on the surface cools to 4°C, away it sinks to the bottom. In fact, none of the water in the lake can start to freeze until all has cooled beneath 4°C. This can take months of freezing weather.

Not so the puddle. One good overnight frost can cool it all beneath 4°C. Then freezing soon sets in.

If a lake *does* freeze over, water at the bottom can still be at 4°C. Fish can survive a severe winter by staying in this deeper warmer water.

1 If you are filling a bottle with a drink, why should you leave a space at the top before putting on the cap?

2 Copy the boxes. Write in the FIRST letter of each answer. The result is a word which tells you what happens to water when it is warmed from 0°C to 4°C.

?	Abbreviation for Celsius
?	A thermostatic valve does this when the temperature falls
?	Does water at 0°C expand when heated?
?	Device that controls temperature
?	It warms a room
?	Liquid used in a thermometer
?	When a liquid does this, it usually contracts
?	2°C is an example
?	Water at 4°C does this when surrounded by cooler or warmer water

3 Explain why fish in a lake can survive a harsh winter, even though the surface of the lake is frozen.

4 Study the diagrams of the thermostatic radiator valve on the opposite page.
Turning the control knob raises or lowers the oil container and piston. This makes the valve shut at a different temperature.
If the oil container and piston are RAISED, will this give you a WARMER room than before? Or a COOLER one?

2.16 Expanding gases

Why shouldn't you . . .

throw aerosols on the fire?

leave a fully inflated dinghy in the Sun

heat an unopened tin of baked beans in the oven?

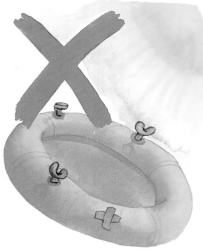

Gases are squashy. So it is easier to stop a gas expanding than a liquid or a solid. But if a trapped gas isn't allowed to expand, its pressure rises. And the container may not be strong enough to resist it.

Why the pressure rises

In a gas, molecules are always on the move. They travel very fast, hitting each other, and the sides of their container. Struck by billions of molecules, the container feels an outward pressure. If the temperature rises, the molecules move faster. The collisions become more violent. And the pressure rises.

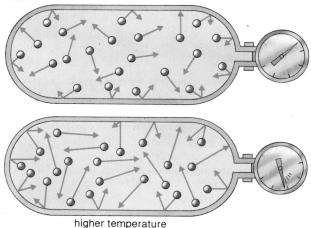

higher temperature
faster molecules
higher pressure

Using gas expansion

If a gas *can* expand, its expansion can be put to work:

In these cylinders, the heat from burning petrol causes more than forty violent gas expansions every second. The force is enough to accelerate the motor cycle to over 50 m/s.

You can use the expansion of gas to undent your table tennis ball.
Dip the ball in very hot water. And wait. The extra air pressure inside the ball should push out the dent.

Two gas laws

Facts and figures about how temperature affects a gas:

This mass of gas is trapped in a container. Its VOLUME doesn't change.

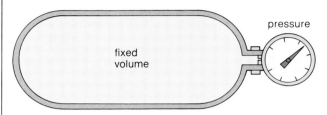

If its TEMPERATURE is increased, its PRESSURE rises like this:

TEMPERATURE in K	200	400	600	800
PRESSURE in mm of mercury	100	200	300	400

These figures follow some simple rules:

1 If the KELVIN TEMPERATURE doubles, the PRESSURE doubles, and so on.

2 Dividing the PRESSURE by the KELVIN TEMPERATURE gives the same value every time – in this case, 0.5.

Put another way,

The PRESSURE is directly proportional to the KELVIN TEMPERATURE
(provided the VOLUME doesn't change)

This is sometimes called the **Pressure law**.

This mass of gas is free to expand. Its PRESSURE doesn't change.

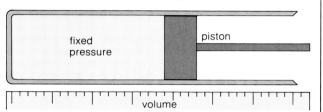

If its TEMPERATURE is increased, its VOLUME rises like this:

TEMPERATURE in K	200	400	600	800
VOLUME in cm³	300	600	900	1200

These figures follow some simple rules:

1 If the KELVIN TEMPERATURE doubles, the VOLUME doubles, and so on.

2 Dividing the VOLUME by the KELVIN TEMPERATURE gives the same value every time – in this case, 1.5.

Put another way,

The VOLUME is directly proportional to the KELVIN TEMPERATURE
(provided the PRESSURE doesn't change)

This is sometimes called **Charles' law**.

---

1 Explain why
a a beach ball may burst if left in the Sun
b air bubbles come out of an empty washing-up liquid bottle if you hold it in hot water without squeezing.

2 Sponge cakes contain thousands of tiny trapped gas bubbles. Explain why a sponge ...

looks like this after it has been left standing for a while:

3 Here is some information about the compressed air in a cylinder, before and after warming:

	cold cylinder	warm cylinder
temperature in K	300	400
pressure in mm of mercury	600	?
pressure ÷ temperature	?	?

Copy the chart and fill in the missing information.

2.17 Squashed gases

Pressure problems

This diver is hunting for pearl oysters. At 30 metres, she is ten times deeper than the bottom of a swimming pool. She has been underwater for over two minutes. And she isn't using any breathing apparatus. The pressure on the diver is around four times atmospheric. To survive such a pressure, she has to expand her lungs to the limit before she dives. Even so, when she reaches the sea bed, her lungs are so squashed that the air in them takes up only a quarter of its normal volume.

More squashed air

Pump air into a motor-cycle tyre, and it is squashed into about one third of its normal space. Then, the tyre is full of air at roughly three times the outside pressure. Like all gases, air has a greater pressure when its volume is reduced.

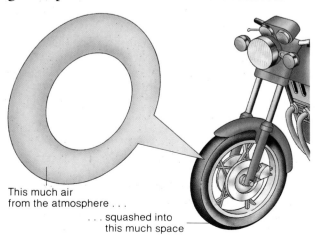

This much air from the atmosphere . . .

. . . squashed into this much space

How pressure and volume are linked

This is the equipment you might use to find the connection between the pressure of a gas and its volume:

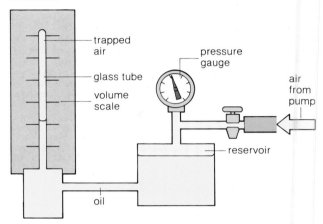

trapped air

glass tube

volume scale

pressure gauge

air from pump

reservoir

oil

The gas is air, trapped above the oil in the glass tube. The volume of the air is reduced in stages by pumping outside air into the reservoir. This forces more oil up the glass tube. Every time the volume is reduced, the pressure of the trapped air is measured on the gauge. Squashing the air warms it slightly, so you have to wait a few moments after each reading for the air to settle to its original temperature.

Here are some typical readings:

VOLUME in cm³	50	40	25	20	10
PRESSURE in mm of mercury	800	1000	1600	2000	4000

There are two connections between the readings:

1 if the VOLUME is HALVED then the PRESSURE is DOUBLED, and so on.

2 multiplying the PRESSURE by the VOLUME gives the same value every time – in this case, 40 000.

The air obeys **Boyle's law:**

If a fixed mass of gas is kept at a steady temperature, PRESSURE × VOLUME stays the same

Most others gases obey this law too.

Using Boyle's law

This is the type of problem you could solve using Boyle's law:

A diver working on the sea bed is breathing out air bubbles. The air in each bubble has a volume of 2 cm³, *and a pressure of* 3 atmospheres. *Up on the surface, the pressure is* 1 atmosphere. *What is the volume of a bubble when it reaches the surface?*

If the temperature doesn't change,
PRESSURE × VOLUME stays the same. So,

pressure × volume = pressure × volume

at 20 m   at 20 m   at surface   at surface

Filling in the figures,

3	×	2	=	1	×	volume
atm		cm³		atm		at surface

Rearrange this, and the volume of the bubble at the surface works out to be 6 cm³.

Concentrating the molecules

The diagrams show why the pressure rises when a gas is squashed:

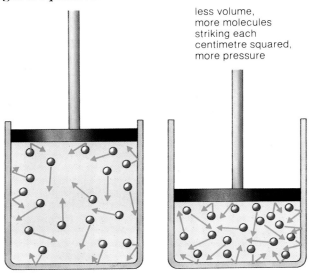

less volume, more molecules striking each centimetre squared, more pressure

The pressure is caused by fast-moving gas molecules colliding with the sides of the container. If the gas is compressed into a smaller space, the molecules become more concentrated. Each square centimetre of the container sides has more molecules striking it. So the pressure is greater.

1 Copy, and fill in the blanks:
According to __'s law, if a gas is squashed into a quarter of its original __, its __ rises to __ times its original value, provided the __ doesn't change.
2 This question is about the experiment and the table of readings on the opposite page.
a If the VOLUME of the gas were only 5 cm³, what would the PRESSURE be?
b Plot a graph of PRESSURE (side axis) against VOLUME (bottom axis).
c From your graph, read off the PRESSURE of the gas when the VOLUME is 30 cm³.
3 Sue's bicycle pump takes in 100 cm³ of air from the atmosphere at each stroke.
Her bicycle tyre has a volume of 1000 cm³.
The pressure in the tyre is just 1 atmosphere, the same as the pressure of the air outside. In other words, the tyre needs pumping up.
She pumps up the tyre using 20 strokes of the pump.
a What total volume of air is taken from the atmosphere by the pump?
b If all the air now in the tyre were free in the atmosphere, what volume would it occupy?
(Remember to include the volume of the air in the tyre before the pump was connected.)

c Copy and complete the table:

	Air, if free in atmosphere	Air, when squashed in tyre
PRESSURE in atm	1	?
VOLUME in cm³	? (answer b)	1000
PRESSURE × VOLUME	?	?

d From your table, write down the final pressure of the air in the tyre.
e In making your calculations, what assumption have you made about the temperature of the air? Is this assumption true in practice? How would you find out?

2.18 Conducting heat

Walking on burning coals at 700 °C. Mind over matter? Not necessarily. It may work because coal is a very poor conductor of heat. The firewalker's feet only touch each coal for a short time. So not enough heat flows out to damage the skin. Best not try it yourself however...

How things conduct

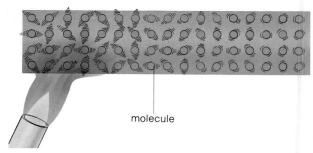

molecule

Heat one end of a metal bar, and the molecules will vibrate faster. Eventually the molecules will vibrate faster all along the bar. Heat has been conducted. The quicker this happens, the better the bar is as a conductor.

Conducting ability – best at the top, worst at the bottom		
Good conductors	metals	copper aluminium iron
Bad conductors (insulators)	glass water plastics wood materials with air trapped in them air	aerated concrete wool fibre glass expanded polystyrene

Good and bad conductors

Metals are the best conductors of heat. Non-metals like wood and plastic are bad conductors. So are most liquids. Gases are worst of all. You can sometimes tell how well something conducts just by touching it. A metal door handle feels cold because it quickly conducts heat away from your hand. A polystyrene tile feels warm because it hardly conducts away any heat at all.

Poor conductors of heat are called **insulators**. Many materials are good insulators because they have tiny pockets of air trapped in them.

Insulating the house

In a house, good insulation means lower fuel bills. Here are some of the ways in which insulating materials are used to cut down heat loss:

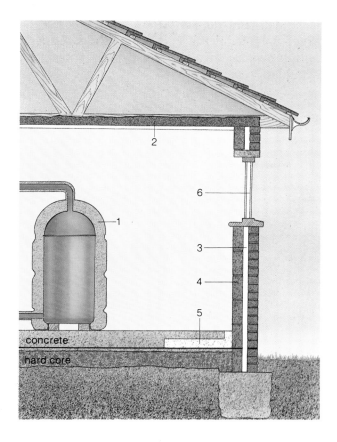

1 Fibreglass lagging round the hot water tank.
2 Fibreglass insulation in the loft.
3 Air cavity between the inner and outer walls.
4 Inner wall built from highly insulating aerated concrete blocks. The concrete has tiny bubbles of air trapped in it.
5 Polystyrene insulation under the edge of the floor.
6 Double-glazed windows. Two sheets of glass, with an insulating layer of air trapped between them.

1 Explain why:
a an aluminium window frame feels cold when you touch it, but a wooden frame feels warm;
b aerated concrete is a better insulator than normal concrete;
c it is much safer picking up hot dishes with a dry tea-towel than with a wet one;

U-values

To calculate likely heat losses from a house, architects need to know the **U-values** of different materials. For example:

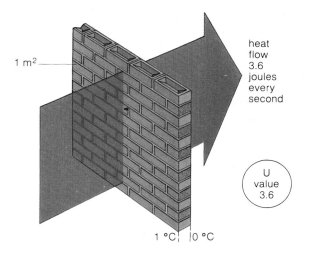

A single brick wall has a U-value of 3.6 W/(m^2°C). This means that the 1 square metre wall, with a 1°C temperature difference across it, will conduct heat at the rate of 3.6 joules every second.

The heat flow would be greater if
a the temperature difference were higher
b the area was greater
c the wall was thinner

This is how the U-values of different materials compare. The lower the U-value, the better the insulation.	U-value: W/(m²°C)
Single brick wall	3.6
Double wall, with air cavity	1.7
Double wall, with insulating foam in cavity	0.5
Glass window, single layer	5.7
Double glazed window	2.7

d Dave feels cold in his string vest, but warm if he puts a tight shirt over it.
2 Look at the table of U-values on this page. Then explain why houses with small, single layer windows are likely to lose less heat than those with larger windows. Is this true if the windows are double glazed and the wall cavities are insulated?

2.19 Convection

Unless the pilot can find a thermal, this glider isn't likely to stay airborne for very long. Thermals are rising currents of warm air. They can occur above hilltops, over factories, or under clouds. The problem is finding them. Experienced pilots keep a look out for circling birds. Birds discovered the secrets of thermal soaring many millions of years before people.

Whenever warm air rises, cooler air moves in to take its place. The result is a circulating current of air called a **convection current**. Convection doesn't only happen in air. It can occur in all gases and liquids.

Two simple experiments show convection in air and in water:

Hot air rises above the candle. Cooler air flows in to replace it. The smoke from the burning straw shows the current of air.

Hot water rises above the bunsen flame. Cooler water flows in to replace it. Potassium permanganate crystals colour the water so that you can see the current.

card

low flame

purple crystals

Why warm air rises

When air is heated it expands. This makes it less dense because the same mass now takes up a larger volume. Being less dense, the warm air floats upwards through the denser, cooler air around it.

Weather convection

In a cloud like this, warm damp air can rise at speeds of 30 metres per second or more. As the air rises, it cools. This forms new cloud. Read page 93 to find out why.

Cutting convection

It works for eggs as well as heads. Put an insulated cover over any warm surface, and the circulation of air is cut down. Also, the outside air isn't heated so much. Either way, the heat lost by convection is reduced.

Using convection

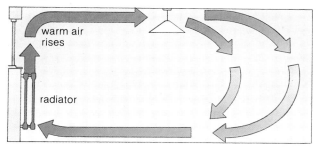

warm air rises

radiator

Most of the heat from a radiator is circulated by convection. Warm air rises above the radiator. It carries heat all round the room.

In a 'fridge, cold air sinks below the freezer compartment. This sets up a circulation which cools all the food in the 'fridge.

freezer compartment

cold air sinks

main supply

overflow pipe to allow for expansion

header tank

storage tank

hot water rises

boiler

Supplying your taps with hot water –
Water is heated in the boiler. It rises to the storage tank. Cooler water flows in to replace it. It too is heated. In time, a supply of hot water collects in the tank from the top down. The header tank provides the pressure to push the hot water out of the taps.

1 Explain why
a the freezer compartment in a 'fridge is placed at the top.
b a 'fridge doesn't work properly if the food is too tightly packed inside.
c a radiator quickly warms all the air in a room, even though air is a very poor conductor of heat.
d warm water rises when surrounded by cooler water.
2 This person feels a draught when the bonfire burns fiercely. Why?

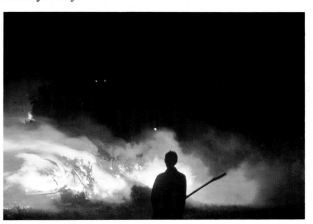

Draw a diagram to show the flow of air.
3 Two freshly poured cups of hot tea:

One is covered, the other isn't.
This is how the temperature of each drops with time:

TIME in minutes	0	2	4	6	8	10
TEMPERATURE (covered) in °C	80	73	66	61	56	52
TEMPERATURE (uncovered) in °C	80	67	56	48	42	37

a Plot a graph of TEMPERATURE (side axis) against TIME (bottom axis) for each cup. *Use the same axes for both graphs.*
b What is the difference in temperature between the two cups after 5 minutes?
c Most people don't like drinking tea which is cooler than 45°C. Estimate to the nearest half minute how long you could leave the uncovered drink before drinking it.

2.20 Holding heat

June, Newquay. The beach may be warm. But the sea most definitely isn't. In fact, it will take so much heat energy to warm up the sea, that it won't reach its maximum temperature until the end of September. However, there's good news for winter swimmers. With so much heat absorbed, it will then take the sea a long time to cool down again. Chances are that, in January, you'll find the sea warmer than the beach.

Specific heat capacity

It takes 4200 joules of heat energy to heat 1 kilogram of water just through 1°C:

water has a specific heat capacity of 4200 joules per kilogram per °C (written 4200 J/kg °C)

This is how water compares with other materials:

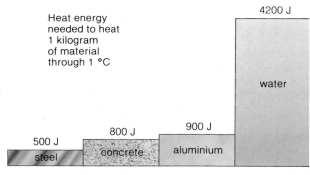

Heat energy needed to heat 1 kilogram of material through 1 °C

4200 J — water
900 J — aluminium
800 J — concrete
500 J — steel

This is also the heat energy given **out** when 1 kilogram **cools** by 1 °C

Calculating heat energy

For water, 4200 joules heats 1 kilogram through 1°C

so, 8400 joules heats 2 kilograms through 1°C

and, 84 000 joules heats 2 kilograms through 10°C

You could have calculated these results using an equation:

$$\text{heat energy gained} = \text{mass} \times \text{specific heat capacity} \times \text{temperature rise}$$

(J) (kg) (J/kg °C) (°C)

The equation works for other things as well as water. You can also use it to calculate the heat energy lost when the temperature falls.

Storing heat

Water has a high specific heat capacity. This makes it a very useful material for storing and carrying heat energy:

A hot water bottle can keep your feet warm for an hour or so.

Water carries heat from the boiler to the radiators around the house.

Water carries unwanted heat from the engine of a car to the radiator.

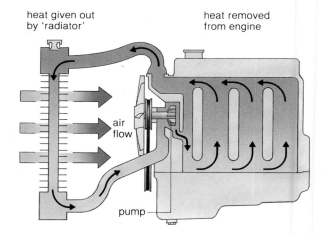

heat given out by 'radiator'

heat removed from engine

air flow

pump

Night storage heaters use concrete blocks to store heat. Concrete doesn't have as high a specific heat capacity as water. But it is more dense, so the same mass takes up less space. Heating elements warm the blocks overnight when electricity is cheap. The blocks give out heat through the day as they cool down.

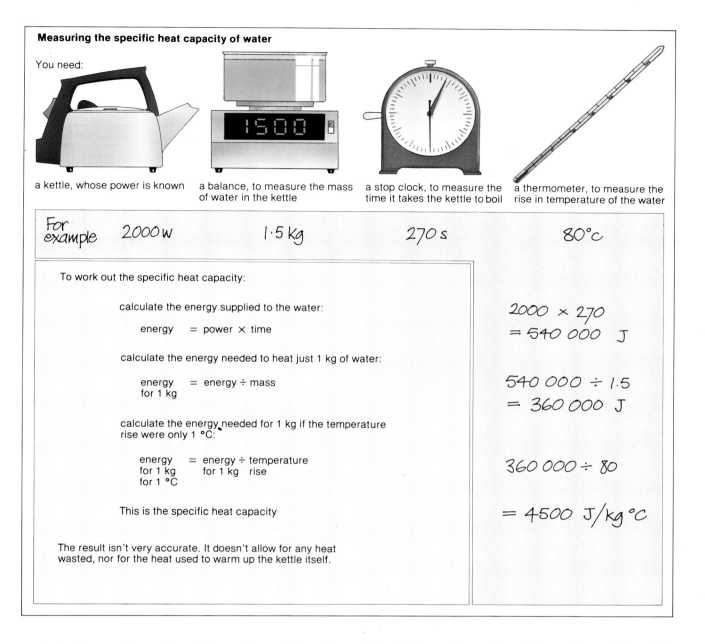

Measuring the specific heat capacity of water

You need:

a kettle, whose power is known | a balance, to measure the mass of water in the kettle | a stop clock, to measure the time it takes the kettle to boil | a thermometer, to measure the rise in temperature of the water

For example 2000 W 1·5 kg 270 s 80°C

To work out the specific heat capacity:

calculate the energy supplied to the water:

energy = power × time

$$2000 \times 270$$
$$= 540\ 000 \quad J$$

calculate the energy needed to heat just 1 kg of water:

energy = energy ÷ mass
for 1 kg

$$540\ 000 \div 1.5$$
$$= 360\ 000 \quad J$$

calculate the energy needed for 1 kg if the temperature rise were only 1 °C:

energy = energy ÷ temperature
for 1 kg   for 1 kg   rise
for 1 °C

$$360\ 000 \div 80$$

This is the specific heat capacity

$$= 4500 \quad J/kg\,°C$$

The result isn't very accurate. It doesn't allow for any heat wasted, nor for the heat used to warm up the kettle itself.

---

1 Eating a jam tart straight from the oven – the jam is at the same temperature as the pastry, but it's more likely to burn your tongue:
● Nick says this is because there's a greater mass of jam than pastry.
● Deborah says it's because the jam has a higher specific heat capacity than the pastry.
● Razia says that it's a combination of both reasons. Who is right?

2 Steve has a bright idea. Instead of filling his hot water bottle with water, he will fill it with hot air from the hair dryer. Then he won't have to worry about leaks.

Here is some information about the water or air he could use in the bottle:

	water	air
mass in kg	0.5	0.0005
specific heat capacity J/kg °C	4200	1000
temperature in °C	75	75

a Calculate the heat given out when a water-filled bottle cools to 25°C.
b Explain why you think that Steve's idea is a good one or not.

2.21 Coping with cold

Cold hands. But at least the core of his body is warm. And if his temperature drops beneath the normal 37°C, then his automatic temperature control system goes into action:

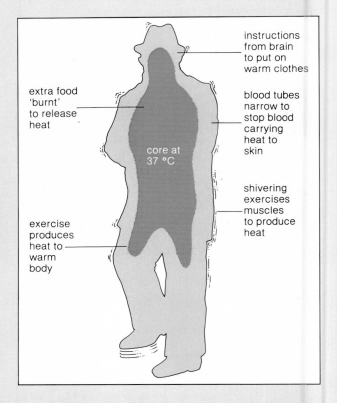

instructions from brain to put on warm clothes

blood tubes narrow to stop blood carrying heat to skin

core at 37 °C

shivering exercises muscles to produce heat

extra food 'burnt' to release heat

exercise produces heat to warm body

At risk

If the body loses too much heat, the core temperature starts to drop. If it drops more than 2°C, the body stops working properly. The condition is called **hypothermia**.

Old people are especially at risk from hypothermia. Every winter, thousands of old people die because they are unable to heat their homes properly.

Young babies also find it difficult to cope with the cold. They don't store as much body heat as adults, so a loss of heat can have a more drastic effect. And they can't adjust to sudden heat losses because their temperature control system isn't fully developed.

Survival on the hills

Early March. A mild sunny day suddenly turns cold wet and windy. Down in the town, the weather is just a nuisance. But for walkers up on the hills, it can be a killer.

Water evaporating from wet clothes quickly takes heat from the body. And a sharp wind makes matters worse. A 30 mph wind has the same chilling effect as a 40°C drop in air temperature. Accidents bring extra problems, because the risk of hypothermia ('exposure') is much greater if someone is injured and can't move.

To face the weather, hill walkers need to be properly equipped:

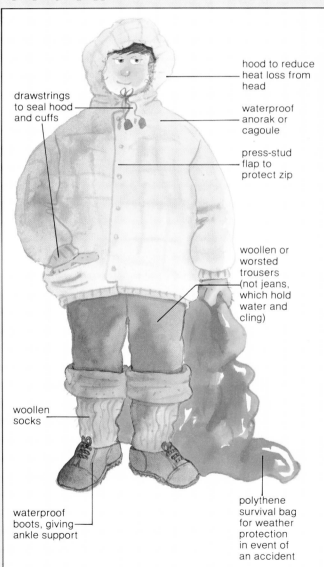

drawstrings to seal hood and cuffs

hood to reduce heat loss from head

waterproof anorak or cagoule

press-stud flap to protect zip

woollen or worsted trousers (not jeans, which hold water and cling)

woollen socks

waterproof boots, giving ankle support

polythene survival bag for weather protection in event of an accident

Survival at sea

Without an insulating suit this North Sea diver would be suffering from hypothermia in a matter of minutes. In a cold sea, the human body loses heat over 20 times faster than in cold air.

The wet-suit is worn with a layer of water trapped between the suit and the diver's skin. The water is an insulator. More insulation comes from the thousands of tiny nitrogen bubbles trapped in the suit lining.

Can you think of reasons why:
- babies store less body heat than adults?
- old people are more at risk from hypothermia than younger people?
- hill walkers and climbers are more at risk from hypothermia if they are injured?
- a swimming pool changing room is kept at a temperature of 25°C, but the pool itself is kept at 30°C?

2.22 Melting and freezing

Ice is a marvellous substance for keeping things cool. Not just because it is cold – but because it absorbs so much heat when it melts.

The quick way to cool a drink. Just add a couple of ice cubes and stir. As the ice melts, it absorbs so much heat from the drink that the temperature falls to near-freezing.

Ice pack in a cool box. As the ice melts, it absorbs so much heat that the food stays as cool as in a fridge, for 24 hours or more.

Arctic icebergs like this have been found drifting as far south as Florida. It would take more than 10 000 000 000 000 joules of heat energy to completely melt this iceberg.

Latent heat

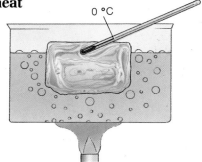

0 °C

Putting heat into ice at 0°C.
The ice melts. But it doesn't get any hotter. The temperature stays at 0°C until all the ice has melted.

The heat absorbed when a solid melts is called **latent heat of fusion**:
fusion means *melting*; *latent* means *hidden*.
The effect of the heat seems to be hidden because the temperature doesn't rise. In fact, the heat absorbed is used to wrench the molecules of the solid apart, so that they are free to move around as a liquid.

For ice to melt, each kilogram has to absorb 330 000 joules of heat energy:
water has a **specific latent heat of fusion** of 330 000 joules per kilogram.

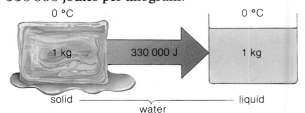

0 °C   0 °C
1 kg   330 000 J   1 kg
solid ——————— water ——————— liquid

This means that it takes nearly as much energy to change ice into water as it does to heat the water right up to boiling point.

Volume changes

When it melts,

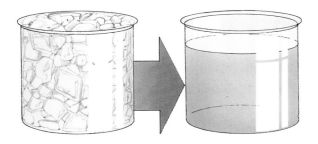

this much ice . . . . becomes this much water.
Water takes up less space as a liquid than as a solid.

This is because of the way the molecules stick together. In ice the molecules are grouped in rings. This takes up a lot of space. When the ice melts, the rings are broken. So the molecules can pack together more closely.

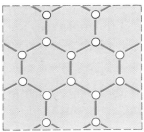

molecules in ice

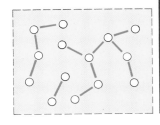
molecules in liquid water

When water changes to ice, it expands. If the ice is trapped, the expansion produces a huge force. This can
– burst pipes
– lift paving stones
– crack stonework off buildings
– split pieces of rock from a rock face.

Lowering the freezing point

Adding salt to water makes the freezing point go down. Damp roads which would be completely frozen over at $-10°C$, will stay clear of ice if salt is sprinkled over them.

Adding antifreeze to water keeps it liquid down to $-25°C$ or lower.

Finding a melting point

Melting point means the same as **freezing point**. It is the temperature at which a solid turns liquid, or a liquid turns solid. This is how you can find the melting point of wax:

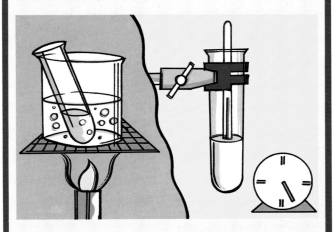

Put some candle wax in a test tube.
Melt the wax by putting the tube in boiling water.
Let the melted wax cool.
Measure the temperature every minute.
While the wax is liquid, the temperature falls; while the wax is solid, the temperature falls.
But while the wax is changing from liquid to solid, the temperature stays the same.
This temperature is the melting point.

1 Explain why, in winter
a a car engine may be damaged if antifreeze isn't added to the water in its cooling system.
b heaps of snow may still be standing at the roadside days after the weather has become warmer.
2 Water has a specific latent heat of fusion of 330 000 J/kg. How much heat energy is needed to melt
1 kg of ice? 2 kg of ice? 10 kg of ice?
3 This is how the temperature of some melted wax changed when it was left to cool:

TIME in minutes	0	1	2	3	4	5	6	7	8
TEMPERATURE in °C	83	70	60	53	53	53	53	48	43

a Plot a graph of TEMPERATURE against TIME.
b How long was it before the wax started to turn solid?
c How long was it before the wax had all turned solid?
d What is the melting point of the wax?

2.23 Making vapour

It happens every time you put the kettle on. Heat energy is absorbed by the water. The temperature rises to 100°C but no further. If you leave the kettle switched on, the extra energy just turns more and more of the water into a gas called **water vapour** or **steam**. But the temperature stays at 100°C.

The heat energy absorbed when a liquid changes into a gas is called **latent heat of vaporization**. The energy is needed to wrench the molecules apart so that they can move around freely as a gas.

Each kilogram of water has to absorb 2 300 000 joules of heat energy to change into vapour: water has a **specific latent heat of vaporization** of 2 300 000 joules per kilogram.

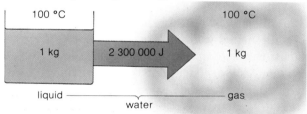

Compare this with the specific latent heat of fusion of water on page 88. It takes around seven times as much heat energy to change water into vapour as it does to change ice into water.

Getting back the latent heat.
Jet of steam meets cold coffee.
Steam condenses – it changes back to a liquid.
Result: large release of heat. Hot coffee in next to no time.

Evaporation

A liquid doesn't have to boil to change into a gas. Even on a cool day, rain puddles can vanish and wet clothes can dry out.

If a liquid is changing into a gas, it is **evaporating**. Liquids evaporate because some of their molecules move faster than others. Most of the molecules stick together. But faster ones close to the surface may escape from the others and form a gas.

How to make a liquid evaporate more quickly:

Increase the temperature
Wet clothes dry better on a warm day because more of the water molecules have enough energy to escape.

Increase the surface area
Water in a puddle dries out more quickly than water in a cup because more of the molecules are close to the surface.

Blow air across it
Wet clothes dry better on a windy day because the moving air carries escaping molecules away more quickly.

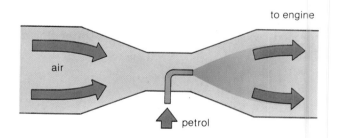

Turn it into a spray
A spray is made up of millions of tiny liquid droplets. It gives the liquid a much larger surface area.
The idea is used in the carburettor of a car engine. Here, petrol evaporates as it is sprayed into a moving stream of air. The mixture of air and petrol vapour is sucked into the engine to be burnt.

Boiling

Boiling is a very rapid form of evaporation. When water boils, you can see bubbles forming deep in the liquid. They grow, rise, and burst from the surface, carrying large amounts of vapour with them.

Even a cold liquid has tiny vapour bubbles inside it. But these are squashed by the pressure of the atmosphere pushing on the water. As the temperature rises, the pressure inside the bubbles grows stronger. Eventually, it is strong enough to overcome atmospheric pressure. The bubbles grow quickly. The liquid boils.

A lower boiling point

A higher boiling point

At the top of Mount Everest, water boils at only 70 °C. Atmospheric pressure is much lower than at sea level. So the vapour bubbles don't have to be so hot to overcome the pressure.

In a pressure cooker, water boils at about 120 °C. Trapped steam puts the pressure up, and this raises the boiling point of the water. The higher temperature means faster cooking.

Adding plenty of salt to water raises the boiling point by several degrees. It may mean slightly faster cooking, but it isn't good for your taste or your health.

---

1   [?]   A gas becomes this when it condenses.

  [?]   The surface of a puddle of water has more of this than a beaker of water.

  [?]   If this rises, water becomes vapour more quickly.

  [?]   A liquid does this when it becomes a gas.

  [?]   Does water have to boil to become vapour?

  [?]   This stays the same when water is boiling.

Copy the boxes. Fill in the first letter of each answer to make a word. This is the heat absorbed when a liquid becomes a gas.

2 Explain why
a food cooks faster in a pressure cooker
b once the water in a kettle has boiled, it doesn't go on getting hotter and hotter, even if the kettle is left switched on.

3 A kettle has a power output of 2300 W. It is full of boiling water.
The specific latent heat of vaporization of water is 2 300 000 J/kg.
a How much heat energy is needed to change 1 kg of water into steam?
b How much heat energy is put into the water every second?
c How long will it take the kettle to produce 1 kg of steam?

4 Mike and Janet have used a kettle to boil drinking water while climbing in the Alps, sea water on the beach, and tap water at home. They have measured the three temperatures: 100°C, 95°C, and 103°C. But they can't remember which is which. Decide for them.

2.24 Cooling by evaporation

Evaporation has a cooling effect.
You only have to stand around in wet clothes to discover that. The water has to absorb latent heat to evaporate. So when your clothes dry out, heat is taken from your body. If there is a wind blowing, the water evaporates faster, and you chill even more.

Sometimes, your body needs to lose heat. Sweating does this for you automatically. You start to sweat if your body temperature rises more than $1/2°C$ above normal. The sweat comes out of tiny holes in your skin. As it evaporates, it takes heat away from your body.

Dogs don't sweat through their skin. To lose heat, they hang out their tongues and pant. As moisture evaporates from the tongue, it takes heat away from the bloodstream. The panting speeds up evaporation because it blows air across the tongue.

Cool in the 'fridge

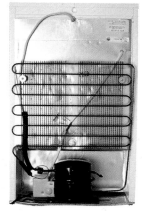

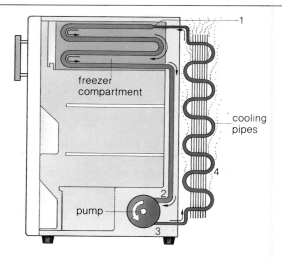

A refrigerator takes heat from the food inside, and gives it out at the back. Put your hand over the back and you can feel the warm air rising.

Evaporation keeps food cool in the 'fridge.
Many refrigerators use a liquid called Freon, which evaporates easily.

Follow the Freon round the circuit:

1. Freon evaporates in pipes in freezer compartment. Heat taken from food and air in 'fridge.
2. Vapour drawn away by electric pump.
3. Electric pump compresses vapour. Vapour turns liquid. Latent heat is released.
4. Hot liquid forces through cooling pipes. Heat given off.

Vapour in the air

On 'close' or **humid** days, the air is so full of water vapour that other water evaporates very slowly. Sweat tends to stay on your skin. There is hardly any cooling effect. So you feel hot and uncomfortable.

Warm air can hold more water vapour than cold air.

If warm humid air sudden cools, some of its vapour has to condense.

It may become billions of tiny water droplets in the air. You see these as white cloud, steam or mist. It may become condensation on any cold surface. If condensation freezes, the result is frost.

warm air

cold air

These all have something in common:

clouds of steam from a kettle . . .   frost . . .

condensation on windows . . .   fog, mist, and clouds . . .

They are all formed when humid air cools.

1

evaporation	latent heat	condensation
water vapour	humidity	clouds

Choose one item from the table to match each of the following:
a warm air can hold more than cold air;
b formed when water vapour meets a cold surface;
c absorbed when a liquid evaporates;
d millions of tiny water droplets in the air.
2 Explain why:
a if you tip white spirit on the back of your hand, the spirit vanishes and your hand feels cold;
b on a humid day, you feel hot and uncomfortable;
c . . . but you don't feel so uncomfortable if there is a breeze blowing.

3 In a refrigerator:
a what happens to the Freon when it absorbs latent heat?
b where does it absorb latent heat?
c what happens to the Freon when it releases its latent heat?
d where does it release its latent heat?
4 Sue goes to check her car one morning. She finds that there is condensation on the INSIDE surface of the windows.
Say whether each of the following is TRUE, or FALSE, or whether you CAN'T TELL without more information.
A It is cooler outside the car than inside.
B It is cooler inside the car than outside.
C There is humid air outside the car.
D There is humid air inside the car.

2.25 Changing the weather

Summer all the year round.
This weather is made by technicians.
Outside, the weather happens naturally.
But it can still be changed by human activity

Do-it-yourself weather

Gardeners create their own 'microclimates' using greenhouses, cloches, and windbreaks.

Living in a heat island

Towns are warmer than the country. And less windy.
But they get less sunshine and more rain.
Here are some of the reasons:

- Towns produce heat. It comes from factories, vehicles and heating systems.

- Towns have huge surfaces to absorb the Sun's heat. And they are full of materials like bricks, stone and concrete which are good at storing heat.

- Smoke and exhaust gases from vehicles collect above towns and act as a huge insulating blanket.

- Towns are windbreaks. They slow the air, so that heat isn't carried away. Each town becomes an 'island' of heat. As warm air rises from it, clouds and thunderstorms may develop.

Central London gets almost twice as much thundery rain as its suburbs. On a summer's evening, it can be as much as 10°C warmer. And it has at least one more frost-free month every year.

Too hot to bear

Heat and humidity can make life very uncomfortable. This chart shows the 'zone of comfort' which suits people best:

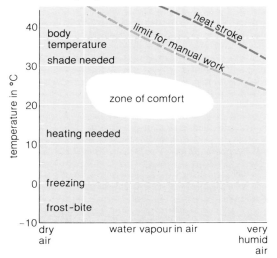

Many people think that city violence comes from frustration, unemployment, and poor housing. And statistics show that it is most likely to erupt on hot summer evenings when the build-up of heat in an overcrowded city can make life unbearable.

Outlook: warmer, but wetter:

That's the world outlook for the next few centuries. But it isn't good news. The tropics will be wetter, but countries like Ethiopia and Sudan, which already have severe drought problems, are likely to be even drier.

The main cause of the change is the slow build-up of carbon dioxide gas in the atmosphere. All living things give off carbon dioxide. Plants absorb it. But extra carbon dioxide is pouring out of power stations, homes and vehicles as fuels are burned. And that is upsetting the balance, because plants can't absorb the extra.

Carbon dioxide in the air is like the glass in a greenhouse. It lets the Sun's radiated heat reach the ground, but traps heat radiated from the ground. Scientists expect the 'greenhouse effect' to lift world temperatures by about 4°C over the next few hundred years. It isn't much. But it will be enough to change the world's climate. How we use fuels today is going to affect the lives of many generations in the future.

Look at the 'zone of comfort' chart on this page. What is the maximum comfortable temperature for manual work when the air is very humid? How does this change if the air is drier? Can you explain why?

This map shows a block of houses and the different heat-absorbing materials around. Draw a map like this for your home and its surroundings. Mark on anything that acts as a windbreak. Then mark on the most windy places, the most sheltered places, and the places you would choose if you were going to sunbathe.

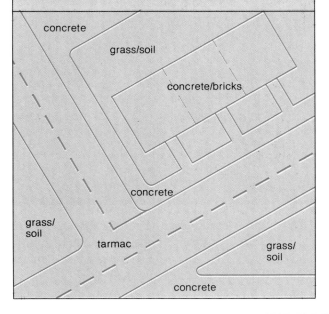

3.1 Rays of light

Almost anything can give out light.

You see some things because they give off their own light: the Sun, for example.

You see other things because daylight, or other light, bounces off them. They **reflect** light into your eyes: this page, for example.

Rays and beams

In diagrams, **rays** are lines with arrows on them. They show you which way the light is going.
A **beam** is drawn using several rays side by side.

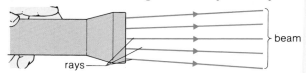

Some facts about light

Light carries energy. This calculator doesn't need a battery to keep it going. Just plenty of sunlight.

Light waves can travel through empty space. Otherwise it wouldn't be possible to see the Sun and the stars. The waves travels very fast – about 300 000 kilometres every second.

Light travels in straight lines. The edge of a laser beam shows you this. You can see the path of the beam because dust in the air glints when light reflects from it.

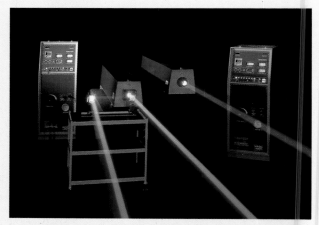

Light is made up of waves. Throw a stone into a pond and ripples spread across the surface of the water. Light travels in much the same way. But the 'ripples' are tiny electric and magnetic vibrations. And they don't need water to travel across.

Holograms

The picture on the credit card is called a **hologram**. It looks three-dimensional. And its colour changes as you look at it from different angles. The image is actually a pattern of light waves reflecting from the surface of the card. The hologram is put on the card to make it difficult for a forger to copy.

Lasers

Lasers give out a very intense beam of light. The beam is extremely narrow. It is just one colour.

Surgeons use laser in delicate operations on eyes and nerves. The fine beam gives a concentrated heat which can seal blood vessels and cut tissue very accurately.

Lasers are used in compact disc players. Like records, compact discs 'store' music in coded form. But they don't have a groove for a stylus to travel along. Instead, a tiny laser beam travels over thousands of tiny pits on the surface of the disc. A detector picks up the reflected beam, and the light 'pulses' are changed into sound.

At many supermarket check-outs, the price of each item is 'read' by passing its bar-code over a laser. A detector picks up the reflected beam. The light 'pulses' are changed into electrical signals for the till.

1 Which of the following give off their own light?
A page of a book
B the Sun
C traffic lights
2 Write down *three* uses of lasers.

3 Pia isn't convinced that light is a form of energy. She wants evidence for this as well. What can you suggest?
4 What is the speed of light through space?

3.2 Flat mirrors

The door isn't as smooth as the mirror. It scatters light in every direction.
Mirrors reflect light in such a way that they produce images.

Laws of reflection

A ray of light bounces off a flat mirror. Here are some of the words used to describe the reflection of the ray:

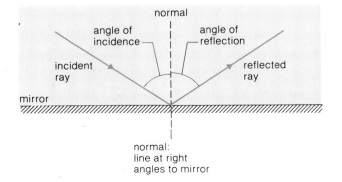

When a ray of light is reflected from a mirror, it obeys two simple rules:

1 The angle of reflection is equal to the angle of incidence. The ray is reflected from the mirror at the same angle as it arrives.

2 The ray striking the mirror, the reflected ray, and the normal all lie in the same plane. You can draw all three on one flat piece of paper.

These are the **laws of reflection**.

How a flat mirror makes an image

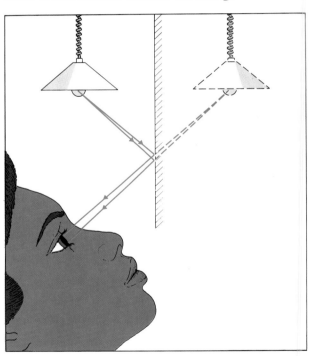

Thousands of rays could be drawn from the lamp. But to keep things simple, only two are shown. The rays are reflected into the eye. They seem to come from a position behind the mirror. This is where you would see an image of the lamp.

Rays don't actually pass through the image. They just *seem* to come from it. The image is called a **virtual image**. It can't be put on a screen.

Finding the image

You can find the position of an image by experiment:

1 Stand a mirror along the middle of a piece of paper. Draw a pencil line along the back of the mirror. Place a pin upright in front of the mirror. Mark its position.

2 Line up one edge of a ruler with the image of the pin in the mirror. Do this again from another position. Mark the position of the ruler edge each time.

3 Take away the mirror, pin and ruler. Find out where the ruler lines would cross. This is the position of the image.

More rules

When something is put in front of a flat mirror, its image is

the same size;

the same distance from the mirror, and in a matching position;

laterally inverted – 'left' becomes 'right' and 'right' becomes 'left'.

1 Copy the diagram.

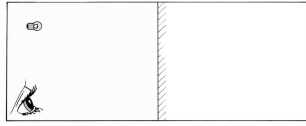

Mark the position of the image of the bulb. Draw two rays which leave the bulb, reflect from the mirror and enter the eye.

2 Someone stands 5 metres in front of a flat mirror. How far is she from her image?
She walks 2 metres towards the mirror.
Now how far is she from her image?

3 This is a plan of a room.

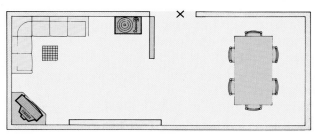

There is a mirror on the wall. If you stood in the doorway, would you be able to see the television? the record deck?

4 Police cars sometimes have the word STOP on them. It is written in 'mirror writing', so that drivers can read it in their driving mirrors. Write the word STOP as it appears on the police car.

3.3 Curved mirrors

Magic spoons

The same spoon. But very different images.
Try it for yourself. Then put your thumb really close to each side of the spoon and see how the images compare.

Concave mirrors

Concave mirrors curve inwards.
They can form two types of image:

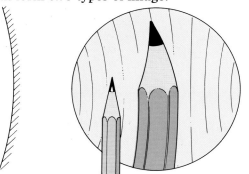

If the light rays come from something close, the image is upright and magnified.
It is a **virtual** image, like the one in a flat mirror.

If the light rays come from something distant, they come to a focus after reflection.
They **converge** (come together) to form a small upside down image which can be picked up on a screen.
This type of image is called a **real** image.
The rays of light actually meet to form it.
Rays from very distant things are nearly parallel to each other. A concave mirror brings parallel rays to a focus at a point called the **principal focus**. The distance from the mirror to the principal focus is called the **focal length**.
Highly curved mirrors have short focal lengths.

Convex mirrors

Convex mirrors bulge outwards. They only give one type of image. It is always small, upright and virtual.

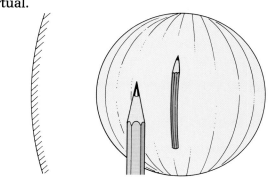

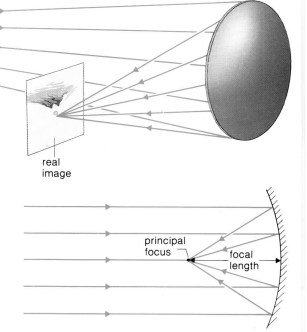

real image

principal focus

focal length

Light isn't the only thing to be reflected by a curved surface. Curved reflectors are also used for sound, radiated heat, and radar and TV signals.

Concave reflectors

A concave mirror is very useful when making up or shaving, because it can magnify.

Not just for decoration. The concave ears are just the job for focusing distant sounds.

Radar pulses from a distant aircraft are focused by this concave dish.

Convex reflectors

Convex mirrors give you a much wider view. They are used as driving mirrors and shop security mirrors.

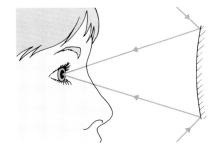 

1 Which kind of mirror
a can magnifiy **b** always gives a small upright image **c** can give a real image on a screen?
2 Copy and complete the table to show which type of mirror you would pick for each job.

Use	type of mirror	reason for choice
Shop security mirror		
make-up mirror		
headlamp reflector		

3 This portable gas fire is used by campers.

What type of reflector does it have?
Why does it have a reflector?
Where is the principal focus of the reflector?

3.4 Bending light

It doesn't hurt!

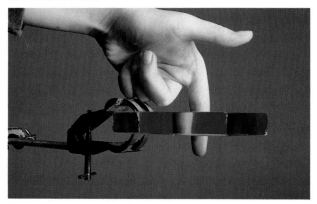

Turn the glass block, and out comes a piece of finger. Or so it seems. In fact, it is the light rays which move, not the finger.

This is how a ray of light passes through a glass block:

The ray is bent, or **refracted**, when it goes into the block. It is bent again when it leaves the block. So, the block moves the ray sideways.
The only time the ray doesn't bend is when it strikes the face of the block 'square on', at right angles.

When light goes into glass, water, or other transparent material, it bends towards the normal. In other words:

the angle of refraction is less than the angle of incidence.

When light leaves a transparent material, it bends away from the normal.

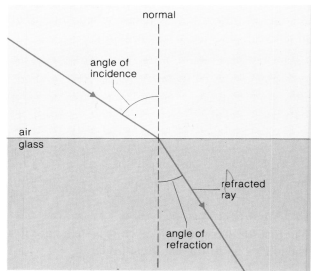

Deeper than it looks

Water never looks as deep as it really is:

Light rays from the pebble bend away from the normal when they leave the water. From above, the rays seem to come from a point which isn't so deep, and is slightly to one side. So, the pebble seems closer than it actually is.
Because of this, objects seem larger underwater. When scientists or archaeologists are working on marine life or wrecks, they overestimate sizes and must measure for accuracy.

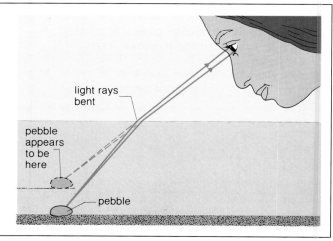

Colour

Where colours come from:

When a narrow beam of white light passes through a prism, the beam splits into all the colours of the rainbow. White isn't a single colour at all, but a mixture of colours. The colours enter the prism together but are bent different amounts by the glass. The effect is called **dispersion**.

The range of colours is called a **spectrum**. Most people think they can see six colours in the spectrum:

red, orange, yellow, green, blue, violet,

though really, there is a continuous change of colour from beginning to end.

The different colours are actually light waves of different wavelengths. Red light has the longest wavelength, blue the shortest.

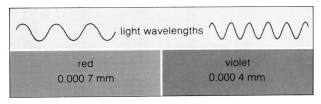

1 Copy the diagrams below. Complete them to show what happens to each ray of light as it passes through the glass block.

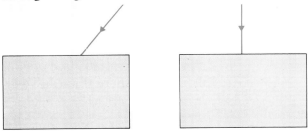

2 A game for the school fête. Scatter some 20p coins over the bottom of a bowl.

Why light bends

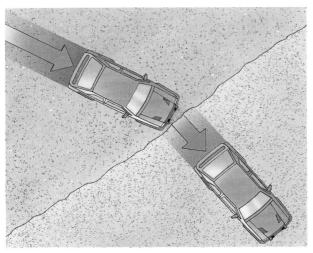

A fast car drives at an angle into sand.
One front wheel strikes the sand before the other.
So one side of the car is slowed down before the other.
The path of the car is bent.
Light isn't solid like a car.
But it too bends because it is slowed down.
The more it is slowed, the more it bends.

In air, light travels at about 300 000 kilometres/second.
This is its speed in some other materials:

Material	Speed of light
water	225 000 km/s
glass	197 000 km/s
Perspex	201 000 km/s
diamond	124 000 km/s

(These speeds vary slightly depending on the colour.)

To play, you take aim from the side, and throw in a 2p coin. You win if your coin covers a 20p coin. Explain why you don't have much chance of winning if the bowl is filled with water.

3 The table on this page gives the speed of light in water, glass, Perspex and diamond.
a Which of these materials bends light the most?
b Compare water with glass. Which of these two bends light more?
c If the blocks in Question 1 were made of Perspex instead of glass, how would your drawings be different?

4 Which colour is
a bent the most by a prism?
b bent the least by a prism?

3.5 Inside reflections

Diamond. The hardest substance known. And probably the most beautiful. It takes a skilled diamond cutter to reveal the true beauty of a diamond. The faces or **facets** have to be cut at carefully chosen angles so that any light going into the diamond is reflected back out again. That is the secret of the sparkle.

Internal reflection

The inside surface of a diamond or a block of glass or water can act like a perfect mirror. It all depends on the angle at which light rays strike it.

Three rays leave a lamp on the bottom of a swimming pool. Each leaves at a different angle:

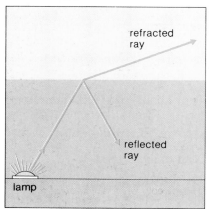

This ray splits.
Some of the light is reflected.
Some is refracted.

This ray splits.
Some of the light is reflected.
Some is refracted. But the angle is so large that the light only just manages to leave the surface of the water.

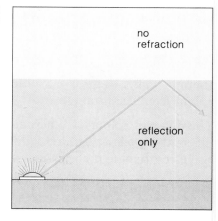

All of the light is reflected.
There is no refracted ray because the light strikes the surface at too great an angle.

In the middle diagram angle C is called the **critical angle**. If light strikes the surface at a greater angle than this, the surface acts like a perfect mirror. The light is **totally internally reflected**.

Different materials have different critical angles:

material	critical angle
water	49°
glass	42°
diamond	24°

For example, any light which strikes the inside face of a diamond at more than 24° will be completly reflected.

Prisms, pipes, and mirages

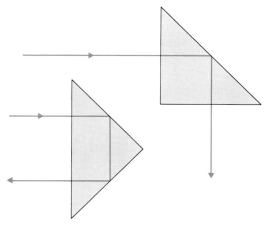

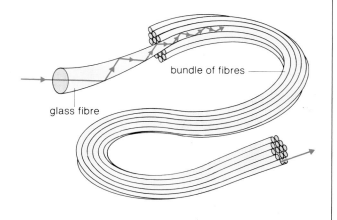

Glass prisms can behave like perfect mirrors. But the light has to strike an inside face at an angle greater than the critical angle.

With a light pipe, you can see round corners. Surgeons use them to inspect the insides of stomachs and wombs. Each pipe is a bundle of fine glass threads or fibres. When a ray enters a fibre at one end, it reflects off the sides until it comes out of the other end.

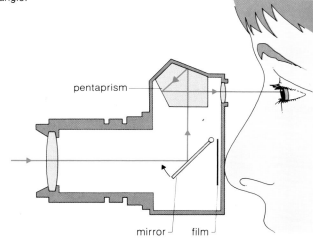

With this camera, you actually look out through the lens when you line up your shot. A five-sided 'pentaprism' relects light from the mirror into your eye. When you press the button, the mirror flicks up out of the way so that light can reach the film.

In a hot desert, you may see pools of water in the distance. Only they aren't really there. The image is just a mirage. Just above the ground there is a layer of very hot thin air. This acts like the inside face of a glass block. It reflects light. You see the reflection of the sky, and think that the ground is wet and shiny.

1 Copy and complete each diagram to show what happens to the ray of light after it reaches the prism.

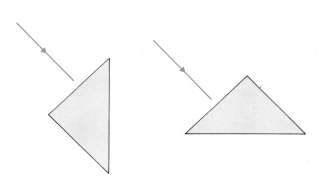

2 A light ray strikes the inside surface of material X.

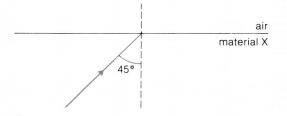

Look at the table of critical angles on the opposite page. Then copy and complete the diagram to show what would happen to the ray of light if material X were
a water **b** glass **c** diamond

3.6 Convex lenses

What do they have in common?

They all have a small upside down image inside them. It's formed by a convex lens.

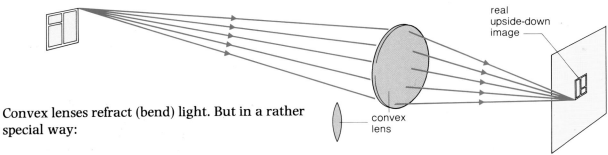

real upside-down image

convex lens

Convex lenses refract (bend) light. But in a rather special way:

Light rays leave a distant window and pass through a convex lens. The rays are bent by the lens. They converge (come together) to form a small upside down image of the window. The image is **real**. It can be put on a screen.

Rays from very distant things are parallel to each other. A convex lens brings parallel rays to focus at a point called the **principal focus**.
The distance from the lens to a principal focus is called the **focal length**.

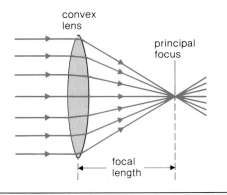

convex lens

principal focus

focal length

How to measure a focal length

- Place a convex lens several metres from a window.
- Focus the image of a distant building on a screen.
- Measure the distance from the lens to the screen. This is the focal length.

Do the experiment twice, with a thick lens and a thinner lens. Which has the longer focal length? Which gives the larger image?

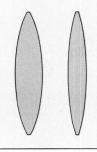

Finding the image

Move something closer to a lens, and its image moves too. You can find the image position by experiment.

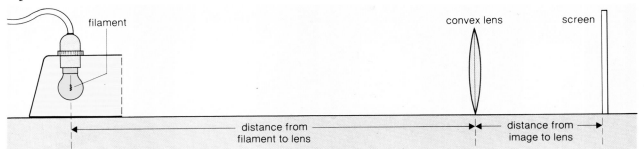

- Place a ray box so that the filament is one metre away from a convex lens.

- Move the screen until you focus the image of the filament.

- Measure:
  the distance from the filament to the lens;
  the distance from image to the lens.
  The length of the image.

- Move the ray box closer to the lens, 10 cm at a time.
  Take measurements as before.
  Enter your readings in a table.

Distance from filament to lens in cm	Distance from image to lens in cm	Length of image in cm
100		
90		
80		
...		

As the filament moves closer to the lens, what happens to the image distance? what happens to the image size?

To answer these questions, you will need to have done the two experiments on this double page.

1 Copy and complete the diagram to show what happens to the rays of light when they pass through the lens.

Mark on the principal focus of the lens and the focal length.

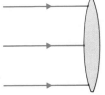

This lens is thicker and more highly curved than the previous one. Copy and complete the diagram.

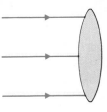

2 Dave did an experiment like the one on this page. Unfortunately he wrote down the image distances on a piece of rough paper. Then he copied them into his book in the wrong order:

Reading	Distance from filament to lens in cm	Distance from image to lens in cm
1	100	24
2	60	60
3	40	30
4	30	20
5	20	18

a Rewrite Dave's table so that the image distances are in the correct order.
b For which reading would you expect the image to be biggest?
c For which reading would you expect the image to be smallest?
d What is the shortest distance between the image and the filament?

3.7 Lenses at work

The projector

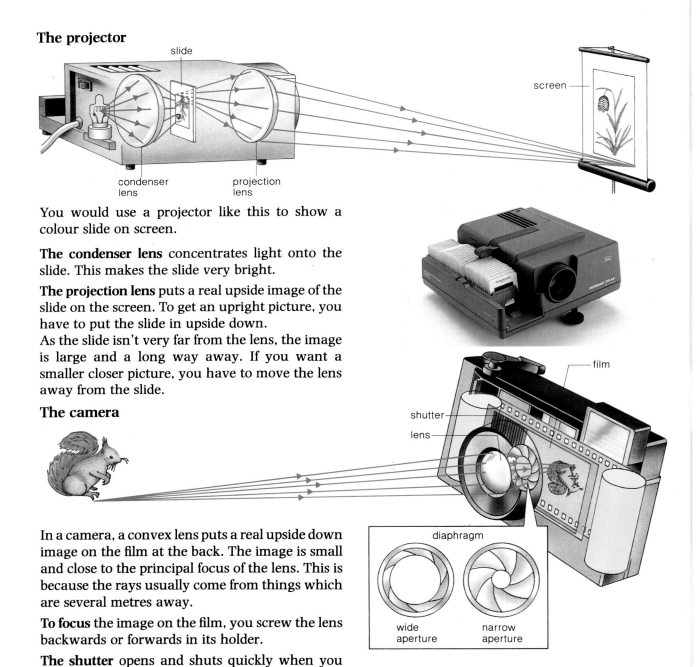

slide
screen
condenser lens
projection lens

You would use a projector like this to show a colour slide on screen.

The condenser lens concentrates light onto the slide. This makes the slide very bright.

The projection lens puts a real upside image of the slide on the screen. To get an upright picture, you have to put the slide in upside down.
As the slide isn't very far from the lens, the image is large and a long way away. If you want a smaller closer picture, you have to move the lens away from the slide.

The camera

film
shutter
lens

diaphragm

wide aperture

narrow aperture

In a camera, a convex lens puts a real upside down image on the film at the back. The image is small and close to the principal focus of the lens. This is because the rays usually come from things which are several metres away.

To focus the image on the film, you screw the lens backwards or forwards in its holder.

The shutter opens and shuts quickly when you press the button. This lets a small amount of light into the camera.

The film is coated in chemicals which are sensitive to light. The chemicals are changed by the image. Later, the changes can be 'fixed' to form the photograph.

The diaphragm is a ring of sliding metal plates. When you adjust it, you change the size of the hole of **aperture** through which the light rays pass. In bright sunshine, you might use a small aperture. This would cut down the amount of light reaching the film.

The human eye

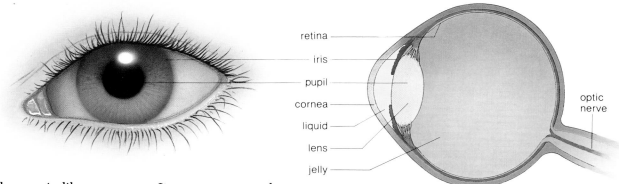

retina — iris — pupil — cornea — liquid — lens — jelly — optic nerve

The eye is like a camera. It uses a convex lens system to form a small upside down image of anything in front of it.

The iris controls the amount of light going into the eye. If you walk into a dark room, the hole in the middle of the iris (the **pupil**) grows larger.

The cornea and the watery liquid behind it do most of the focusing of the rays.

The lens itself makes small focusing adjustments. It doesn't move backwards or forwards like the lens in a camera or projector. Instead it becomes thinner or fatter.

The retina is the 'screen' which detects the image. It contains millions of tiny cells which are sensitive to light. The cells send signals along the optic nerve to the brain.

Your brain gives you an upright view of the world. But it isn't always the same as the image in your eye. Look at the examples below.

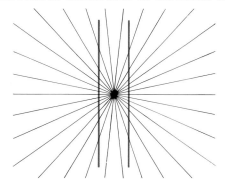

The brown lines look bent. Now check them with a ruler.

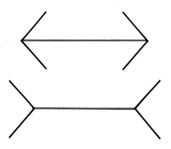

The brown lines look the same length. Now check them with a ruler.

1

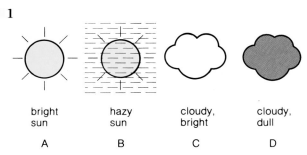

bright sun	hazy sun	cloudy, bright	cloudy, dull
A	B	C	D

Some cameras have weather symbols marked on them. The symbol changes when you turn a dial. This changes the aperture.
Which symbol, A, B, C, or D, gives the largest aperture?
Which symbol gives the smallest aperture?

2 Copy and complete the chart to show which parts of the camera and the eye do similar jobs:

camera	eye	job done
		focuses rays
diaphragm		
		picks up image

3 Explain why:

a the image from a projector is much bigger than the image in a camera;

b the pupils of your eyes become smaller if you walk out into bright sunshine.

3.8 Waves

Havoc in Alaska

The after effects of a tsunami or 'tidal wave'. It started with a violent underwater earthquake thousands of kilometres away. This set waves racing across the ocean. Far out at sea, the waves were small. Ships moved up and down a metre or so, but no more. But as the waves approached the coast, they grew to an enormous size. Finally, taller than a house, they hit the shore. As they collapsed, they caused a forward rush of water which carried trees, boulders and boats hundreds of metres inland.

Waves carry energy from one place to another.

They don't only move across water. Sound, light, and radio signals all travel in the form of waves.

There are two main types of wave. You can study them using a stretched 'slinky' spring.

Transverse waves

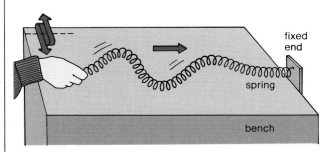

Keep moving one end of the spring from side to side, and waves travel along the spring. Each coil moves from side to side but a little later than the one before. Waves like this, where the movements are sideways (or up and down) are called transverse waves.

Longitudinal waves

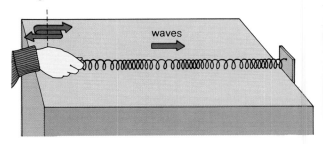

Keep moving one end of the spring backwards and forwards, and waves travel along the spring. Each wave is a compression followed by a stretched out section. Waves like this, where the movements are backwards and forwards, are called longitudinal waves.

How to draw waves

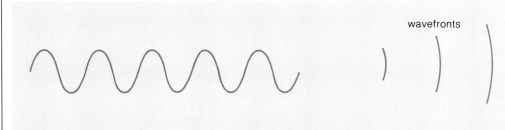

Transverse waves can be drawn like this.

You can also draw waves using lines called wavefronts. Think of each wavefront as the top of a transverse wave, or the compression of a longitudinal wave.

Describing waves

The **wavelength** is the distance between wave-fronts . . . or between any place on one wave and the same place on the next.

The number of waves passing every second is called the **frequency**. It is measured in **hertz (Hz)**. A frequency of 100 Hz means that 100 waves are passing every second.

This height shown on the right is called the **amplitude** of the wave.

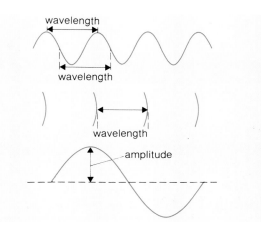

An equation for waves

Imagine waves travelling across the sea . . .

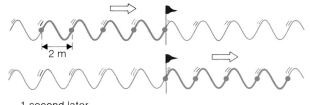

1 second later

speed = frequency × wavelength
This equation is true for all waves.

Here, 4 waves pass the flag in one second . . .
                          so the frequency is 4 Hz
Each wave is 2 metres long . . .
                          so the wavelength is 2 m

This means that
the waves travel 8 metres in one second . . .
                          so the speed is 8 m/s
In this example,

| 8 | = | 4 | × 2 |
| m/s | | Hz | m |

a What type of wave is A?
b Using a ruler marked in millimetres, measure:
the wavelength of A;
the amplitude of A;
the wavelength of B.
2 Three waves travel at the same speed, but they have different frequencies and wavelengths. Copy the chart, then fill in the blank spaces:

	speed in m/s	frequency in Hz	wavelength in m
wave 1		8	4
wave 2		16	
wave 3			1

3 These waves all travel at the same speed:

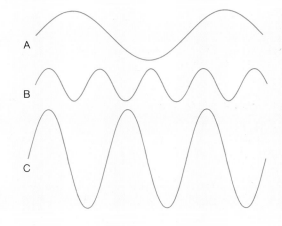

Which has:
a the highest frequency?
b the longest wavelength?
c the greatest amplitude?

3.9 Ripples of water and light

A **ripple tank** – for studying how waves behave. The shallow tank is filled with water.

The vibrating dipper sends ripples across its surface.

You place different shapes in the water to reflect or bend the wave 'beam'.

The ripples seem to behave in much the same way as a beam of light. It's one good reason for thinking that light is made up of waves.

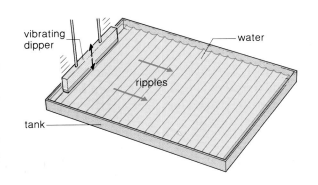

In water

In light

Reflection

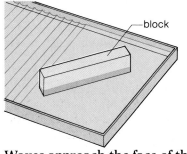

Waves approach the face of the block.

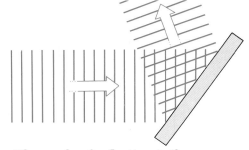

The angle of reflection is the same as the angle of incidence – as with a beam of light.

A beam of light is reflected by a mirror.

Refraction

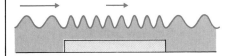

A flat piece of plastic makes the water less deep. This slows down the waves. As they slow down, they bend – just like a

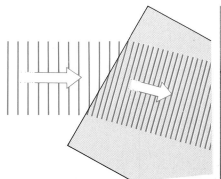

beam of light. Use a lens-shaped piece of plastic, and the waves are focussed.

A beam of light bends when it enters glass.

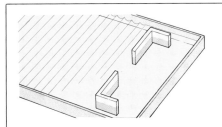

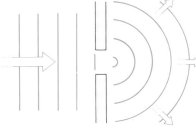

Diffraction

Waves bend when they pass through a narrow gap. This is called **diffraction**. It works best if the width of the gap is about the same as the wavelength. Wide gaps don't cause much diffraction.

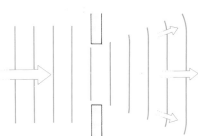

Try looking at a street light through the cover of an umbrella. You will see many images. These are caused by diffraction. The light is bent off course as it passes through the tiny holes in the material.

Gaps have to be extremely small to diffract light. What does this tell you about the wavelength of light waves?

Interference

Surfers know the problem well. Sometimes sea waves combine together to produce a very large wave. Sometimes, they cancel each other out. This is called interference:
To see interference in a ripple tank, you sent out ripples from two points. You get an **interference pattern**. In some places, the ripples add together; in others they cancel out.

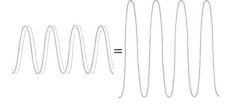

waves add

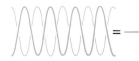

waves cancel

Try looking hard at a soap bubble just before it pops. You should see dark patches spread across it. This is because of interference. Light waves reflected from the outside of the bubble are cancelled by waves reflected from the inside surface.

1 Waves in a ripple tank approach a rectangular block of plastic. The water covers the plastic.
a What happens to the speed of the waves when they reach the plastic? What happens to the waves?
b Copy and complete the diagram to show what happens to the waves.
c The plastic is replaced by another block which is deeper than the water. Draw a diagram to show what now happens to the waves.

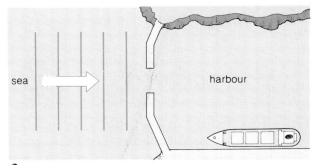

sea   harbour

2
a Copy and complete the diagram to show what happens to the waves when they pass through the harbour entrance.
b What is this called?
c What difference would there be if the harbour entrance were wider?

3.10 Electromagnetic waves

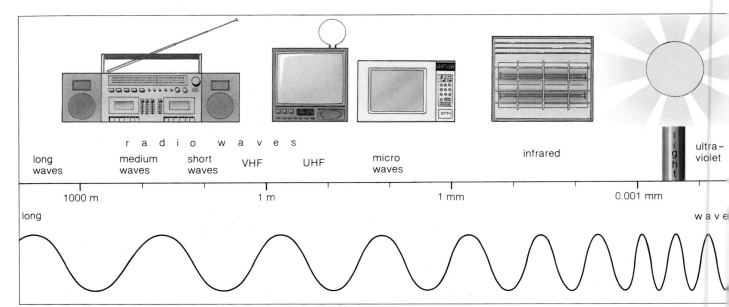

Radio waves

Radio waves are produced by making electrons vibrate in an aerial. They can't be seen or heard. But they can be sent out in a special pattern which tells a TV or radio what pictures or sounds to make.

Long and medium waves will diffract round hills. Your radio will pick them up, even down in a valley.

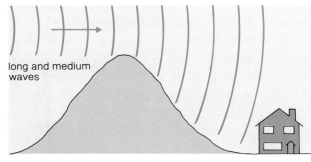

VHF **waves** are used for high quality stereo radio; UHF **waves** are used for television. They aren't diffracted much by hills. So, you don't get good reception unless there is a straight route from the transmitter to your radio or TV aerial.

Microwaves are very short wavelength radio waves. They are used for radar, and for sending signals to satellites. They are also used for beaming television and telephone signals round the country.

Some microwaves are absorbed strongly by food. This produces heat. The idea is used in microwave ovens.

Infrared radiation

Hot things like fires and radiators all give off infrared radiation. In fact, everything gives off some infrared. Usually it comes from molecules which are vibrating rapidly.

As molecules get hotter, infrared wavelengths get shorter. When something is 'red hot', some wavelengths are so short that they can be picked up by the eye.

Ultraviolet radiation

Your eyes can't detect ultraviolet radiation, though there is plenty present in sunlight. This is the type of radiation that gives you a sun tan. But too much can damage your eyes and your skin.

Some chemicals glow when they absorb ultraviolet. The effect is called **fluorescence**. This is the secret of 'whiter than white' washing powders. They absorb the ultraviolet in sunlight. Then they glow to make your clothes look brighter than normal.

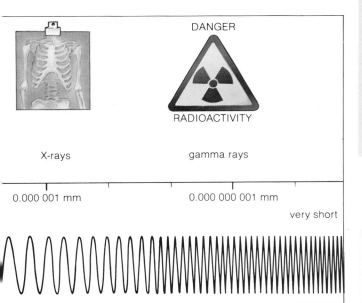

X-rays   gamma rays

0.000 001 mm   0.000 000 001 mm

very short

X-rays

X-rays can be produced using an X-ray tube. The X-rays come out when fast moving electrons smash into a metal target.

Short wavelength X-rays are extremely penetrating. They can even pass through dense metals like lead.

Long wavelength X-rays are less penetrating. They can pass through flesh but not bone. So, bones will show up on an X-ray photograph.

All X-rays are dangerous because they can damage living cells deep in the body.

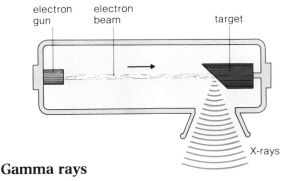

Gamma rays

These are given off by radio-active materials. They have the same effects as X-rays and are extremely dangerous.

Light is a member of a whole family of waves called the **electromagnetic spectrum**. These waves have several things in common:

- they can travel through empty space
- they travel through space at the same speed; 300 000 km/s
- they are electric and magnetic ripples, mostly given off by electrons or molecules as they vibrate or lose energy. (Electrons are tiny electrical particles that come from inside molecules – see page 128.)

1 When the beam from the filament passes through the glass prism, two other types of radiation can be detected, as well as light.
Which type of radiation is at X?
Which type of radiation is at Y?

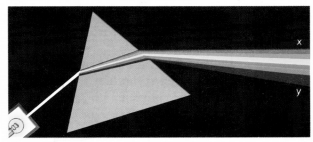

2 Name a type of electromagnetic wave which:
a can cause fluorescence;
b is diffracted by hills;
c is used for radar;
d can pass through metals;
e is given off by hot materials;
f can be detected by the eye.

3

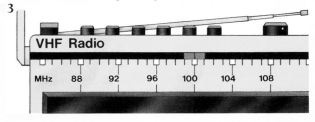

| Speed of electromagnetic waves = 300 000 000 m/s |
| 1 MHz = 1 000 000 Hz |
| Speed = frequency × wavelength |

Use the information above to calculate the wavelength of the waves being picked up by the radio.

3.11 Heat radiation

Taking it in ...

Absorbing electromagnetic waves.
The waves come from the Sun. They are mostly infrared, light and ultraviolet. And they warm up anything (or anyone) that absorbs them. They're known as 'heat radiation' – or just 'radiation' for short.
Some surfaces are better at absorbing radiation than others:
Standing in the sunshine, a black car warms up more quickly than any other. Touch the bodywork to test it for yourself.

... sending it out

Radiating electromagnetic waves in London.
Hot marathon runners give off radiation after the race. The more they radiate the more body heat they lose. And that means a risk of chilling. Silvery sheets solve the problem. They're a quick and easy way of keeping everybody warm.

Some surfaces are better at sending out or **emitting** radiation than others:

A black saucepan cools down more quickly than any other. Could you design an experiment to test it for yourself?

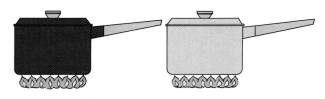

Good absorbers of heat radiation are also good emitters. This is how different surfaces compare:

Dull black surfaces are the best absorbers of radiation. They reflect hardly any radiation at all.

Shiny silvery surfaces are the worst absorbers of radiation. They reflect nearly all the radiation that strikes them.

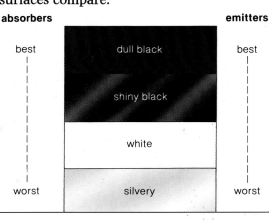

absorbers

| best |
| dull black |
| shiny black |
| white |
| worst | silvery |

emitters

| best |
| worst |

Dull black surfaces are the best emitters of radiation.

Silvery surfaces are the worst emitters of radiation.

Keeping your food warm

Shiny aluminium foil helps keep food dishes warm when they're out on the table.

Keeping your plants warm

How a greenhouse traps heat:

Short wavelength radiation from the Sun passes easily through the glass of a greenhouse. It warms the plants inside. The warm plants also radiate heat, but the wavelengths are longer and don't pass so easily out through the glass.
Result: a build up of heat in the greenhouse.

1

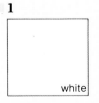

white

dull black

shiny black

Which of these surfaces is best at:
a absorbing heat radiation;
b emitting heat radiation;
c reflecting heat radiation?
2 All three kettles are the same except for their outside surfaces. All are full of boiling water.

dull black

silvery

shiny black

Keeping your drinks warm

outer glass skin

inner glass skin

gap: air removed

silvery surfaces

Shiny kettles keep their heat longer than other sorts.

This Thermos flask has two glass 'skins' with a gap between them. Air has been removed from the gap to stop heat escaping by conduction. The silvery surface stops heat escaping by radiation.

> Heat can travel in three ways;
> by conduction, by convection, and by radiation.
> Read about the other two on pages 80 to 83.

When the kettles are left to cool, this is what happens to their temperature:

	temperature in °C		
	kettle A	kettle B	kettle C
	100	100	100
after 5 min	85	90	80
after 10 min	73	82	65

a Which kettle has the silvery surface?
b Which kettle has the dull black surface?
3 Explain why:
a in hot countries, houses are often painted white;
b on a hot summer's day, the inside of a white car is cooler than a dark one;
c if you use a lens to focus the Sun's rays on newspaper, the print burns more easily than the white paper.

3.12 Sound waves

When these vibrate . . .

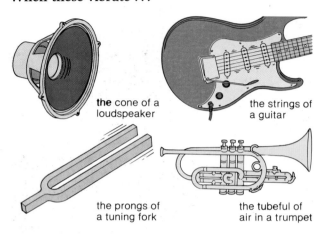

the cone of a loudspeaker

the strings of a guitar

the prongs of a tuning fork

the tubeful of air in a trumpet

. . . they give off sound waves.

Sound waves are vibrations.
When a loudspeaker cone vibrates it moves in and out very fast. This stretches and squashes the air in front. The 'stretches' and 'squashes' travel out through the air as waves. When they reach your ears, they make your ear drums vibrate and you hear a sound.

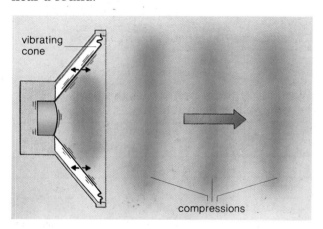

vibrating cone

compressions

Sound waves are longitudinal waves; the vibrations are backwards and forwards (see page 110).

The 'squashes' are called **compressions**; the air pressure here is higher than normal.

The 'stretches' are called **rarefactions**; the air pressure here is lower than normal.

Sound waves can travel through solids.
They can travel through doors, floors, ceilings and brick walls.

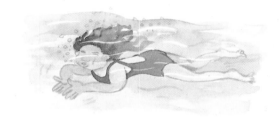

Sound waves can travel through liquids. You can still hear sound when you are swimming underwater.

Sound waves can travel through all gases. This flask has air in it. But, you would still hear the bell ringing whatever type of gas was in the flask.

Sound waves can't travel through a vacuum (empty space). If the air is pumped out of the flask, the sound stops, even though the bell goes on working. Sound waves can't be made if there is nothing to be squashed and stretched.

Seeing sounds

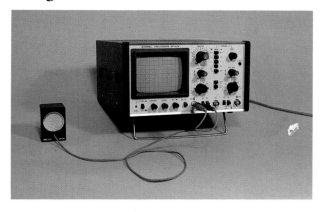

You can't see sounds. But with a microphone and an oscilloscope, you can show sounds as wave shapes on a screen.

When sound waves reach the microphone, they make a tiny sheet of metal vibrate. The microphone changes the vibrations into electrical vibrations. The oscilloscope uses these to make a spot vibrate up and down on the screen. It moves the spot steadily sideways at the same time. The result is a **waveform.**

The waveform looks like a series of transverse waves. But it is really a graph of pressure against time. It shows how the air pressure near the microphone rises and falls as sound waves pass.

If the sound gets louder, the amplitude of the waveform increases:

Waveforms on disc. The grooves on an LP. When you play a record, a tiny stylus moves along the groove. The groove makes the stylus vibrate. The vibrations are changed into electrical vibrations. These make a loudspeaker cone vibrate. You hear a copy of the original sound.

1 Someone blows a whistle near a microphone. This is the waveform produced on the screen of an oscilloscope.

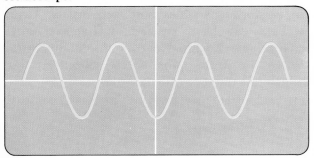

a Use a ruler marked in millimetres to measure the amplitude of the waveform.
b Redraw the waveform so that it has an amplitude of 15 mm. Would the whistle that produced this be louder than the one before?
2 Copy the sentences and fill in the blanks:
a Sounds are caused by __.
b Sound waves can't travel through a __.
c Sound waves are __ waves.
d When sound waves pass, the __ of the air rises and falls rapidly.
3 Using things you might find around the house, how could you show someone that sound can pass through solid materials?

3.13 Vibrations

Vibrations don't only make sounds. They can have other effects as well:

Old brickwork is easily damaged by the vibrations from heavy traffic.

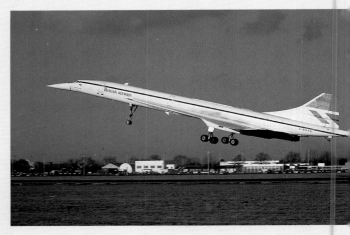

Supersonic aircraft aren't allowed to fly fast over populated areas. When planes fly faster than sound they cause air vibrations which can shatter windows.

If car wheels are out of balance, they vibrate when the car moves. This 'wheel wobble' makes the steering wheel judder and can damage the suspension. To prevent it, the wheels have to be balanced by fixing small lead masses to them.

Here, damaging vibrations are being put to work – to crack concrete.

In washing machines and spin dryers, 'drum wobble' can be a problem. It happens when clothes aren't spread evenly inside the drum. When the drum spins, severe vibrations start which can damage the machine.

Road vibrations can make a journey uncomfortable and tiring. But not for this truck driver. That's because the driving seat is suspended on a cushion of air.

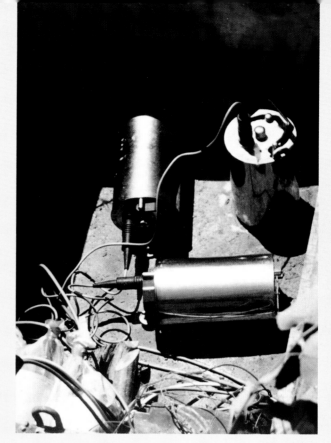

This is a **seismometer**. It can detect the vibrations from earthquakes thousands of miles away. It can also pick up the vibrations from distant nuclear bomb tests. Governments use the readings to check that international test-ban agreements haven't been broken.

> What vibrates in each of these?
> And what is the effect used for?

Problem: how to get cider apples out of a tree.
Solution: vibrate the tree.
A clever invention that saves time and money. But it does a job that once provided work for people.

3.14 Speed of sound

Lightning strikes. You see the flash. The crash comes later. Much later if you're lucky.

Sound is very much slower than light. So you always hear things after you've seen them. Over short distances, you don't notice the difference. But with distant lightning, there can be a delay of several seconds. The longer the delay, the further away the lightning – it's about 3 seconds for every kilometre (half mile).

In air, the speed of sound is about 330 metres/second. That's about four times faster than a racing car, but slower than Concorde.

The speed of sound depends on the temperature of the air. Sound waves travel faster through hot air than through cold air.

The speed of sound doesn't depend on the pressure of the air. If the pressure rises the speed of the waves stays the same.

The speed of sound is different through different materials. Sound waves travel faster through liquids than through gases. They travel fastest of all through solids.

speed of sound

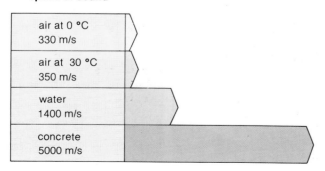

air at 0 °C 330 m/s	
air at 30 °C 350 m/s	
water 1400 m/s	
concrete 5000 m/s	

Echoes

Hard surfaces like walls reflect sound waves. When you hear an **echo**, you are hearing a reflected sound a short time after the original sound.

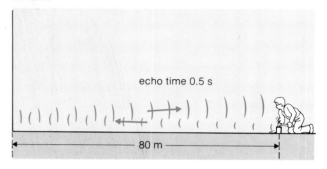

echo time 0.5 s

80 m

This girl is 80 metres from a large brick wall. She is hammering a block of wood. Every time she hits the block, she hears an echo 0.5 seconds later. This is the **echo time**.

She could use this information to calculate the speed of sound:

$$\text{speed} = \frac{\text{distance travelled}}{\text{time taken}}$$

so

$$\textbf{speed of sound} = \frac{\textbf{distance to wall and back}}{\textbf{echo time}}$$

$$= \frac{2 \times 80}{0.5} = \frac{160}{0.5} = 320 \, \text{m/s}$$

Do-it-yourself

If there's a large wall around, you can find the speed of sound for yourself. Just fit your own distance and time measurements into the equation above.

To make your time measurement more accurate, measure the time for 20 echoes instead of just one. Bang the block repeatedly so that each blow is made just as an echo returns. If it takes 10 seconds to make 20 hammer blows, then the echo time is 10 ÷ 20 seconds, or 0.5 seconds.

Using echoes

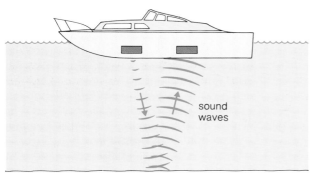

sound waves

Ships use **echo sounders** to measure the depth of water underneath them. An echo sounder sends bursts of sound waves towards the sea bed. Then it measures the time taken for the echoes to return. The longer the time, the deeper the water.

For example:

If – a burst of sound takes 0.1 seconds to reach the sea bed and return,

and – the speed of sound in water is 1400 m/s.

then – distance travelled = speed × time

$$= 1400 \times 0.1 \, \text{m}$$
$$= 140 \, \text{m}$$

But – the sound has to travel down *and* back,

so – the depth of water is 70 m.

		distance travelled in m	time taken in s
	rocket	900	3.0
	aircraft	1000	2.0
	bullet	100	0.5
	meteorite	3000	0.1

1 If the speed of sound in air is 330 m/s, which of the above are travelling faster than sound?

2 If the speed of sound in air is 330 m/s, how far does sound travel in

a 1 second

b 2 seconds

c 10 seconds

d 0.1 seconds?

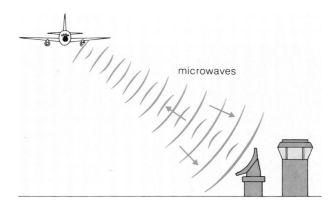

microwaves

Radar works rather like an echo sounder. Except that microwaves are sent out rather than sound waves. The microwaves are reflected by aircraft. The longer they take to return, the further away the aircraft.

Losing echoes

Echoes can be a nuisance. In empty rooms, cinemas and concert halls, reflected sounds can take so long to die away that it is sometimes difficult to hear anything clearly. Carpets, curtains and soft chairs help to solve the problem. Modern concert halls are designed so that sounds are neither muffled nor echoing around.

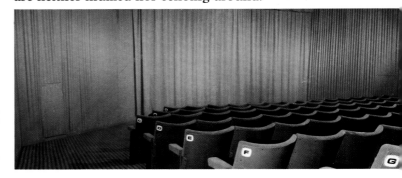

3 Jeff thinks that his cassette player sounds clearer in the bedroom than it does in the kitchen. Is he imagining things? Or could he be right? Explain.

4 The echo sounder in this ship sends a burst of sound waves towards the sea bed. 0.2 seconds later, reflected waves are picked up by the ship.

a How long did it take the waves to reach the sea bed?

b If the speed of sound in water is 1400 m/s, how far is it to the sea bed?

3.15 Sounds high and low

She doesn't necessarily sing better than him.
But she can reach higher notes.
She can give out more sound waves every second.

Frequency and pitch

The number of waves per second is called the **frequency**. It is measured in **hertz (Hz)**.
If a singer gives out 200 sound waves every second, the frequency is 200 Hz.

Different frequencies sound different to the ear.
You hear *high* frequencies as *high* notes.
They have a **high pitch**.
You hear *low* frequencies as *low* notes.
They have a **low pitch**.

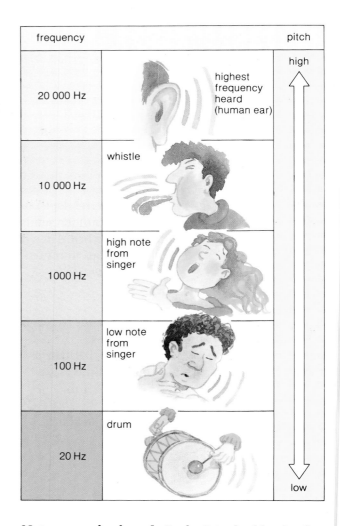

Changing note

The notes from many musical instruments are all based on **octaves**.
Each time the pitch goes up an octave, the frequency doubles.

Notes on a keyboard. Each C is double the frequency of the one to its left. This is also true for any other notes that are an octave apart.

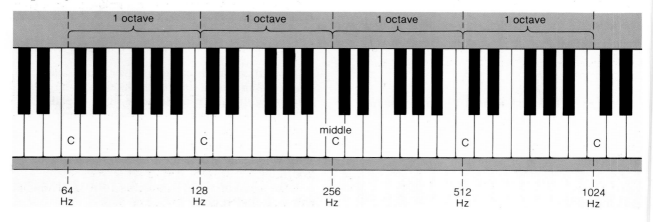

length halves
frequency doubles

A vibrating guitar string.
To make the pitch of the note higher, you could
– tighten the string
– shorten the length of string which can vibrate by
  pressing the string against a fret.

If you halve the vibrating length of the string, the
frequency doubles and pitch goes up by an octave.

The note from this clarinet comes from a vibrating
column of air inside. As you uncover the air holes,
the vibrating column gets shorter and the pitch
goes up.

Quality

Middle C on a guitar doesn't sound quite the same
as Middle C on a piano – and its waveform looks
different on an oscilloscope screen. The two
sounds have a different **quality**.

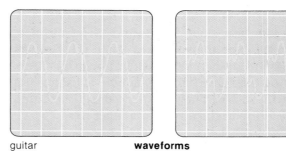

guitar   **waveforms**   piano

In fact, each sound has a strong **fundamental
frequency**, giving Middle C. But other weaker
frequencies are mixed in as well. These are called
overtones. They differ from one instrument to
another. With a synthesiser, you can choose
which frequencies you mix together, and make
the sound of a piano, guitar or any other instrument you want.

---

speed = frequency × wavelength
speed of sound in air = 330 m/s
1000 hertz = 1 kilohertz (kHz)

1 Copy the chart below. Fill in the blanks to show
the frequencies and wavelengths of the different
sounds:

frequency in Hz	wavelength in m
?	10
?	2
330	?
660	?

2 What happens to the pitch of a guitar string if you:
a shorten the string;
b slacken the string?
3 Four instruments are giving out four different
notes:

instrument	flute	guitar	trumpet	keyboard
frequency	400 Hz	150 Hz	500 Hz	200 Hz

a Which has the highest pitch?
b Which two notes are one octave apart?
c A saxophone plays a note 2 octaves higher than
the guitar. What is the frequency of the note?
d Explain why the saxophone doesn't sound like the
guitar even if both play the same note.

3.16 Noise

LIVING WITH NOISE

The people who live here don't need any scientist to tell them what noise is. It is any sound they don't like. Especially the sound of jet airliners taking off over their garden. Since the runway was extended, the value of their house has dropped. And they have had to fit double-glazing to cut down the noise. They are very dissatisfied, and keep writing to the airport manager to say so.

The Airport Manager, thinks that they are being unreasonable. Pilots have to follow special rules during take off to limit engine noise. And at night, there's a complete ban on flights altogether. Besides which, jets are much quieter than they used to be. Modern jets push out air more smoothly than old ones. So they produce less noise.

WHAT NOISE? Debbie is protected from noise by the Safety at Work Act. When she is working in the machine shop, her company has to provide her with ear protectors.

NOISE DAMAGE Strickly speaking it isn't noise at all. Just high quality rock music. But if you keep the volume turned up for hours on end, it can damage your ears. In extreme cases, it can lead to deafness.

ESCAPING FROM NOISE? This 'dead room' has a special lining on its walls. It absorbs over 99% of the sound energy striking it. So it seems like the perfect place for peace and quiet. But there is a snag. The room is so quiet that you can hear the food churning in your stomach and the blood pumping through your veins. Perhaps a little noise isn't such a bad thing after all.

WARNING NOISES

Noise is often used to give warnings. Here are some examples:

'Bleepers' on this vehicle warn people behind that it is reversing.

The high frequency, rapidly changing sound from an ambulance is easily heard above the noise of other traffic.

Foghorns give out low frequency sounds that can be heard many miles out to sea. They warn shipping that rocks are close.

You want to play your stereo loud. Your next-door neighbour doesn't like your type of music. Write down the ways in which you could reduce the amount of noise reaching your neighbour.

Most cinemas have several films on show in the same building. Try to find out how the noise from one studio is prevented from reaching another.

Spin dryer, motor cycle, electric drill.
Design an experiment to test which of these makes most noise.
What must you do to be sure that your experiment is a fair test?
Would you expect the loudest noise to be the most annoying?

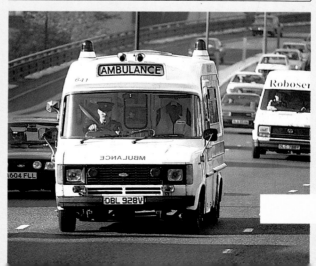

4.1 Electric charge

It makes cling-film stick to your hands, and dust stick to your records. It causes crackles and sparks when you comb your hair. It can even make your hair stand on end.

Where charge comes from

Records, combs, hair, and all other materials are made up of tiny particles called **molecules**. Molecules are built from **atoms**.
A molecule may be just a single atom.
Or it may be several atoms stuck together.
It all depends on the material.

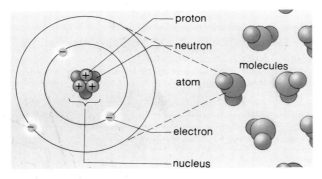

Atoms all have electric charges inside them.
In the centre of each atom there is a **nucleus**. This is made up of **protons** and **neutrons**. Even tinier particles orbit round this nucleus. These are **electrons**.

Protons and electrons both carry an electric charge. But the charges are of opposite types:

Electrons have a negative (−) charge.

Protons have a positive (+) charge, equal in size to the charge on the electron.
Neutrons have no charge.

Normally, atoms have equal numbers of electrons and protons. So the − and + charges cancel each other out. But electrons don't always stay attached to atoms. They can be removed by rubbing.

Charging by rubbing

If two materials are rubbed together, electrons may be transferred from one to the other. This upsets the balance between + and −.

A polythene comb is pulled through hair.
The polythene pulls electrons from atoms in the hair.
This leaves the polythene with more electrons than normal, and the hair with less.
The polythene becomes *negatively* charged.
The hair becomes *positively* charged.

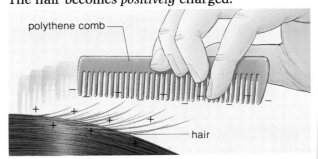

A Perspex comb is pulled through hair.
This time, the hair pulls electrons from the Perspex.
The hair becomes *negatively* charged.
The Perspex becomes *positively* charged.

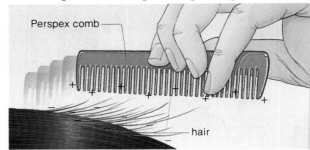

Forces between charges

Like charges repel
Hold two strips of cling-film together at one end. Charge them up by pulling them between your fingers.
Both strips have the same type of charge on them. They try to push each other apart.

Unlike charges attract
Pull a piece of cling-film across your hand. Both become charged up. But the charges are opposite. The cling-film is attracted to your hand.

Charge attraction

A positively charged comb is put just above a small piece of kitchen foil. Electrons in the foil are pulled upwards. This makes the top end of the foil negative. But it leaves the bottom end short of electrons, and therefore positive.

The comb attracts the negative end of the foil strongly, because it is close. It repels the positive end . . . but less strongly because it is further away. The attraction wins. The foil is pulled to the comb.

This is an example of something charged (a comb) attracting something uncharged (foil). The charges which appear on the foil are called **induced** charges.

1 Say whether the things below will attract each other, repel each other, or do neither:

a

b

c

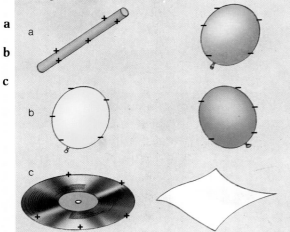

2 A balloon becomes negatively charged when rubbed against someone's sleeve.

Explain:
a how it becomes charged;
b why it will then stick to a wall.

4.2 Charge on the move

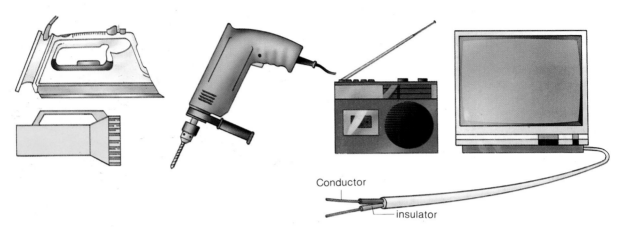

Conductor

insulator

When electric charge passes through these, they can give you anything from heat to moving pictures:

When you switch on a television, the 'electricity' passing through the cable is actually a flow of electrons. The flow is called a **current**.

Electrons flow easily through the copper wire in the cable. Copper is a good **conductor**. But the electrons can't pass through the PVC plastic coating round the wire. PVC is an **insulator**.

Conductors		
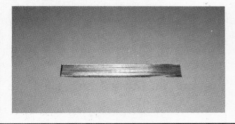	In conductors, some electrons aren't very tightly held to their atoms. They can move through the material by passing from atom to atom. Good conductors of electricity are also good conductors of heat (see page 80).	Conductors can't easily be charged by rubbing. Any electrons gained or lost immediately flow through the material to restore the balance.
Semiconductors		
	Semiconductors behave like insulators when cold. When warm, they become poor conductors.	
Insulators		
	In insulators, the electrons are all tightly held to atoms.	Insulators can be charged by rubbing. If electrons are gained or lost, they can't flow back through the material.

Charge movers

Cells and batteries are a useful source of electric charge. They change chemical energy into electrical energy.

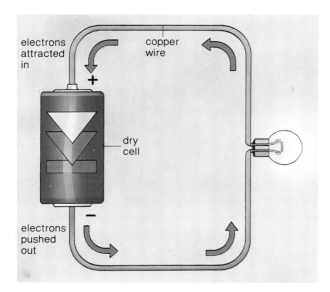

This is a **dry cell**, connected to a light bulb by two copper wires. In the cell, chemical reactions move electrons to the outside case. This makes the case negative (−) and leaves the central terminal positive (+). Electrons are pushed out of the − and attracted round to the +. As they pass through the filament of the bulb, they make it so hot that it gives out light.

When the chemicals in the cell have been used up, no more electrons can be pushed out. The cell is then 'flat'.

1 Battery Charge Current Insulator
   Conductor Cells Semiconductor

Which word describes each of the following?
a A material through which electrons can flow.
b A flow of electrons.
c A material which doesn't allow a current to pass through.
d A collection of cells.
e A material which acts as an insulator when cold, but conducts when warm.

2 Mike uses a metal comb, Rachel uses a nylon one. Explain why one of them may see sparks when they comb their hair, but the other one won't.

A **battery** – made by joining several cells together. It can push electrons out with more force than one cell by itself.

A battery really means a collection of cells, though the word is often used for just one cell.

There are six cells in this lead-acid car battery. The battery is rechargeable. Electrons can be passed back through it to reverse the chemical reactions. Then the charge can be pushed out all over again.

For their size, batteries are poor storers of energy. It's one reason why electrically powered cars have never been very successful.

3 The chart gives information about a cassette player and the cells needed to make it work.

Number of cells needed	6
Cost of each cell	50p
Energy stored in each cell	10 000 joules
Energy used by cassette played in 1 hour	20 000 joules

a What is the total energy stored by the cells?
b For how long will the cassette player run on one set of cells?
c What is the cost of running the cassette player for one hour?

4.3 A simple circuit

When you dry your hair, 20 million million million electrons pass along the cable every second.

The hair dryer and cable are part of a huge conducting loop which passes right out of the house.

The loops on this page are much smaller. But the principles are just the same.

Current

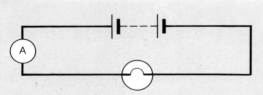

A bulb, wire, meter and battery – all drawn using electrical symbols.

The complete loop is known as a **circuit**.
The meter is measuring the flow of charge.
The meter is called an **ammeter**.
The flow of charge is called a **current**.

Current is measured in amperes (A)

A current of 1 ampere means that about 6 million million million electrons are flowing round the circuit every second.

Typical current sizes	
current through ... .. a small torch bulb __	0.2 A
.. a hair dryer __	3 A
.. a car headlight bulb __	4 A
.. an electric kettle __	10 A

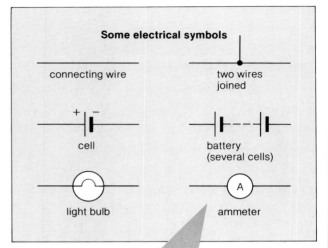

Some electrical symbols

connecting wire — two wires joined — cell — battery (several cells) — light bulb — ammeter

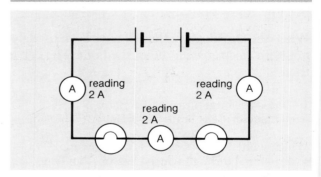

reading 2 A — reading 2 A — reading 2 A

This circuit has three ammeters and two bulbs in it. When electrons leave the battery, they flow through each of the ammeters in turn. So the readings are all the same. In a simple circuit, **the current through every part is the same.**

Putting ammeters in the circuit doesn't affect the current. As far as the circuit is concerned, the ammeters are just like pieces of connecting wire.

Which way?

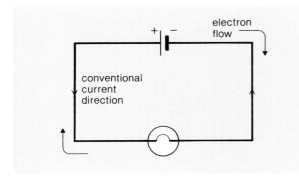

Some circuit diagrams have arrowheads marked on them. These *don't* show a flow. They just give the direction from positive (+) to negative (−) round the circuit. This is called the **conventional current direction**. The electrons actually flow the opposite way.

Current and charge

If a current is flowing, then electric charge is passing round a circuit.
Amounts of charge are measured in **coulombs**:

If a current of	flows for	then the charge passing is
1 ampere	1 second	1 coulomb
2 amperes	1 second	2 coulombs
2 amperes	3 seconds	6 coulombs
. . . and so on.		

You can use an equation to calculate charge:

charge = **current** × **time**
(coulombs)   (amperes)   (seconds)

Use it to check the examples above.

If you think of a current as a flow of charge, then

this current	*means* this flow of charge
1 ampere	1 coulomb every second
2 amperes	2 coulombs every second
. . . and so on	

1 What is the reading on each of these ammeters?

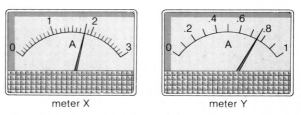

meter X   meter Y

2 Copy the diagram below.

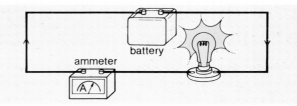

a What do the arrows on this diagram show?
b Mark in the positive and negative terminals of the battery.
Mark in the direction of electron flow, using an arrow alongside the wire.
c Redraw the diagram using the correct electrical symbols.

3 The current through the bulb is 3 A.

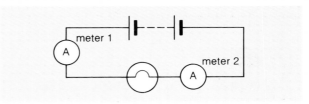

What is the current through the battery?
What is the current through meter 1?
What is the current through meter 2?

4

appliance	time switched on in s	current in A
electric drill	20	2
food mixer		1
hairdryer	8	

The electrical appliances in the chart were all switched on for different times.
a How much charge was taken by the electric drill?
b If the food mixer took the same charge as the electric drill, how long was it switched on for?
c If the hairdryer took the same charge as the other two, what current was flowing through it?

4.4 Voltage

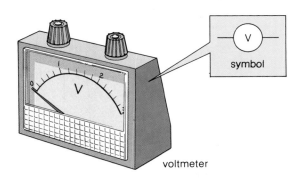

voltmeter

Anyone who attacks this fish is likely to get a shock – in more ways than one. When an electric eel senses danger, it turns itself into a living battery – pushing out electrons with nearly double the energy of those from a mains socket.

Energy from a battery

When electrons are pushed out of a battery, they carry energy with them.

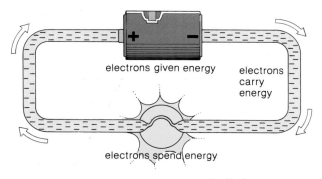

electrons given energy   electrons carry energy

electrons spend energy

In the circuit, the electrons spend all their energy passing through the bulb. The energy is changed into heat and light. When the electrons reach the battery again, all their energy has gone.

Battery voltage

Some batteries give electrons more energy than others. The higher the **voltage**, the more energy is given to each electron.

Voltage is also known as **potential difference (p.d.)**. It is measured in **volts (V)**.

Voltage is measured by connecting an instrument called a **voltmeter** across the battery terminals. The voltage produces inside a battery is called the **electromotive force (e.m.f.)** of the battery.

Voltages round a circuit

Three bulbs connected to a 12 volt battery. The battery gives the electrons energy.

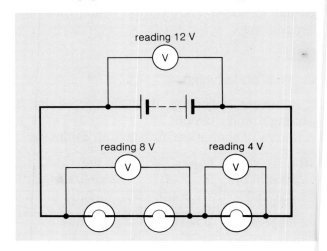

reading 12 V

reading 8 V   reading 4 V

The electrons spend some of their energy in the first bulb, some in the second, and the rest in the third.

Connect a voltmeter across any of the bulbs and it shows a reading. The higher the voltage, the more energy each electron spends as it passes through that part of the circuit.

Between them, the bulbs give out all the energy supplied by the battery:

The voltages across the bulbs add up to equal the battery voltage.

Connecting a voltmeter has almost no effect on the current flowing in the circuit. As far as the circuit is concerned, the voltmeters might as well not be there.

Cells in series and parallel

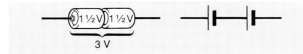

3 V

These cells are connected in **series**.
They give twice the voltage of a single cell.

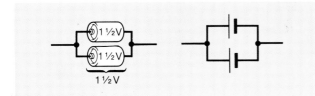

1½V

These cells are connected in **parallel**.
They give the same voltage as a single cell.
But they last twice as long as a single cell.

Volts, coulombs, and joules

There is an exact link between voltage, charge and
energy:

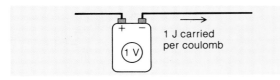

1 J carried
per coulomb

Voltage across cell: 1 volt.
This cell gives 1 joule of energy to every coulomb
of charge it pushes out.

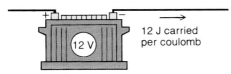

12 J carried
per coulomb

Voltage across battery: 12 volts.
This battery gives 12 joules of energy to every
coulomb of charge it pushes out.

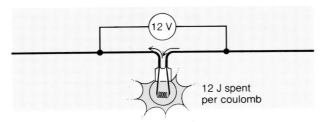

12 J spent
per coulomb

Voltage across bulb: 12 volts
12 joules of energy are spent by every coulomb of
charge passing through.

1 In which section of this circuit do the electrons
have:
a most energy; **b** least energy?

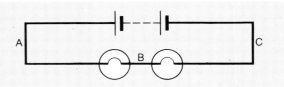

What happens to the energy they lose?
2 What is the voltage across each arrangement of
cells?

3 a What is the reading on the voltmeter across
bulb B?

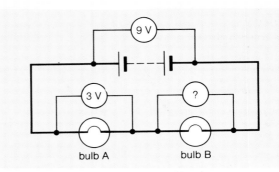

b How much energy does the battery give each
coulomb of charge it pushes out?
c How much energy is spent by each coulomb of
charge as it passes through bulb A?
4 To answer this question, you may need to look up
information in the previous section.

	A Battery of dry cells	B car battery	C watch battery
e.m.f. in V	15	12	1.5
maximum current in A	6	100	0.01

a Which battery can push out the most electrons
every second?
b Which battery pushes out electrons with most
energy?
c How much charge can the car battery push out in
10 seconds?
d How much energy can the car battery deliver in
10 seconds?

4.5 Resistance

Current passes easily through a piece of copper connecting wire. But it doesn't pass so easily through the thin nichrome wire of an electric fire element. This wire has much more **resistance**. Energy has to be spent to force electrons through it. And heat comes off as a result.

All conductors have some resistance. But:

long wires have more resistance than short wires;

thin wires have more resistance than thick wires;

nichrome wire has more resistance than copper wire of the same size.

Resistance is calculated using this equation:

$$\text{resistance} = \frac{\text{voltage}}{\text{current}}$$

Resistance is measured in **ohms (Ω)**.

For example:

If there is a voltage of 12 volts across this piece of nichrome, then a current of 4 amperes flows through. So:	If there is a voltage of 12 volts across this piece of nichrome, then a current of 2 amperes flows through. So:
$\text{resistance} = \dfrac{12}{4} \text{ ohms}$ $= 3 \text{ ohms}$	$\text{resistance} = \dfrac{12}{2} \text{ ohms}$ $= 6 \text{ ohms}$

The *higher* the resistance, the *less* current flows for each volt across the wire.

Heaters...

Like electric fires, kettles and hairdryers have heating elements made from coils of thin nichrome wire. The wire gives off heat when a current passes through.

... and resistors

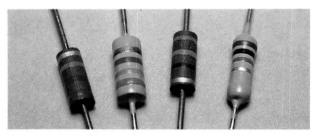

These are **resistors**. They also give off heat when a current passes through. But that isn't their job. In some circuits, they are used to reduce the current. In radio or TV circuits, they keep currents and voltages at the levels needed to make other parts work properly.

In a **variable resistor** there is a sliding contact which moves along a coil of nichrome wire. By moving the contact, you can change the resistance.

Variable resistors like this are used as volume controls in TVs and radios, and in computer joysticks.

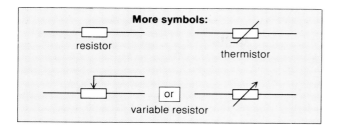

More symbols:

resistor

thermistor

variable resistor   or

Measuring resistance – Ohm's law

This is an experiment to measure the resistance of a length of nichrome wire when different currents are flowing through it:

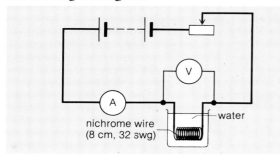

nichrome wire
(8 cm, 32 swg)

water

The voltmeter measures the voltage across the wire. The ammeter measures the current flowing through. The water keeps the wire at a steady temperature. To change the voltage across the wire, you move the sliding contact on the variable resistor. This gives the wire a different share of the battery voltage. You increase the voltage in stages, and measure the current each time. For example:

Voltage across wire in V	Current through wire in A	voltage ÷ current in Ω
3.0	1.0	3
6.0	2.0	3
9.0	3.0	3
12.0	4.0	3
		= resistance

Here, the voltage and current are in *proportion*. The resistance has the same value every time. Like all other metals the nichrome obeys **Ohm's law**:

The resistance of a metal conductor is the same, whatever current is flowing – provided the temperature doesn't change.

Resistance and temperature

If the temperature changes, so does the resistance.

If a *metal* is warmed, its resistance goes *up*.

If a *semiconductor* is warmed, its resistance goes *down*. Carbon behaves in the same way.

This is a **thermistor**, made from semiconducting materials. When it is warmed, its resistance falls sharply. Thermistors are used in electronic circuits which have to be 'switched' on or off by a temperature change (see page 198).

1 When a kettle is plugged into the 240 V mains, a current of 8 A flows through its element. What is the resistance of the element?
2 A piece of nichrome wire is kept at a steady temperature. Different voltages are applied across the wire, and the current measured each time. Copy the table, and fill in the missing values.

voltage in V	current in A	resistance in Ω
8	2	?
4	?	?
2	?	?

3 A headlamp bulb has a filament made of tungsten metal. This is how the current through the bulb rises when the voltage across it is increased:

voltage in V	2	4	6	8	10	12
current in A	1.8	2.8	3.5	4.1	4.6	5.0

Plot a graph of *current* (side axis) against *voltage* (bottom axis). Use your graph to find:
a the current flowing when the voltage is 9 V.
b the resistance of the bulb when the current is 2 A.
c the resistance of the bulb when the current is 4 A.
d the highest resistance of the bulb.
Mark on your graph the point where the temperature is highest.

4.6 Danger! Electricity

A 132 000 volt overhead cable can push more than enough current through someone to kill them. To prevent accidents, the cables are suspended way above roof-top height. And the pylons are built so that people can't climb them. However, accidents have occurred when kite lines have touched cables.

A deadly playground

Every year, over 50 children are killed or seriously injured while playing on railway lines. With more and more track being electrified, the problem is getting worse. Contact with the live rail doesn't always kill. But it can cause serious burns as current flows through arms or legs to the ground.

Lightning doesn't always kill. But it too can cause serious burns. You are most at risk on open ground, or near an isolated tree or buildings. But the chances of being struck are still very small – much less than a big win on the football pools for example.

It's only a 12 volt battery. So most people don't expect it to be dangerous. But if a spanner is accidently connected across the wires from the battery, the surge of current could be enough to burn you or start a fire. Wise mechanics disconnect the battery before starting work.

Fire hazards

In the home people are more at risk from electrical fires than they are from electric shocks. Here are some of the causes:

Old, frayed wiring.
Broken strands of wire can mean that a cable has a high resistance at one point. So heat is given off when current flows through. It may be enough to melt the insulation and cause a fire.

Dirty plug pins.
These give a high resistance where they connect with the socket. When a current flows through, the plug may overheat.

Too many appliances connected to one socket. If all the appliances are switched on at once, the supply cable may become overloaded.

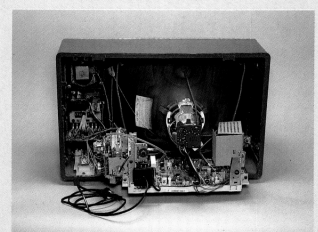

The TV is probably the most dangerous piece of equipment in the house. When a TV set is working, the voltages inside can reach 20 000 V or more. And parts inside are still live even when the set is switched off.

For safety's sake:

NEVER take the back off.

ALWAYS switch off at the plug overnight.
Unless you do this, there is still a live connection through to the set. If a fault develops, a current could flow, and a fire could start.

Can you explain why, for safety, you should disconnect the battery before working on a car engine?
Can you explain why you should NOT:

- fly kites near overhead cables?
- connect too many appliances to one socket?
- leave a television set plugged in overnight?

Try to find out why:

- bathroom lights have to be switched on and off by a pull-cord;
- extension leads shouldn't be coiled up tightly when in use;
- electric drills and food mixers are 'double insulated'.

4.7 Series and parallel

How do you run twenty dodgems from one fairground generator? Or two lamps and a hair-dryer from one mains socket? In much the same way as you run two light bulbs from one battery.

Connected to a battery, a single bulb glows brightly.

Here are two ways in which you could add a second bulb to the circuit:

Bulbs in series

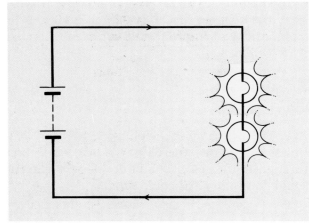

These bulbs are connected in **series**.
They have to share the battery voltage. So each glows dimly.

If one bulb is removed, the circuit is broken. The other bulb goes out.

Bulbs in parallel

These bulbs are connected in **parallel**.
Each has direct connections to the battery.
Each gets the full battery voltage. So each glows brightly. But together, the bulbs take twice as much current as a single bulb. Energy is taken from the battery at a faster rate, so the battery goes 'flat' more quickly.

If one bulb is removed, there is still an unbroken circuit through the other bulb. So it continues to glow brightly.

Switches

A **switch** breaks a circuit by moving two contacts apart.
In this circuit, each bulb is controlled by a switch. To find out which:
trace a route with your finger from one side of the battery, through a bulb, to the other side.
Your finger will pass over a switch.
This is the switch that turns the bulb on and off.

Two of the bulbs are controlled by the same switch. Can you tell which?

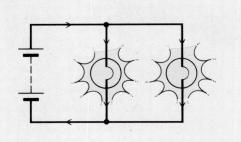
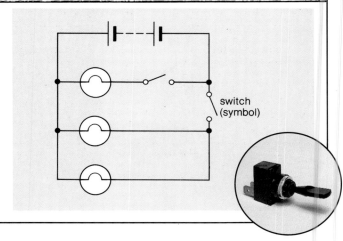

switch
(symbol)

Resistors in series

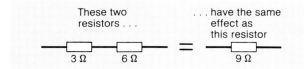

These two resistors . . . = . . . have the same effect as this resistor

3 Ω   6 Ω   9 Ω

Two resistors in series.
Together, they give a higher resistance than either resistor by itself. The effect is the same as joining two short lengths of nichrome wire together to make a longer length.

To find the combined resistance, just add up the resistance values:

combined = **first** + **second**
resistance   **resistance**   **resistance**

The rule works for three or more resistances as well.

If one bulb breaks they all go off. What does this tell you about the way that these lights are connected?

Resistors in parallel

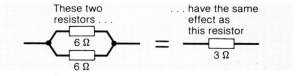

These two resistors . . . = . . . have the same effect as this resistor

6 Ω
6 Ω   3 Ω

Two resistors in parallel.
Together, they give a lower resistance than either resistor by itself. The effect is the same as putting two pieces of nichrome wire side by side. They behave like a wider piece of wire.

If the two resistances are the *same*, the combined resistance is *half* a single resistance.

If the two resistances are different, you have to use an equation find the combined resistance:

$$\text{combined resistance} = \frac{\text{first resistance} \times \text{second resistance}}{\text{first resistance} + \text{second resistance}}$$

For example:

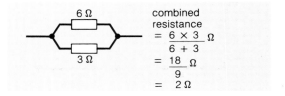

6 Ω
3 Ω

combined resistance
$= \dfrac{6 \times 3}{6 + 3} \, \Omega$
$= \dfrac{18}{9} \, \Omega$
$= \; 2 \, \Omega$

1 The chart give you information about three different sets of bulbs: A, B, and C. In each case, say whether the bulbs are arranged in SERIES or in PARALLEL. Then copy and complete the last column.

	power source	bulbs connected	voltage across each bulb	effect of removing one bulb
A	240 V mains	3 ceiling bulbs	240 V	others stay ON
B	240 V mains	20 Christmas tree bulbs	12 V	?
C	12 V battery	2 headlamp bulbs	12 V	?

2 Match the resistors!

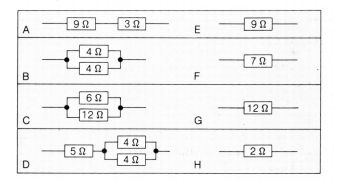

Somewhere in the right-hand column is a resistor with the same resistance as a combination in the left-hand column. Find the matching pairs.

4.8 Solving circuits

Useful equations

This equation: **resistance** $= \dfrac{\text{voltage}}{\text{current}}$

can be written using symbols: $R = \dfrac{V}{I}$

where R is the **resistance** in **ohms**
        V is the **voltage**   in **volts**
and I is the **current**   in **amperes**

You can rearrange the equation in two ways:

$$I = \dfrac{V}{R} \quad \text{and} \quad V = I \times R$$

These are useful if you know the resistance, but need to find the current or voltage.

This triangle gives you all three equations. If you want the equation for I, just cover up I, and so on. . . .

For example:
A current of 2 A flows through a 6 Ω resistor. To find the voltage across the resistor:

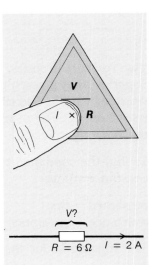

Select the equation for V and fill in the values of I and R:
$$V = I \times R$$
$$= 2 \times 6$$
$$= 12 \text{ V}$$

When resistors are in series . . .

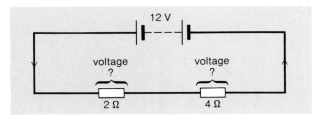

the current is the same through each.

But the voltage is shared.

Problem: to find out the voltage across each resistor in this circuit:

● Find the total resistance in the circuit:
  resistance $= 2\,\Omega + 4\,\Omega = 6\,\Omega$

● Use $I = V \div R$ to find the current in the circuit:
  current $= 12 \div 6 = 2$ A

● Now you know the current, use $V = I \times R$ to find the voltage across each resistor:
  voltage across 3 Ω resistor $= 2 \times 2$
                               $= 4$ V
  voltage across 6 Ω resistor $= 2 \times 4$
                               $= 8$ V

● Check your answers:
  the voltages across the resistors should add up to equal the battery voltage (12 V)? Do they?

When resistors are in parallel . . .

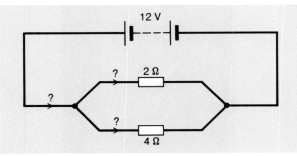

the voltage is the same across each.

But the current is shared.

Problem: to find the currents flowing in the different sections of this circuit:

● Use $I = V \div R$ to find out the current through each resistor
  Both resistors have 12 V across them, so
  current through 2 Ω resistor $= 12 \div 2$
                                $= 6$ A
  current through 4 Ω resistor $= 12 \div 4$
                                $= 3$ A

● Add the currents together to find the current in the main circuit:
  current in main circuit $= 6$ A $+ 3$ A
                           $= 9$ A

Simpler than it looks...

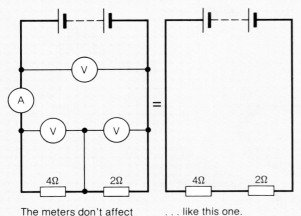

The meters don't affect the circuit. This circuit behaves ...

... like this one.

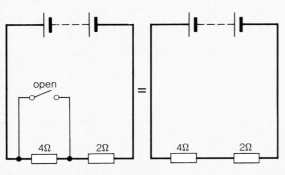

If the switch is open, this circuit behaves ...

... like this one.

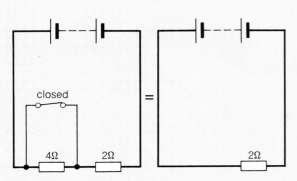

But, if the switch is closed, all the current takes the 'short circuit' route through the switch. It's just as if the 4 Ω resistor wasn't there.

1 In each of the following, the *resistance, voltage* or *current* needs to be calculated. Find the missing value:

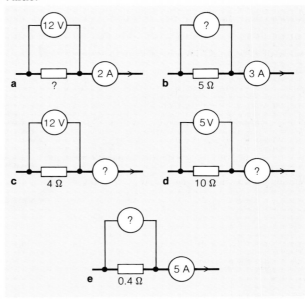

2

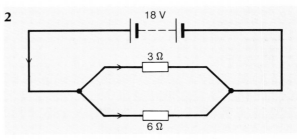

a In the circuit above, what is the current through the 6 Ω resistor?
b What is the current through the 3 Ω resistor?
c What current flows from the battery?
d Redraw the circuit, replacing the two parallel resistors by a single resistor.
If the current from the battery is the same as before, what is the resistance of this resistor?
e Use the equation for parallel resistances on page 141 to calculate the combined resistance of the resistors in the diagram above.

3

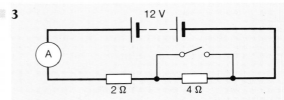

In the circuit above, what is the reading on the ammeter when the switch is **a** open **b** closed?

4.9 Mains electricity

When you plug in an electric kettle, you are connecting it into a circuit. The circuit hasn't got a battery in it. But the mains supply is doing much the same job.

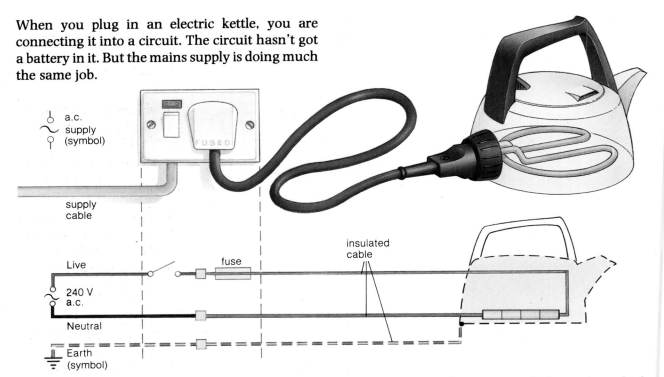

The current from a mains socket isn't a one-way flow like the current from a battery. Instead, it is pushed and pulled forwards and backwards round the circuit 50 times every second.

The current is known as **alternating current** or **a.c.**

The **mains frequency** is 50 Hz.

Power stations supply a.c because it is easier to generate than one-way **direct current (d.c.)**.

In Britain, the supply voltage is 240 V.

The connecting wires to the kettle are insulated. They are all contained in a single cable or 'flex'.

The live wire goes alternately − and + as electrons are pushed and pulled around the circuit.

The neutral wire is earthed by the Electricity Board. It is connected to a metal plate buried in the ground. Current passes through the wire. But the voltage is zero. If you accidentally touch the neutral wire, you should not get a shock.

The switch on the mains socket is fitted in the live wire. This is to make sure that none of the wire in the flex is live when the switch is turned off.

The fuse is a short piece of thin wire which overheats and melts if too much current flows through it. If a fault develops, the fuse 'blows' and breaks the circuit before anything else can overheat and catch fire. The fuse is inside a small cartridge in the plug. Like the switch, it is placed in the live wire.

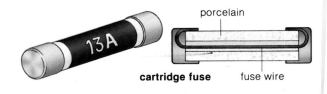

cartridge fuse   fuse wire

The earth wire is a safety wire. It connects the metal body of the kettle to earth, and stops the kettle ever becoming 'live'. For example:

A fault develops − the live wire works loose and touches the metal body of the kettle.

Results − a large current flows to Earth, and blows the fuse. So the kettle isn't dangerous to touch.

Your hairdryer or radio probably doesn't have an earth wire connected to it. This is because it has an insulating plastic case, and not a metal one.

Three pin plugs

Plugs are a simple and safe way of connecting things to a mains circuit. In Britain, the square-pin fused plug is the most commonly used type:

When wiring a plug, check that

- the three wires are connected to the correct terminals:

  brown to **Live**
  blue to **Neutral**
  yellow and green to **Earth**

- there are no loose strands of wire.
- the cable is held firmly by the grip.
- a fuse of the correct value is fitted.

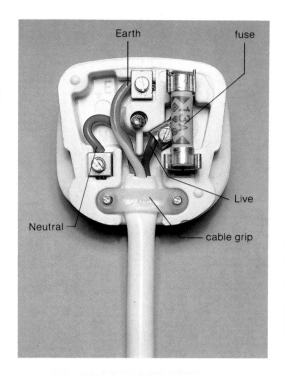

Earth · fuse · Live · cable grip · Neutral

If a fuse blows

- switch off at the socket and pull out the plug.
- don't fit a new fuse until the fault has been put right.

Choosing a fuse

Plugs are normally fitted with 3 A or 13 A fuses. The value tells you the current needed to 'blow' the fuse.

If a TV takes a current of 0.5 A, its plug should be fitted with a 3 A fuse.

If a kettle takes a current of 10 A, its plug should be fitted with a 13 A fuse.

The fuse value should always be more than the actual current, but as close to it as possible. The TV will still work with a 13 A fuse fitted. But it might not be safe. If something goes wrong, the circuits could overheat and catch fire, without the fuse blowing.

---

1 LIVE NEUTRAL EARTH
Which of these wires
a has a brown covering
b is a safety wire
c goes alternately + and −
d has a blue covering
e has a yellow and green covering
f forms part of the circuit, but has no voltage on it?
2 Copy and complete the table to show whether a 3 A or 13 A fuse should be fitted to the plug connected to each appliance. The first is done for you.

Appliance	current taken in A	fuse value in A
radio	0.1	3
hair dryer	4	
refrigerator	0.5	
cassette player	0.2	
fan heater	12	
food mixer	2	

3 This circuit has been wrongly wired.

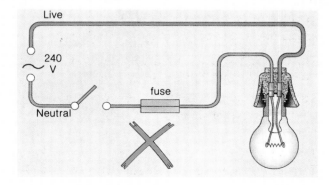

Live · 240 V · Neutral · fuse

If the bulb is taken out of its socket, the circuit isn't safe. Explain why not. Redraw the circuit, showing the correct wiring.

If your circuit were used to supply current to a metal fan heater, an earth wire should be fitted. Why?

4.10 Electrical power

They both change electrical energy into sound energy. But hers has more **power** than his.
It changes more energy every second.

Power is measured in joules per second, or **watts (W)**.

A power of 1 watt means that 1 joule of energy is being changed every second.

Typical powers

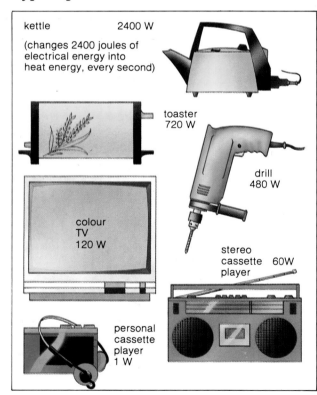

kettle   2400 W

(changes 2400 joules of electrical energy into heat energy, every second)

toaster 720 W

drill 480 W

colour TV 120 W

stereo cassette player 60W

personal cassette player 1 W

Power is sometimes given in **kilowatts**:
1 kilowatt (kW) = 1000 watts
The kettle has a power of 2.4 kW

An equation for electrical power

You can calculate electrical power using the equation:

power = voltage × current
(watts) (volts) (amperes)

For example:
if a 240 V hairdryer takes a current of 2 A, power = 240 × 2 = 480 W

- a higher voltage gives more power because each electron carries more energy.
- a higher current gives more power because there are more electrons to spend their energy every second.

Why the equation works

First, look up the meanings of *current* and *voltage* on pages 133 and 135.

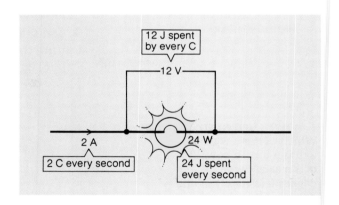

12 J spent by every C

12 V

2 A

2 C every second

24 W

24 J spent every second

This bulb has a current of 2 A flowing through it. It has a voltage of 12 V across it:
So,
2 coulombs of charge are passing through the bulb every second;
each coulomb spends 12 joules of energy as it passes through.

This means that 12 × 2 joules of energy are spent every second.
So, the power is 24 joules per second, or 24 watts.

To get this answer, you multiply the *voltage* by the *current*.

More equations

The power equation can be written using symbols:

$$P = V \times I$$

You can rearrange the equation in two ways:

$$V = \frac{P}{I} \quad \text{and} \quad I = \frac{P}{V}$$

These are useful if you know the power, but need to find the voltage or current.

More about fuses

A kettle has more power than a TV.
It takes more current from the mains.
It needs a higher value fuse in its plug:

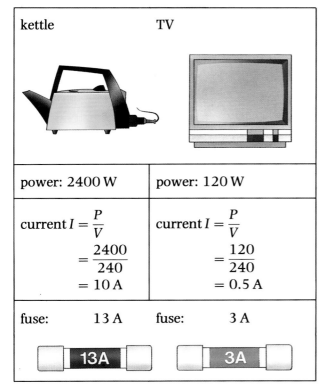

kettle	TV
power: 2400 W	power: 120 W
current $I = \dfrac{P}{V}$ $= \dfrac{2400}{240}$ $= 10\,\text{A}$	current $I = \dfrac{P}{V}$ $= \dfrac{120}{240}$ $= 0.5\,\text{A}$
fuse: 13 A	fuse: 3 A

1 Julie is setting up a lighting display in a shop window. The cable to the window can take a maximum current of 5 A. If the mains voltage is 240 V
a what is the maximum power which can be carried by the cable?
b how many 60 W light bulbs can Julie run from the cable?

2

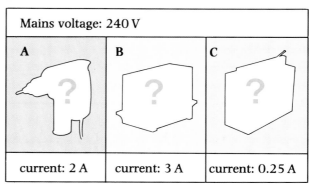

Mains voltage: 240 V		
A	B	C
current: 2 A	current: 3 A	current: 0.25 A

You will find these three appliances in the chart on the opposite page. Calculate the power of each one. Then work out what they are.

3

Mains voltage 240 V		
A	480	watt vacuum cleaner
B	960	watt iron
C	1200	watt fan heater
D	24	watt cassette player
E	40	watt video recorder

a What is the power of each appliance in kilowatts?
b What current is taken by each appliance?
c What fuse (3 A or 13 A) should be fitted to each plug?

4

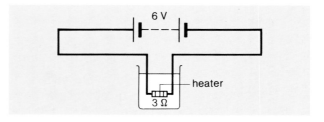

A small heater is being used to warm some water.
a What is the current through the heater?
b What is the power of the heater?

A different battery is put in the circuit. This has *twice* the voltage of the old one.
c What is the current through the heater?
d What is the power of the heater?

4.11 Circuits around the house

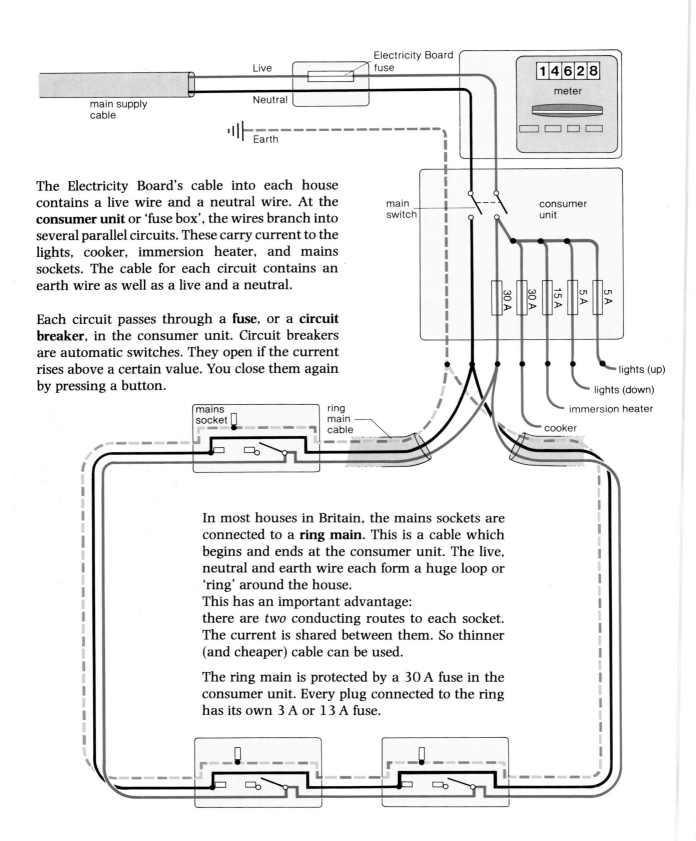

main supply cable

Live

Neutral

Earth

Electricity Board fuse

1 4 6 2 8
meter

main switch

consumer unit

30 A   30 A   15 A   5 A   5 A

lights (up)
lights (down)
immersion heater
cooker

mains socket

ring main cable

The Electricity Board's cable into each house contains a live wire and a neutral wire. At the **consumer unit** or 'fuse box', the wires branch into several parallel circuits. These carry current to the lights, cooker, immersion heater, and mains sockets. The cable for each circuit contains an earth wire as well as a live and a neutral.

Each circuit passes through a **fuse**, or a **circuit breaker**, in the consumer unit. Circuit breakers are automatic switches. They open if the current rises above a certain value. You close them again by pressing a button.

In most houses in Britain, the mains sockets are connected to a **ring main**. This is a cable which begins and ends at the consumer unit. The live, neutral and earth wire each form a huge loop or 'ring' around the house.
This has an important advantage:
there are *two* conducting routes to each socket. The current is shared between them. So thinner (and cheaper) cable can be used.

The ring main is protected by a 30 A fuse in the consumer unit. Every plug connected to the ring has its own 3 A or 13 A fuse.

Two-way switches

In most houses, you can turn the landing light on or off using upstairs or downstairs switches. These aren't the simple 'on-off' type. They have two contacts instead of one. They are **two-way switches:**

If the switches are both up or both down, then a current flows through the bulb. But if one switch is up and the other down, the circuit is broken. Move either switch and you reverse the effect of the other one.

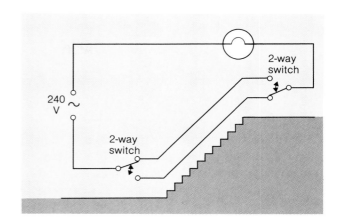

Safety first
If an accident happens ...

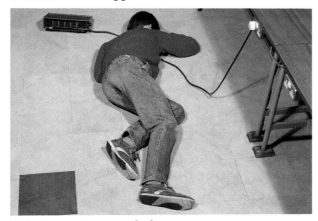

before you give any help
- **switch off at the socket**
- **pull out the plug**

To prevent accidents ...

fit an **earth leakage 'power breaker'.**
This compares the currents in the live and neutral wires. They should be the same. If they're different, then current must be flowing to earth – perhaps through someone touching a faulty wire. The power breaker senses the differences and switches off the power before any harm can be done.

---

1 If an accident occurs, and someone is electrocuted, what should you do before giving any assistance?

2 When you switch on a hairdryer, the current flows through three fuses. Where are these fuses?

3 Copy and complete the diagram to show how the sockets can be connected to the consumer unit using a ring main.

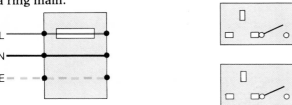

What is the main advantage of the ring main?

4 Copy and complete the diagram to show how the light bulb can be controlled by either of the switches.

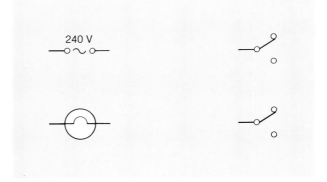

4.12 Buying electricity

Electrical energy costs money. And it can be expensive. The energy needed to keep a cassette recorder running for 24 hours costs:

about 2p,
on the electricity bill

about £20,
buying batteries

Working out the energy ... in joules

A heater with a power of 1 watt (W) changes 1 joule of electrical energy into heat energy every second.
So,

with 1 joule of energy,
you could run a 1 watt heater for 1 second.

with 6 joules of energy,
you could run a 2 watt heater for 3 seconds,
or a 6 watt heater for 1 second.
And so on.

To calculate energy in joules, use the equation:

energy = power × time
(joules)   (watts)   (seconds)

Working out the energy ... in kilowatt hours

The 'units' on an electricity bill are units of energy called **kilowatt hours (kWh)**. The Electricity Board charges you a set amount for each kWh bought.

With 1 kWh of energy,
you could run a 1 kilowatt heater for 1 hour.
With 8 kWh of energy,
you could run a 1 kilowatt heater for 8 hours,
or a 2 kilowatt heater for 4 hours.

To calculate energy in kilowatt hours, use the equation:

energy = power   × time
(kWh)   (kilowatts)   (hours)

CENTRAL ELECTRICITY BOARD V.A.T. Registration No. 338 7449 45

UNITS USED	PRICE PER UNIT P	V.A.T. RATE	£
1220	8.00	0	97.60
QUARTERLY CHARGE		0	10.50
		AMOUNT DUE NOW	108.10

The cost of drying your hair

If a 1 kW hairdryer is switched on for 15 minutes,
the power   = 1 kW
the time   = 0.25 hours
So, using the energy equation,
the energy bought = 1 × 0.25
                  = 0.25 kWh

If each kWh *or 'unit' costs* 8p,
then the total cost = 0.25 × 8
                    = 2p

If each kilowatt hour of energy costs 8p, then it will cost about....
A 4p to watch TV all evening.
B 12p to bake a cake.
C 24p to wash one load of clothes.
D 192p to leave a fan heater running all day.

A bath a day

Don is horrified by his electricity bill.
Should he stop taking hot baths and buy air
fresheners instead? How much is his daily bath
costing him?

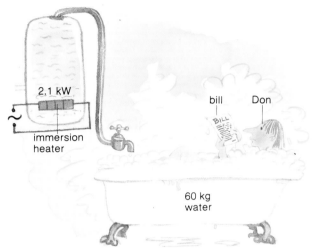

In his bath, he uses 60 kg of water.
From cold, the water has to be heated through
30°C.
The water has a specific heat capacity of
4200 J/(kg °C):
4200 joules of energy are needed to heat every kg
through each °C.
So,
the heat energy needed = 4200 × 60 × 30
= 7 560 000 joules

An immersion heater warms his water.
It has a power of 2.1 kW:
it supplies 2100 joules of heat energy every
second.
But, 7 560 000 joules are needed altogether.

So, the time taken = $\dfrac{7\,560\,000}{2100}$

= 3600 seconds
= 1 hour

This is how long the immersion heater has to be
switched on for.

The cost can be worked out from the following:
power of heater: :   2.1 kW
time: 1 hour
cost of each kWh: 8p

Can you finish the calculation?

1

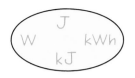

Which of these are units of energy?

2

Electric fire	
Power, in kilowatts:	1 kW
Time switched on, in hours:	1 h
Power in watts:	?
Time switched on, in seconds	?
Energy bought, in kilowatt hours	?
Energy bought, in joules	?

a Copy the table and fill in the missing values.
b If you can buy 1 kWh of energy for 8p, how many
joules of energy can you buy for 8p?
3 In the chart on the opposite page, how much
energy is bought in each case (A to D)? Give your
answers in kWh.
4

Appliance	Power	Time
Mains radio	10 W	16 hours
Electric blanket	100 W	8 hours

Donna likes to leave her radio on all day. Her father
keeps his electric blanket switched on all night. Each
thinks that the other is wasting electricity. But who
is adding most to the bill? Use the information in the
chart to find out.
5 If each kWh of energy costs 8p, what is the cost of
a leaving a 2 kW fire on for 5 hours.
b leaving a 100 W lamp on for 10 hours.
c using a 800 W microwave oven for 15 minutes?
6 Finish the calculation on the left to find out the
cost of Don's daily bath.
Don decides to take showers instead of baths.
If the water temperature is the same, but he only
uses 6 kg of water each time,
a how much energy is needed to heat the water?
b how long must the 2.1 kW heater be switched on
for?
c what is the cost of each shower?

4.13 Magnets

Is it worth buying? Check it with a magnet:

Ordinary steel is attracted to a magnet. But the very best quality stainless steel isn't. If the cutlery is expensive, it shouldn't do this.

If the bodywork isn't attracted to the magnet, then plastic filler has probably been used to cover up rust or crash damage.

Poles of a magnet

Iron filings cling to a bar magnet. The magnetic pull seems to come from two points near the ends. These are the **poles** of the magnet.

If you hang a bar magnet up with a piece of thread, it swings round until it lies roughly north-south. This effect gives the poles their names – the **north pole** and the **south pole**.

Pushes and pulls

Bring the ends of two identical bar magnets together and there is a force between the poles:

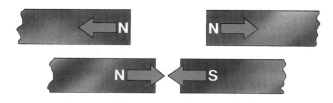

If the poles are the same, they repel (push each other apart).
If the poles are different, they attract each other.

Permanent and temporary magnets

Pieces of iron and steel *become* magnets if you place them near a magnet. The magnet **induces** magnetism in both metals. The magnet attracts the pieces of metal because the poles nearest each other are different.

When the pieces of metal are pulled away, the steel keeps its magnetism, but the iron does not. The steel has become a **permanent** magnet. The iron was only a **temporary** magnet.

Magnets inside magnets

In a piece of iron or steel, every atom is a tiny magnet. Normally, these tiny magnets point in all directions. So their effects cancel out. But when the iron or steel is magnetized, the atoms are turned so that they line up. Billions of tiny magnets then act as one big magnet.

If you hammer a magnet, atoms are thrown out of line again. Strong heating has the same effect. The magnet becomes **demagnetized**.

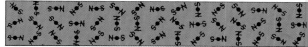

unmagnetized steel

magnetized steel

Hard or soft?

Iron and steel can both be magnetized. They are **ferromagnetic materials**. One is **hard**. The other is **soft**. But the words don't have their usual meanings.

Hard magnetic materials

These are difficult to magnetize. But they are also difficult to demagnetize. Once magnetized, they keep their magnetism.

Steel is used to make permanent magnets. **Alcomax** makes an even stronger magnet than steel.

A cassette tape is coated with tiny particles of **iron oxide**. These become magnetized when you make a recording. The strength of the magnetism varies along the tape, so that the particles form a magnetic 'copy' of the original sound waves.

Soft magnetic materials

These are easy to magnetize. But they quickly lose their magnetism.

Iron and **mumetal** are used in electromagnets because their magnetism can be 'switched' on or off (see page 158).

Most materials are **non-magnetic**. They can't be magnetized.

Many metals are non-magnetic. For example: copper, brass, aluminium, silver, gold.

---

1 Pieces of iron and steel are pulled to the ends of a magnet.

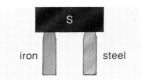

a Copy the diagram. Draw in any magnetic poles on the iron and steel.

b If the lower ends of the iron and steel start to move, which way will they move, and why?
c What happens to each of the metals when it is taken away from the magnet?

2 Which material is the odd one out in each of these lists? Why?

a	copper aluminium steel brass	**b**	steel iron iron oxide alcomax

3 Write down two ways in which a magnet could be demagnetized.

4 This is a magnetically-operated switch.

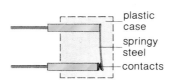

What happens when the magnet is brought close?

12 V alarm bell

12 V battery

door

This door is to be protected by a burglar alarm. Copy the diagram. Show where you would fit a magnetically-operated switch, magnet, and connecting wire so that the alarm bell will ring if the door is pushed open.

4.14 Magnetic fields

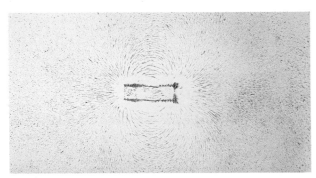

Iron filings, sprinkled on paper over a bar magnet. The filings have become tiny magnets – pulled into position by forces from the poles of the magnet.

Magnetic forces are acting in the space around the magnet. There is a **magnetic field** in this space.

The compass

Magnetic fields can be studied using a small compass. Inside the compass is a tiny magnet called a **needle**. It is on a spindle and can turn freely. The north end of the needle is a pointer. Near a magnet, the needle is turned by forces between its poles and the poles of the magnet. The needle comes to rest with the turning forces balanced.

Field lines around a bar magnet:

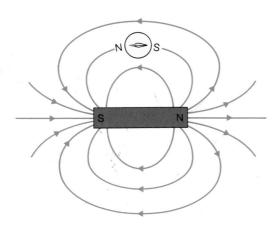

- The lines show the direction a compass needle would point. They run from the north pole of the magnet round to the south.
- The field is strongest where the lines are closest together.

Plotting a field

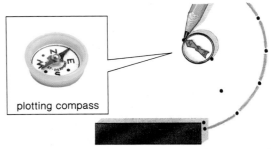

plotting compass

- Put a magnet in the middle of a piece of paper. Draw round it to mark its position.
- Place a plotting compass near one end of the magnet. Mark the position of the needle with two pencil dots.
- Move the compass so that the needle lines up with the last dot you made. Mark the position of the needle again ... and so on until you reach the magnet or the edge of the paper.
- Join up the dots. When you do this, you are drawing a **field line**.
- Repeat, starting at different points round the magnet. You can draw any number of field lines, but it's simplest not too show too many.

Field lines between magnets:

Poles different
The field lines run from north to south.

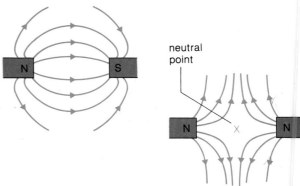

neutral point

Poles the same
At point X, the field from one magnet cancels the field from the other. X is called a neutral point. If you placed a compass at X, the needle wouldn't be turned by the magnets.

The Earth's magnetic field

The Earth has a magnetic field. It isn't very strong. No one knows what causes it. But it is rather like the field around a huge bar magnet.

If there aren't any other magnets around, a compass needle turns into line with the Earth's magnetic field.

The *north* pole of the needle points *North*.
But a *north* pole is always attracted to a *south* pole. So the *south* pole is of the Earth's magnet is actually in the *North*! It lies under a point in Northern Canada called 'magnetic north'.

'Magnetic north' is over 1200 kilometres away from the North Pole. This is because the Earth's magnet isn't quite in line with its true North-South axis.

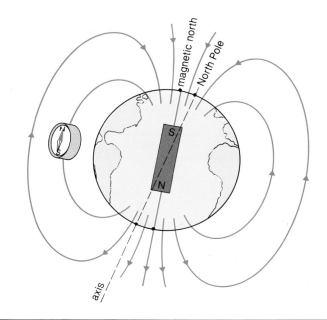

Did you know?

Seamen used to think that there was a huge magnetic mountain in northern seas. It attracted compass needles and pulled ships to their doom.

No one has ever found 'magnetic north'. It moves too fast. Every day, it travels in circles across the ice at about 5 m/s. And no one has ever found 'magnetic south' either.

Racing pigeons probably use the Earth's magnetic field to find their way home. Part of their brain acts like a compass.

---

1 Things are missing from these diagrams.

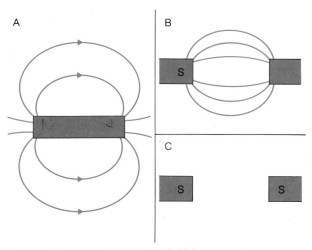

Copy each one, and add any field lines, arrows, or magnetic poles which should be there.
In which diagram could a neutral point be shown?

2

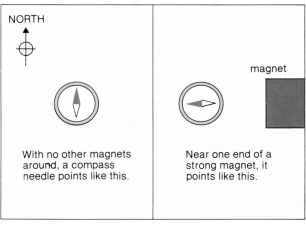

With no other magnets around, a compass needle points like this.

Near one end of a strong magnet, it points like this.

a At which end of the compass needle is there a north pole?
b What type of pole is at the end of the magnet?

4.15 Magnetism from currents

Make a recording on this tape and 45 minutes of sound becomes over 100 metres of varying magnetism along the tape. But the tape isn't magnetized by a magnet. It is magnetized by a current passing through a piece of wire.

Field around a wire

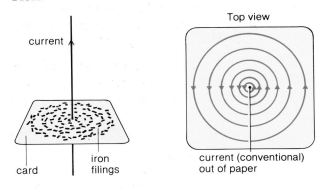

A high current flows through a wire. Iron filings are pulled into circles around it. The current produces a weak magnetic field:

- The magnetic field is strongest close to the wire.
- Increasing the current makes the magnetic field stronger.

Field around a coil

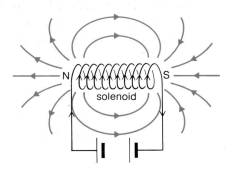

A current flows through a long coil, called a **solenoid**. A magnetic field is produced. The field is like the field around a bar magnet. The solenoid behaves as if it has magnetic poles at its ends.

- Increasing the current makes the magnetic field stronger.
- Increasing the number of turns on the coil makes the magnetic field stronger.

Rules to remember

Current flows from + to −.
This is the conventional current direction.

Magnetic field lines run from N to S.

The right-hand grip rule for field direction:

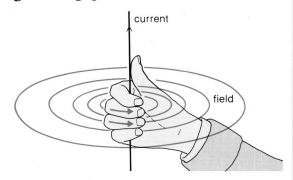

Imagine your right hand gripping the wire so that your thumb points the same way as the current. Your *fingers* curl the same way as the *field* lines.

The right-hand grip rule for poles:

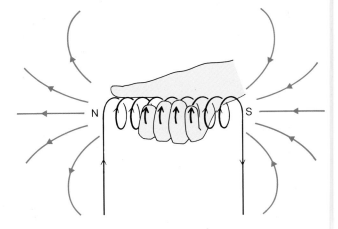

Imagine your right hand gripping the solenoid so that your fingers curl the same way as the current. Your *thumb* then points to the *north* pole of the solenoid.

Making magnets . . .

A current flows through a solenoid. In the solenoid is a bar of steel. The steel becomes magnetized and makes the magnetic field much stronger than before.

When the current is switched off, the steel stays magnetized. It has become a permanent magnet. Nearly all permanent magnets are made in this way.

. . . and demagnetizing them

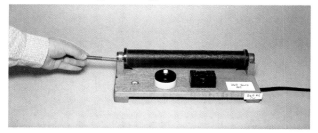

A solenoid can also be used to demagnetize a magnet. The magnet is put in the solenoid. Alternating current (a.c.) is passed through the solenoid. Then the magnet is slowly pulled out.

When a.c. is passing through the solenoid, the magnetic field keeps changing direction very rapidly. This turns the magnetic atoms in the steel out of line.

Making recordings . . .   . . . and removing them

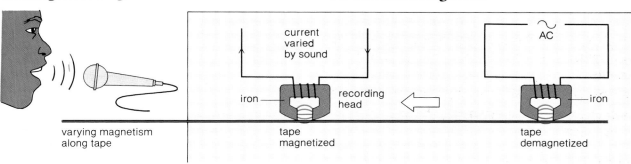

Magnetic tape passes over the recording head in a cassette recorder. The tape is magnetized by the current in the coil. As the sound varies, so does the current – and the strength of magnetism along the tape. Result: a magnetic 'copy' of the original sound waves.

New recordings can't be made until old ones have been removed. This head has a.c. flowing through its coil. It demagnetizes the tape passing over it – ready for the next recording.

---

1 This is the end view of a long length of wire.
A high current is flowing through the wire.
In which direction is the current flowing?
– IN TO the paper? – or OUT OF the paper?
Copy the diagram, and show which way the other compass needles would be pointing.

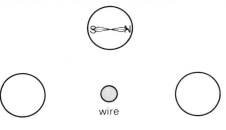

2 All four coils have the same current passing through them.
Which one:
a gives the weakest magnetic field;
b has a north pole at the left hand end;
c will still give a magnetic field when the current is switched off?

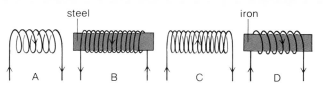

4.16 Electromagnets

Electromagnets can do all the things that ordinary magnets can do. But you can switch them on and off.

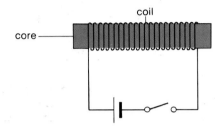

The parts of an electromagnet:

a coil – made from several hundred turns of insulated copper wire. The greater the number of turns, the stronger the field.

a battery – to supply current. The higher the current, the stronger the field.

a core – made from a soft magnetic material like iron. This makes the field much stronger. But its magnetism dies away as soon as the current is switched off.

Using electromagnets

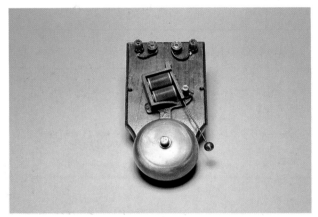

In an electric bell, an electromagnet is switched on and off very rapidly. It keeps pulling the hammer over to the gong, then releasing it.

Sorting scrap metal. Electromagnets are used to separate metals like iron and steel from other metals.

There's an electromagnet in a telephone earpiece. As the current through it varies, the pull on a metal plate varies. This makes the plate vibrate and send sound waves into your ear.

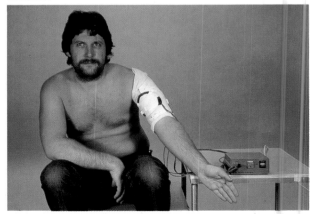

A wrap-round electromagnet. Bursts of magnetism actually help broken bones to mend more quickly. No one is quite sure why.

Switches worked by electromagnets

Problem A car starter motor takes a current of over 100 A. It has to be switched on by a lightweight switch, connected to thin cable. This can't handle the high current.

Solution Use an electromagnetic switch or **relay**. With a relay, a large current in one circuit can be switched ON or OFF by a small current in another circuit.

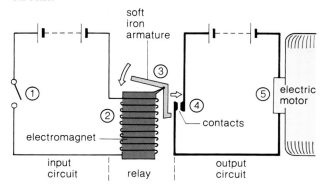

1 When the switch in the input circuit is closed,
2 the electromagnet comes ON
3 and pulls the iron **armature** towards it.
4 This closes the contacts,
5 so the motor in the output circuit is switched ON.

There are two types of relay	
Normally open relay Symbol:	**Normally closed relay** Symbol:
Output circuit is switched ON when input circuit is switched ON	Output circuit is switched OFF when input circuit is switched ON
Example of use: Car starter motor, switched on when switch is turned by key.	*Example of use:* Safety STOP button on electrical machinery. Power is cut when button is pressed.

1 To answer this question, you may need information from the previous section.

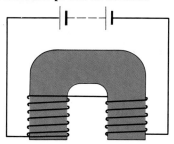

This a U-shaped electromagnet.
a Copy the diagram. Label the COIL and the CORE, and say which material each could be made from.
b Explain why steel wouldn't be a suitable material for the core.
c Explain why the wire in the coil needs to be insulated.
d Which pole is at the left hand end of the electromagnet?
e What two changes could you make to give a stronger magnetic field?

2 This is a shop alarm system. It is switched on by closing the switches X and Y. If anyone tries to steal a radio, the tamper circuit is broken and the alarm bell rings.

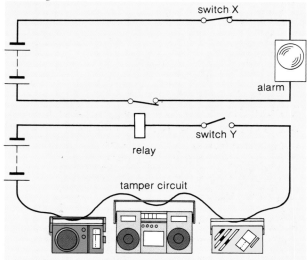

a What type of relay is being used?
b Why will the alarm bell ring if switch X only is closed?
c Why will the alarm bell then stop ringing if switch Y is closed?
d Why will the alarm bell start ringing again if the tamper circuit is broken?
e The shop owner wants a second alarm system fitted. An alarm bell must ring whenever she presses an emergency button. Draw a circuit diagram to show how this could be done using a relay. What type of relay would you use? What is the advantage of using a relay?

4.17 The magnetic force on a current

Put a current into each of these, and something moves:

The loudspeaker
cone vibrates

The pointer moves
up the scale

The motor turns

The movement is caused by a force. A force is produced whenever a current flows with a magnetic field across it.

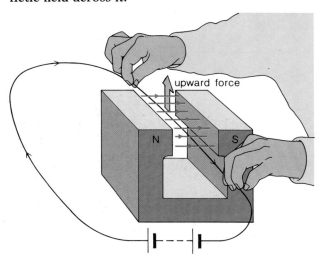

upward force

N   S

A wire is held between the poles of a magnet. When a current flows through the wire, there is an upward force on it.

The force becomes stronger if
- the current is increased
- a stronger magnet is used
- there is a greater length of wire in the field

The force isn't always upwards. It depends on the current and field directions. If the wire is in line with the field, there isn't any force at all.

Fleming's left hand rule

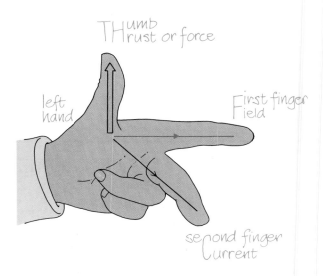

THumb — THrust or force

left hand

First finger — Field

second finger — Current

This is a rule for working out the direction of the force when a current is at right angles to a magnetic field.

Hold the thumb and first two fingers of your left hand at right angles. Point your fingers as shown, and your thumb gives the direction of the force.

When you use the rule, remember
the current direction is from + to −
the field lines run from N to S.

Turning a coil

A coil lies between the poles of a magnet. A current flows through the coil. The current flows in opposite directions along the two sides of the coil. So one side is pushed *up*, and the other side is pushed *down*. There is a turning effect on the coil.

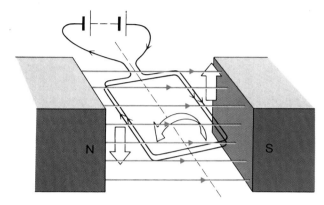

The turning effect is stronger if
- the current is increased
- a stronger magnet is used
- there are more turns on the coil

Using magnetic forces

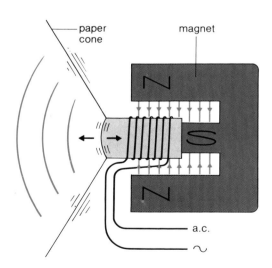

Alternating current passes through the coil of a loudspeaker. The wire in the coil is at right angles to a magnetic field. As the current flows backwards and forwards, the coil is pushed in and out. This makes the cone vibrate and give out sound waves.

1 What is the direction of the force on this wire?

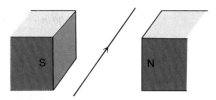

What would be the effect on the force of
a using a higher current?
b reversing the direction of the current?
2 Copy the diagram.

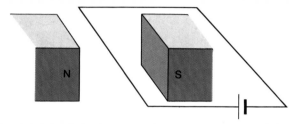

Mark on
a the direction of the current (conventional).
b the direction of the magnetic field.
c the direction in which the wire will move.
3 Leela has made a battery tester. It uses a magnet, flexible wire and a pointer. With it, she can check whether a small battery is 'live' or 'dead', and find out which terminal is which.

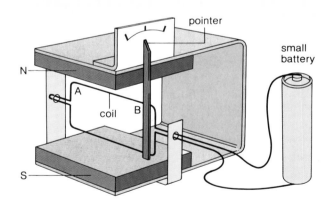

She connects a battery to the tester. The pointer moves to the left.
a Why does the pointer move?
b What is the direction of the magnetic field?
c What is the direction of the current along the top edge of the coil? A-TO-B or B-TO-A?
d Which is the positive (+) end of the battery? TOP or BOTTOM?
e Leela wants to make the tester more sensitive – she wants the pointer to move further when a battery is connected. How could she change her design to make this happen?

4.18 Electric motors

They use the magnetic turning effect on a coil. They can power anything from a model car to a submarine. One simple type is shown on the right.

The poles of the **magnet** face one another.

The **coil** is free to rotate between the poles of the magnet.

The **commutator** or split ring is fixed to the coil, and turns round with it.

The **brushes** are two carbon contacts. They connect the coil to the battery.

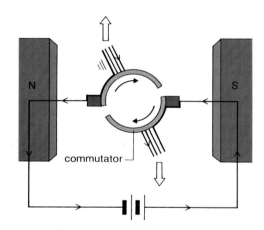

When a current flows through the coil, one side is pushed up, the other side is pushed down. So the coil turns. However, when the coil is vertical, the forces can't turn it any further because they are pointing the wrong way...

... as the coil shoots past the vertical, the commutator *changes* the current direction. Now the forces point the other way. So the coil is pushed round another half turn. And so on.

Practical motors usually have several coils set at different angles. This gives smoother running and a greater turning effect.

Some motors use electromagnets rather than permanent magnets. This means that they can run on alternating current (a.c.). As the current flows backwards and forwards through the coil, the magnetic field changes direction to match it. So the turning effect is always the same way.

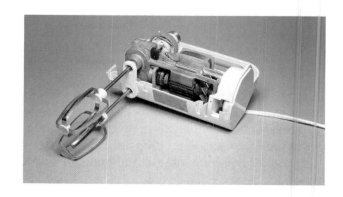

Making a motor

> Using a motor kit, you need:
>
> 3 metres of plastic covered copper wire (26 SWG)
> 1 wooden block with metal tube through centre
> 1 wooden base   1 iron yoke   2 magnets
> 1 metal spindle   2 split pins   4 studs
> 2 rubber rings   3 V battery   Sellotape

1 Insulate one end of the tube with Sellotape.

2 Wind coil on wooden block. You need about 10 turns.

3 Strip plastic from ends of wire.
Fix bare ends of wire to tube using rubber rings.

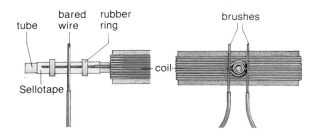

Check the ends are opposite each other and in line with the coil. You have now made the **commutator**.

4 Cut two half-metre lengths of wire.
Bare the ends of the wires.
Fix wires to wooden base using studs.
You have now made the **brushes**.

5 Put split pins into base.

6 Push vertical wires (the brushes) towards each other. Move tube upwards to separate them.

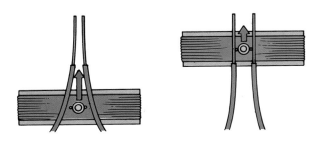

Slide spindle through split pins and tube.
You should now be able to spin the coil.
The brushes should press firmly against the tube and the wire from the coil.

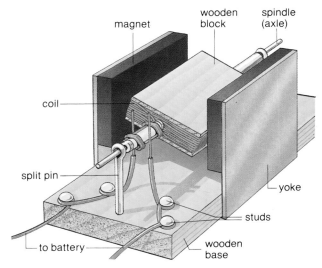

7 Put the two magnets on the yoke to make a single U-shaped magnet. Check that the opposite faces attract each other.

8 Slide yoke into position. Connect wires to battery.
Give the coil a flick to start it turning.

To answer these questions, you will need information from the previous section.

1 COMMUTATOR   BRUSHES   COIL   MAGNET
   SPINDLE

Which of these
a is often made from carbon
b is also known as a split ring
c turns when current flows through it
d connects the battery to the split ring and coil
e changes the current direction every half turn?
2 Someone builds a simple motor following the instructions above. What changes could they make to give the motor a greater turning effect?

3 This is the end view of a simple motor.

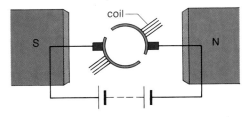

a Copy the diagram and mark on the current direction.
b Which way will the motor turn?
c What is the position of the coil when there is no turning effect on it?
d What is the position of the coil when the current changes direction?

163

4.19 Electricity from magnetism

You don't need batteries to produce a current. Just a wire, a magnet, and movement.

Moving magnets...

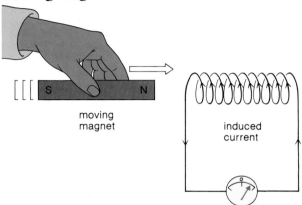

moving magnet

induced current

... and moving wires

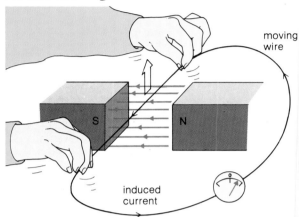

moving wire

induced current

Push a magnet into a coil. Result – electrons in the coil are given a push by the magnetic field. In other words, a voltage is **induced** or **generated** in the coil. It makes a current flow round the circuit.

Move a wire across a magnetic field at right angles.

Results – a voltage is induced in the wire. So a current flows round the circuit.

For a higher voltage (and higher current),

- move the magnet faster
- use a stronger magnet
- put more turns on the coil

When the magnet stops moving, there is no voltage and no current.

> Whenever a conductor cuts through magnetic field lines, a voltage is generated. It doesn't matter whether the conductor moves or the magnet.
> **The faster the field lines are cut, the greater the voltage.**
> This is **Faraday's law**.
> If no field lines are cut there is no voltage.

For a higher voltage (and higher current),

- move the wire faster
- use a stronger magnet

When the wire stops moving, there is no voltage and no current. If the wire is moved sideways there is no voltage and no current.

Playback on a cassette recorder.
Magnetized tape moves over a tiny coil.
A small current is generated.

The current is made bigger by an amplifier.
It makes loudspeakers give out sound waves.

Guitar pickups are rows of magnets with coils round them. The steel springs become magnetized. When vibrated, they generate current in the coils.

Current in a wire – which way?

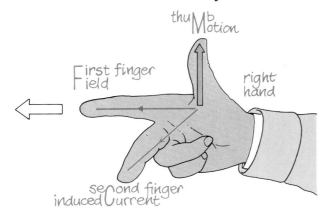

To find which way the induced current flows in a moving wire, use **Fleming's right-hand rule**. Hold the thumb and first two fingers of your right hand at right angles. Point them like this, and the second finger gives you the current direction.

Current in a coil – which way?

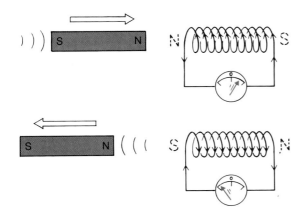

Induced current flows in a coil
– one way when the magnet is pushed in.
– the opposite way when the magnet is pulled out.
Either way, the coil becomes an electromagnet.
It *repels* the magnet when this is pushed *in*.
It *attracts* the magnet when this is pulled *out*.
Whichever way you move the magnet, you have to move against a force – you have put energy in to get electrical energy out.

This is an example of **Lenz's law**:

an induced current always flows to try and stop the movement which started it.

For a wire at right angles to a magnetic field:

If a current is flowing, Fleming's *left*-hand rule tells you the direction of the force on the wire (see page 160)	*If the wire is moving*, Fleming's *right*-hand rule tells you the direction of the induced current (see left)

1 A wire is moved downwards through a magnetic field.

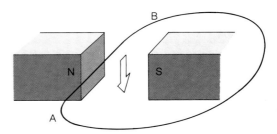

What is the direction of the induced current?
A-TO-B or B-TO-A?
What would be the effect of
a using a stronger magnet
b moving the wire faster
c moving the wire upwards
d moving the wire towards one of the poles?

2 The magnet is being pushed towards the coil

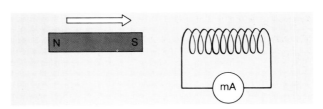

a Copy the diagram. Mark on the type of pole produced at each end of the coil.
b Use the right-hand grip rule (page 156) to work out which way the induced current flows. Mark the direction on your diagram.
c Copy and complete this table to show what happens to the meter when the magnet is moved in and out of the coil:

Magnet pushed in	Needle moves to right
Magnet in coil, but not moving	
Magnet pulled out	
Magnet pushed in again, but faster.	

4.20 Generators

Turn a **generator** and out comes a current . . .

. . . current for the lights on your bike.

. . . current for the circuits in a car.

. . . current to light up a whole city.

In fact, generators provide over 99% of our electrical energy.

A simple alternator

Most generators give out alternating current (a.c.).
A.c. generators are called **alternators**.
This one is providing the current to light up a bulb:

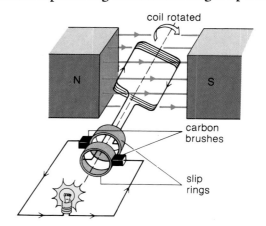

The **coil** is rotated between the poles of a magnet.

The **slip rings** are fixed to the coil and turn round with it.

The **brushes** are two carbon contacts. They rub against the slip rings, so that the rotating coil is connected to the bulb.

When the coil is rotated, it cuts through magnetic field lines. A voltage is generated. This makes a current flow through the bulb.

As the coil rotates, each side travels upwards through the magnetic field, then downwards. So the induced current flows one way, then the opposite way. The current is alternating.

Turning a motor into a generator

You may have made an electric motor like this.
It can be used to generate a current.
Connect the leads to a milliammeter.
Give the coil a spin. The coil cuts through magnetic field lines, and a current is generated.
The milliammeter reading shows that the current is 'one way' direct current (d.c.).
But the flow is very uneven.

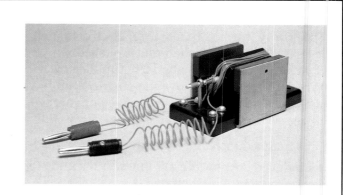

This graph shows how the current from the alternator changes as the coil rotates.
'Forwards' current is plus (+);
'Backwards' current is minus (−):

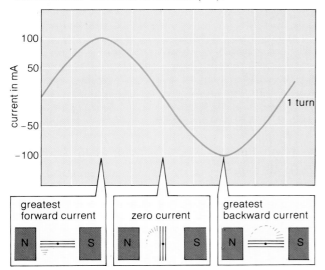

The current is *greatest* when the coil is *horizontal*. The coil cuts field lines most rapidly in this position.

The current is *zero* when the coil is *vertical*. The coil doesn't cut field lines in this position.

The alternator would generate a higher current if

● the coil had more turns

● a stronger magnet was used

● the coil was rotated faster

Alternator facts

● The 'dynamo' on a bike is an alternator. It produces more voltage the faster you pedal. But you would have to travel at over 50 mph to 'blow' all the bulbs.

● Many alternators use electromagnets instead of permanent magnets. These give a stronger field.

● The alternator in a car is fitted with a 'diode block'. This changes the alternating current into 'one way' direct current. The current supplies the car circuits and keeps the battery charged.

● Alternators in power stations have to run at a constant speed. If their speed changed, the mains frequency would change from 50 Hz.

To answer these questions, you will need information from the previous section.

1 Copy the boxes. Fill in the first letter of each answer to make a word. This is an essential part of any generator.

?	It measures small currents;
?	Type of current from an alternator;
?	When turned, they produce currents;
?	Field lines leave this pole;
?	Type of energy from a generator;
?	For more current, a generator coil needs more of these.

2 This is the end view of a simple alternator.

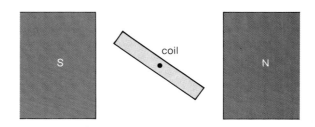

Redraw the diagram to show the position of the coil when the current is **a** greatest **b** zero.

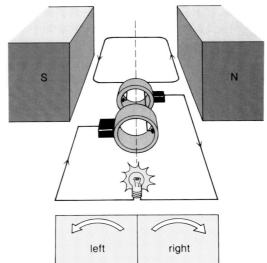

3 This alternator is generating a current.
a Which way is the coil being rotated?
To the LEFT? Or to the RIGHT?
Use Fleming's right-hand rule to find out.
b What changes could you make so that the alternator produced a larger current?
c Explain why the current being generated is a.c. and not d.c.

4.21 Transformers

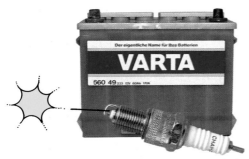

A 12 000 volt spark from a 12 volt battery.
It's needed to ignite the petrol in a car engine.
The high voltage is generated in a coil.
Not by pushing a magnet in and out.
But by switching an electromagnet on and off.

electromagnet

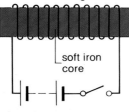

soft iron core

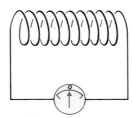

An electromagnet is close to a coil.
Switching on the electromagnet puts a magnetic field around the coil. The effect is the same as pushing a magnet into the coil very fast. A voltage is induced, a current flows, and the meter needle flicks one way. But only for a fraction of a second. When the field is steady, the current stops.

When the electromagnet is switched off, the magnetic field vanishes. The effect is the same as pulling a magnet out of the coil very fast. Just for a moment, the meter needle flicks the other way.

Without the core, the induced voltage would be much less. Can you explain why?

A higher voltage is induced if:

- the core of the electromagnet goes right into the coil.

- the coil has more turns.

The coil in a car engine has many thousands of turns. This gives the thousands of volts needed for the spark plugs. The electromagnet is inside the coil. It runs on only 12 volts. It is switched on and off by a transistor (see page 196) or a set of contacts called 'points'.

Transforming the mains

Problem: how to run a 12 volt bulb from the 240 volt mains.

Answer: use a **transformer.** Easier still – use a labpack. It's already got a transformer in it.

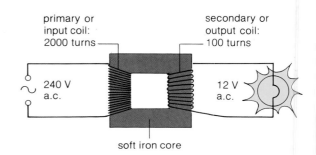

primary or input coil: 2000 turns
secondary or output coil: 100 turns
240 V a.c.
12 V a.c.
soft iron core

This is one type of transformer.
Alternating current flows through the **primary** or **input coil**. This sets up a changing magnetic field in the **secondary** or **output coil**. The effect is the same as moving a magnet in and out of the coil very fast. An alternating voltage is induced. Alternating current flows. The bulb lights up.

There is a connection between the input and output voltages:

$$\frac{\text{input voltage}}{\text{output voltage}} = \frac{\text{turns on input coil}}{\text{turns on output coil}}$$

In this example,

$$\frac{240}{12} = \frac{2000}{100}$$

The input coil has 20 times the turns of the output coil. The **turns ratio** is 20:1.
The input voltage is 20 times the output voltage.

The transformer wouldn't work on d.c. Direct current would give a steady magnetic field. So no voltage would be induced in the output coil.

Stepping down and up

There are two types of transformer:

Step-down transformer	Step-up transformer
Symbol:	Symbol:
Turns on output coil less than turns on input coil	Turns on output coil more then turns on input coil
Output voltage less than input voltage	Output voltage more than input voltage
Used in ...	Used in ...
a mains 'power pack' to supply 9 V for a radio or microcomputer	a television to supply 15 000 V for the picture tube

Transformer power

If a transformer doesn't waste any energy, then it must give out as much energy every second as is put in. In other words – its power output must be the same as its power input. For this to happen, the current must change as well as the voltage. For example:

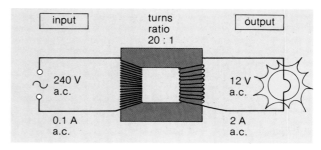

The voltage goes down from
240 V . . . . to 12 V

The current goes up from
0.1 A . . . . to 2 A

The power input = voltage × current	The power output = voltage × current
= 240 × 0.1	= 12 × 2
= 24 watts	= 24 watts

The voltage has gone *down*. The current has gone *up*. But the power has stayed the *same*.

For any transformer that doesn't waste power:

$$\frac{\text{input}}{\text{voltage}} \times \frac{\text{input}}{\text{current}} = \frac{\text{output}}{\text{voltage}} \times \frac{\text{output}}{\text{current}}$$

1

Transformer	A	B	C	D
Input voltage in V	240	120	50	100
Input turns	1000	1000	1000	2000
Output turns	500	100	2000	2000

Which transformer:
a is a step-up transformer;
b has the same output voltage as input voltage;
c has a turns ratio of 10:1;
d has an output voltage of 12 V;
e has the highest output voltage?

2 A 24 V bulb takes a current of 2 A. Its power supply is a transformer connected to the 240 V mains.

You have to choose a suitable transformer. You can assume that the transformer wastes no power.

a What turns ratio is needed?
b What power is taken by the bulb?
c What power is taken from the mains?
d What current is taken from the mains?
e Why wouldn't the transformer work on d.c.?

4.22 Power across the country

Mains power comes from huge alternators in power stations.

Transformers step up the voltage before the power is carried across country by overhead cables.

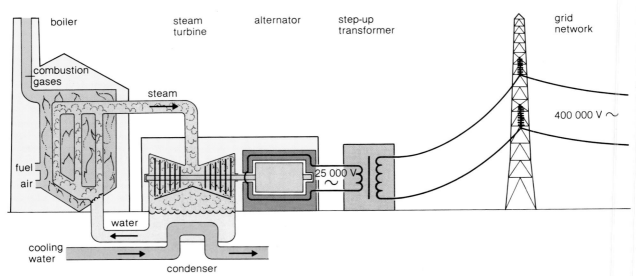

boiler   steam turbine   alternator   step-up transformer   grid network

combustion gases

steam

fuel

air

25 000 V ∿

400 000 V ∿

water

cooling water

condenser

The power station

In the power station, the alternators are driven by huge **turbines**, spun round by the force of high pressure steam. The steam is made by heating water in a boiler. The heat comes from burning coal, gas or oil – or from a nuclear reactor (see page 184).

Huge **cooling condensers** change the steam back into water for the boiler. The condensers need vast amounts of cooling water. So power stations are often built near rivers or the sea.

Why change voltage?

The current from a large alternator can be 20 000 amperes or more. It needs very thick, heavy and expensive cable to carry it. So a transformer is used to *step up* the voltage and *reduce* the current. Then thinner, lighter and cheaper cables can be used to carry the power across country.

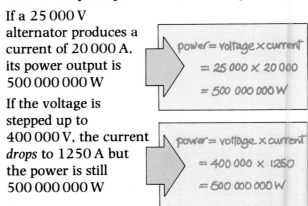

If a 25 000 V alternator produces a current of 20 000 A, its power output is 500 000 000 W

power = voltage × current
= 25 000 × 20 000
= 500 000 000 W

If the voltage is stepped up to 400 000 V, the current *drops* to 1250 A but the power is still 500 000 000 W

power = voltage × current
= 400 000 × 1250
= 500 000 000 W

Why a.c.?

If power stations didn't generate a.c., transformers couldn't be used to change the voltage. D.c. voltages can be changed, but this is difficult and expensive. Transformers don't work on d.c.

Then transformers reduce the voltage . . .   . . . before the power is supplied to homes, offices and factories.

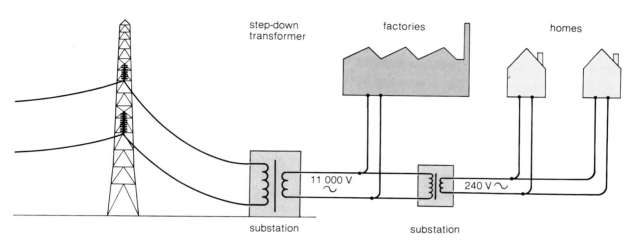

The Grid

Each power station feeds its power to a network of cables and switching stations called the **Grid**. If one area of the country needs more power, it can be supplied by power stations in other areas.

To answer these questions, you may need information from the previous section.

1 MW = 1 000 000 W

1 Explain why:
a steam is needed in a power station;
b power stations are often near a river or the sea;
c the voltage is stepped up before power is fed to the overhead cables;
d power stations generate a.c., and not d.c.
2 The three power stations were built to supply the towns of Newleigh, Extown, and Oldwich.

Each alternator generates at 20 000 V.
Each has power output of 100 MW.
The stations feed their power to the Grid.
The towns take their power from the Grid.

a What is the Grid?
b How many alternators must be working to supply the town of Newleigh?
c Which towns could be supplied by A station alone?
d How much spare power is being supplied to the Grid for use in other areas?

Power from the Grid

Power from the overhead cables is fed to sub-stations. Here, the voltage is stepped down by transformers. Homes take their power at 240 volts. Factories and hospitals take their power at a higher voltages.

e If B station shuts down, how much power must be supplied to the towns from other parts of the country?
f How much energy (in joules) does each alternator supply in 1 second?
g How much current is being generated by each alternator?
h After the voltage has been stepped up to 400 000 V, how much current does each alternator supply to the Grid?

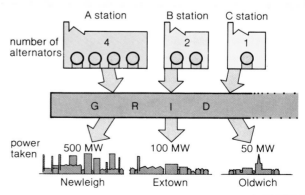

4.23 Power plus

Hidden power

In Snowdonia, the landscape hasn't been spoilt by pylons, because the Electricity Board have put their power lines underground. But this is an expensive way of sending power. Lower voltages have to be used, and that means higher currents and thicker cables. To save the landscape, people have to pay more for their electricity.

Guaranteed power

Power cuts don't happen very often. But when they do, the results can be serious:

A loss of power here – and 200 cows will need milking by hand.

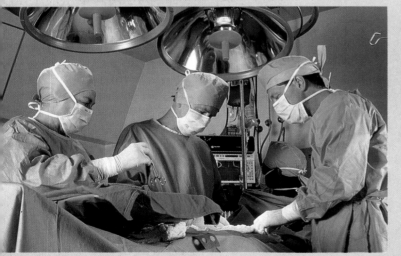

A loss of power here might put someone's life at risk.

For emergencies, most large hospitals and farms have stand-by generators. They are driven by engines which run on petrol, diesel or bottled gas. They start up automatically if there is a mains failure.

Extra power

Battery hens? In Somerset, hens have solved one farmer's electricity supply problems. He saves their droppings in a tank and collects the gas given off. Then he uses the gas to run the engine which drives his generator.

In Florida, the police have collected so much marijuana in drugs raid, that a power station has been specially converted to burn it. One tonne of marijuana gives nearly as much heat as three barrels of oil.

In Edmonton, North London, the council has turned one of its rubbish incinerators into a generating station. Electricity is generated using the heat from burning household rubbish. The council gets rid of its waste. And it keeps its costs down by selling the electricity to the local Electricity Board.

Acid rain

All over Europe, acid rain is falling. The acid in the rain is only weak. But it is killing fish in the lakes of Norway and Sweden, damaging forests in Germany, and eating into the stonework of old buildings.

In Norway, Sweden and Germany, they blame the sulphur fumes from Britain's coal-burning power stations. Winds are blowing the fumes across Northern Europe. And the fumes are making the rain acid.

The Generating Board don't agree. They say that there is no firm evidence to link their power stations with acid rain. Sulphur fumes aren't a new problem – factories and road vehicles have been producing them for years.

And as the argument goes on, the acid rain still falls.

Water power

Hydroelectric power. A river is dammed to form a lake. Water rushes from the lake to turn generators at the foot of the dam. No pollution. But the landscape is changed, and local animal and plant life is disturbed.

In Sweden, much of their electricity comes from hydroelectric schemes. But plans to build more dams have been dropped. The Swedes don't want to see more countryside destroyed.

In Sri Lanka, they're trying to construct a hydro-electric scheme in record time. The power is urgently needed. Without it, they have to borrow money to buy oil. And that keeps the country poor.

Make a list of the buildings where you think an emergency generator is essential.

Here are some of the ways in which a town could get its power:

a hydroelectric power scheme
a coal-burning power station
a small generator in every building.

How many advantages and disadvantages can you think of for each?

Try to find out
– where the power stations in your region are sited
– what fuels they use.

5.1 Inside atoms

34 000 000 000 000 000 000 000

That's the number of atoms in this penny. Everything is made of atoms. They are extremely small. And they're made from particles which are very much smaller.

This is one simple picture or **model** of the atom:
At the centre, is a tiny **nucleus** made up of particles called **protons** and **neutrons**. Around this, orbit much smaller particles called **electrons**.

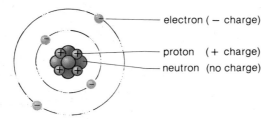

electron (− charge)
proton (+ charge)
neutron (no charge)

The charges on electrons and protons are equal, but opposite. Normally, an atom has the same number of electrons as protons. So the total charge on the atom is zero.

The force of attraction between + and − charges hold the electrons in orbit around the nucleus.
A **strong nuclear force** binds the protons and neutrons together in this nucleus.

The mass of an atom is mainly in its nucleus. Protons and neutrons have about the same mass. But electrons are very much lighter. It takes about 2000 electrons to make up the mass of a proton.

The nucleus is far too small to show in a diagram. If an atom were the size of this concert hall, its nucleus would be smaller than a pea.

Elements, and proton number

All things are made up from about 100 basic materials called **elements**. Each element has a different number of protons in its atoms. It has a different **proton number**. For example:

Element	chemical symbol	proton number
Hydrogen	H	1
Helium	He	2
Lithium	Li	3
Beryllium	Be	4
Boron	B	5
Carbon	C	6
Nitrogen	N	7
Oxygen	O	8
Radium	Ra	88
Thorium	Th	90
Uranium	U	92
Plutonium	P	94

The proton number also tells you the number of electrons in the atom. The electrons control how atoms join together in chemical reactions.

Isotopes, and nucleon number

The atoms of an element aren't all alike.
Some have more neutrons than others.
These different 'versions' of the atom are called **isotopes**. Most elements are a mixture of two or more isotopes. You can see some examples in the chart on the opposite page.

For example:

The metal lithium is a mixture of two isotopes. These are lithium-6 and lithium-7.
Lithium-7 is the more common. Over 93% of all lithium is lithium-7.

The total number of protons and neutrons in each atom is called the **nucleon number**.
Isotopes have *different* nucleon numbers.
But they have the *same* proton number.

Some atoms, elements, and isotopes

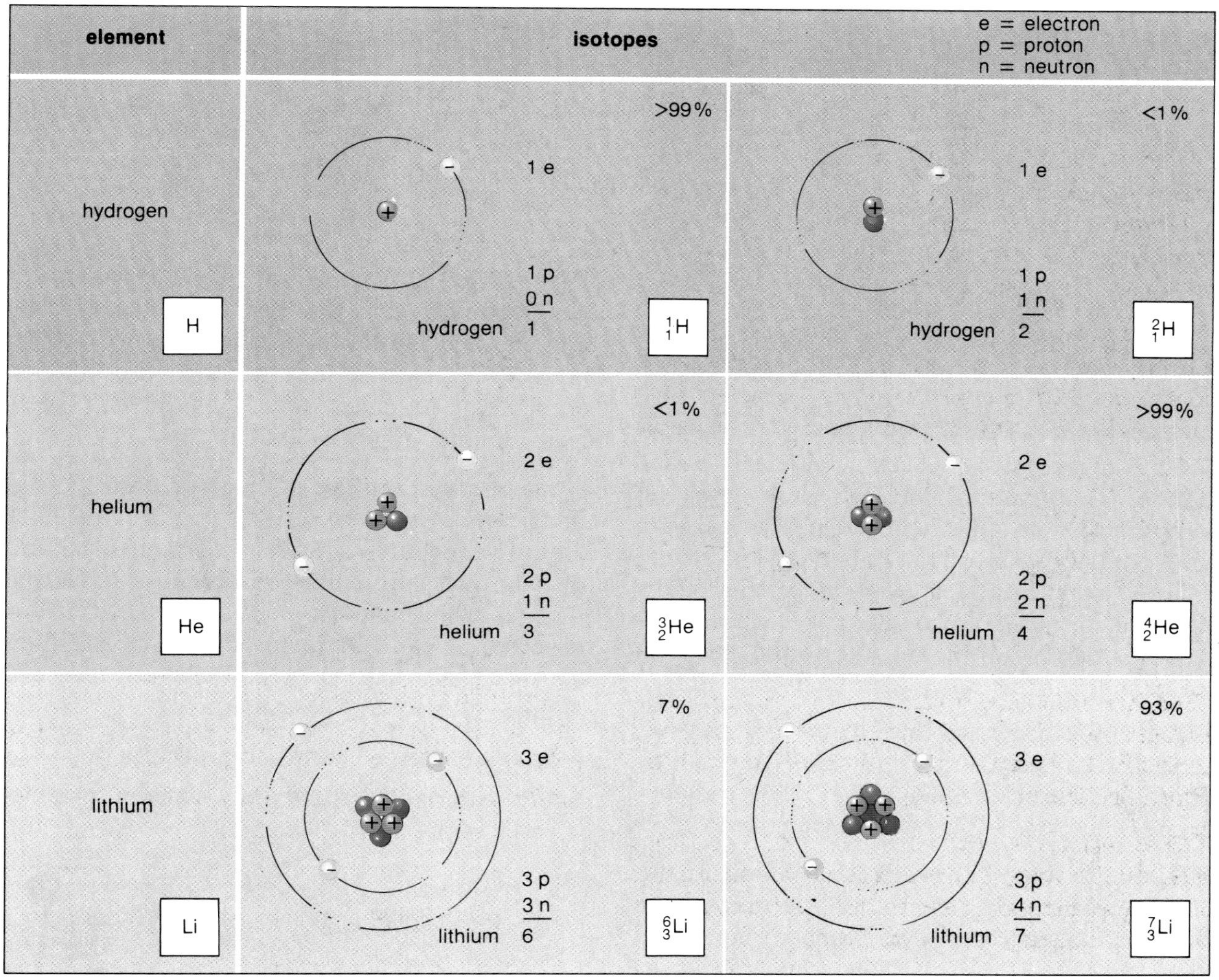

element	isotopes	e = electron p = proton n = neutron

>99%

1 e

1 p
0 n

hydrogen   1 $_1^1H$

<1 %

1 e

1 p
1 n

hydrogen   2 $_1^2H$

hydrogen   H

<1 %

2 e

2 p
1 n

helium   3 $_2^3He$

>99%

2 e

2 p
2 n

helium   4 $_2^4He$

helium   He

7%

3 e

3 p
3 n

lithium   6 $_3^6Li$

93%

3 e

3 p
4 n

lithium   7 $_3^7Li$

lithium   Li

1

electron	proton	neutron	nucleus

Which of these:
a orbits the nucleus;
b is a particle with a + charge;
c is uncharged;
d is lighter than all the others;
e is made up of protons and neutrons;
f has a – charge?

2 Copy the chart and fill in the blanks:

	electrons	protons	neutrons	nucleon number
sodium-23	11			
aluminium-27	13			
strontium-90	38			
cobalt-60	27			

To answer the following questions, you will need information from the table of elements on the opposite page.

3 Nitrogen-14 can be written $_7^{14}N$. How can the following be written?
a Radium-226;   **b** Uranium-235;
c Oxygen-16;   **d** Carbon-12.

4 Here is some information about four atoms:
Atom A: 3 electrons, nucleon number 7;
Atom B: 142 neutrons, nucleon number 232;
Atom C: 3 neutrons, nucleon number 6;
Atom D: 5 electrons, nucleon number 11.
What elements are A, B, C and D?
Which pair of atoms are isotopes? What are the

5.2 Nuclear radiation

DANGER
RADIOACTIVITY

Deadly cargo. Waste from a nuclear power station. The material in each flask gives off **nuclear radiation** – it is **radioactive**. The flasks are thick enough to absorb the radiation. And strong enough to withstand a head-on crash. This is essential. Because if any of the waste leaked out, it could contaminate the air, crops, and the local water supply. And many deaths could result.

Radioactive atoms are unstable atoms. In time, each nucleus breaks up and shoots out a tiny particle or a burst of wave energy. This 'radiates' from the nucleus – it is nuclear radiation.

Radioactive materials aren't only found in nuclear power stations. There are tiny amounts of them in the ground, the atmosphere, and even living things. This is because elements are a mixture of isotopes, and some isotopes are unstable.

For example:

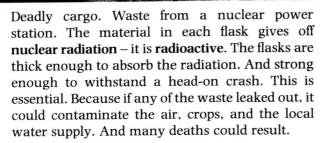

isotopes		found in
stable	unstable, radioactive	
carbon-12 carbon-13	carbon-14	air, plants animals
potassium-39 potassium-41	potassium-40	rocks, plants sea water
	uranium-234 uranium-235 uranium-238	rocks

Danger! Ions

People who work in nuclear power stations wear a film badge like this. This reacts to nuclear radiation rather like the film in a camera reacts to light. Every month, they hand in the film for developing, to check that they haven't been exposed to too much radiation.

Nuclear radiation can damage or destroy vital body cells. An overdose may lead to cancer or incurable radiation sickness. Radioactive gas and dust is especially dangerous because it can be taken into the body with air, food, or drink. Once absorbed, it can't be removed, and its radiation causes cell damage deep in the body. The cell damage is caused by **ionization**:

- Ions are charged atoms or molecules.
- If a material is **ionized**, then some of its molecules carry + or − charges.

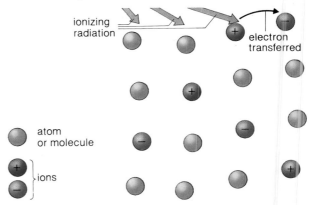

- Nuclear radiation, X-rays, and ultraviolet all cause ionization. When they strike atoms or molecules, they wrench electrons from them, leaving them +. The electrons are caught by other atoms or molecules, making them −.
- Living cells are very sensitive to ionization. It can completely upset their life processes.

There are several types of nuclear radiation. In a nuclear power station, the radiation from the nuclear fuel is mainly a stream of neutrons (see page 184). The radiation from the radioactive waste is mainly **alpha**, **beta** and **gamma** radiation:

type	alpha particles (α)	beta particles (β)	gamma rays (γ)
	each particle is 2 protons + 2 neutrons	each particle is an electron	electromagnetic waves similar to X-rays
charge	+	−	no charge
mass	heavy compared with betas	very light	. . .
speed	up to $\frac{1}{10}$ speed of light	up to $\frac{9}{10}$ speed of light	speed of light
ionizing effect	strong	weak	very weak
penetrating effect	not very penetrating: stopped by thick sheet of paper, or skin	penetrating: stopped by about 5 mm of aluminium	highly penetrating: never fully absorbed but 25 mm of lead halves strength
effect of fields	bent by magnetic and electric fields	bent strongly by magnetic and electric fields	not bent by magnetic or electric fields

1 Copy the boxes. Then use the first letter of each answer to form a word; clue: this is where nuclear radiation comes from.

?	Uncharged parts of an alpha particle.
?	If a material is radioactive, its atoms are . . .
?	Radioactive material in air, plants and animals.
?	Metal used for absorbing gamma rays.
?	Beta particles.
?	Material with nucleon number of 235.
?	If a material isn't radioactive, its atoms are . . .

2

alpha	beta	gamma

Which type of radiation:
a is uncharged;
b can penetrate lead;
c is stopped by a thick sheet of paper;
d has a + charge;
e has most mass;
f isn't bent by electric or magnetic fields;
g is made up of electrons?

3 Explain:
a how an ionized material is different from one that isn't ionized;
b why nuclear radiation is harmful to living things.

177

5.3 Living with radiation

Nuclear power – how safe?

The disaster at Chernobyl nuclear power station, USSR, happened swiftly and without warning. It was in the early hours of April 26 1986 when the cooling system of number four reactor failed. Minutes later, a violent explosion blew the top off the reactor and blasted a huge cloud of radioactive gas high into the atmosphere. Two people were killed outright. Hundreds received massive radiation overdoses. And more than 25 000 had to be evacuated from their homes. Days later, the radioactive cloud had spread as far as Scotland. Its radiation was weak but, all over Europe, radioactive rain was falling. In some areas, people were advised not to eat fresh vegetables, or drink fresh milk, and the sale of meat was banned.

The accident at Chernobyl was the world's worst nuclear accident. In Britain, it convinced many people that all nuclear power stations should be shut down for good. But the Central Electricity Generating Board don't agree. They claim that:

- a similar disaster can't happen in Britain, because the reactors are of a much safer design.
- fewer deaths are caused by using nuclear fuel than by mining for coal or drilling for oil and gas.

- nuclear accidents are rare compared with other types of accident – such as air crashes, fires, or dam collapses.
- more nuclear power stations are essential because the world's supplies of oil, coal, and natural gas are running out.

Britain's worst nuclear accident

Windscale (now called Sellafield) in Cumbria. Here, in 1957, a nuclear reactor overheated and caught fire. No one was killed outright, but fourteen workers received radiation overdoses. And small amounts of radioactive gas and dust were released over the local countryside.

An official report said that accident had nearly become a full-scale disaster. The Nuclear Authorities wanted the report published. But the Prime Minister at the time refused. He thought that it would make people lose confidence in Britain's nuclear industry. Thirty years later, the cabinet records for 1957 were released. Only then did the public discover what had really happened at Windscale.

The search for a nuclear dustbin

The village of Elstow, near Bedford. To the Nuclear Authorities it seemed like the ideal dumping site for Britain's nuclear waste. Firm rocks underneath meant that the containers wouldn't crack open. And the soft clay soil above would absorb the radiation.

When the dumping plans were announced, the residents of Elstow reacted angrily. There was a storm of protests and the plans were dropped. Now, the authorities are searching for other sites. They've considered drilling storage tunnels under the North Sea. But Norway and Denmark are fiercely opposed to this idea. They're afraid that radioactive materials might leak out and contaminate their coastlines. Meanwhile, the waste from Britain's nuclear power stations is piling up. It's going to be radioactive for hundreds of years. And it's got to be stored somewhere . . .

Gammas keep fruit fresher

These strawberries were picked three weeks before the photograph was taken.

So were these. But these were put straight into a beam of gamma radiation. The radiation stopped the rotting process. So the strawberries look as fresh as the day they were picked. They haven't become radioactive. And their taste has hardly changed at all.

Radiating food has many advantages. Or so the food producers claim. The radiation stops vegetables sprouting when they are being stored. It kills off the mould which makes food go off. And it destroys bacteria like *Salmonella* which can give you food poisoning. Many supermarkets want to sell fruit treated with radiation. They claim that it will mean better quality for their customers, less waste and lower prices.

But not everyone likes the idea. The radiation may destroy important vitamins. And it may change some of the chemicals in food – so that they behave like dangerous additives. Irradiated food does last longer. But when you next buy fresh strawberries, how fresh will they really be?

Most people wouldn't want a nuclear waste dump near their homes, even if they were told that the dump was completely safe. Why not? How many reasons can you think of?

Some supermarkets want to sell fruit and vegetables that has been treated with radiation. Make lists of the points for and against this scheme.

5.4 Radiation: detecting it . . .

The Geiger-Müller tube

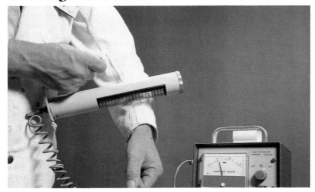

Radiation check on a nuclear laboratory worker. The instrument is a **Geiger-Müller tube**.
If there is any radioactive dust on the clothing, the G-M tube will detect the radiation from it.

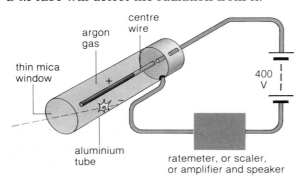

The 'window' at the end of the tube is thin enough even for alpha particles to pass through. If an alpha particle enters the tube, it ionizes the gas inside. This sets off a high voltage spark across the gas, and a pulse of current flows in the circuit. A beta particle or a burst of gamma radiation would have the same effect.

The G-M tube can be connected to

a ratemeter. The needle gives a reading in counts per second. If 50 alpha particles are detected by the tube every second, the reading is 50 counts per second.

a scaler. This counts the total number of particles or bursts of gamma radiation entering the tube.

an amplifier and speaker. The speaker gives a 'click' every time a particle or burst of gamma radiation enters the tube.

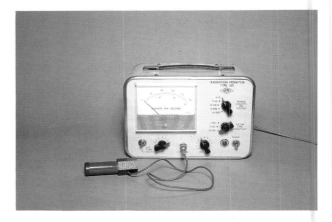

The cloud chamber

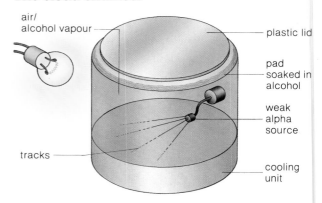

A cloud chamber is particularly useful for studying alpha particles. You can actually see their tracks. The chamber has cold alcohol vapour mixed with the air inside it. The alpha particles make the vapour condense. So you see a trail of tiny droplets where each particle passes through.

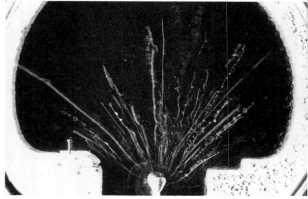

Tracks like this show that alpha particles have a range of only a few centimetres in air.

and using it

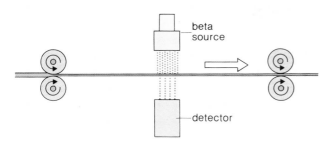

Checking the thickness in a tyre factory.
This moving band of tyre cord has a beta source on one side and a detector on the other. If the detector picks up too much radiation, the cord is being made too thin.

Killing cancer cells.
Gamma rays kill living cells. This machine can concentrate gamma rays on cancer cells in one small area of the body.

Seeing through steel.
Gamma rays are used to take X-ray-type photographs of welded metal joints. Here, the gamma source is inside the pipe. The X-ray film is wrapped round the outside of the pipe.

Checking the lungs with a radioactive tracer. Tiny amounts of radioactive krypton gas are breathed in by the patient. The flow of gas can be 'watched' on a T.V. screen.

To answer these questions you will need some information from the previous unit.

1

ratemeter	cloud chamber	scaler	amplifier

Which of the above would be
a used to show the tracks of alpha particles
b connected to a G-M tube to measure the total number of particles received.
c connected to a G-M tube to measure the number of particles received every second.

2 Explain why
a the window at the end of a G-M tube has to be very thin.
b a cloud chamber has cold alcohol vapour in it.
c a gamma ray source might be put inside a steel pipe.

3 Tracy carries out experiments with three radioactive sources. She puts different absorbing materials in front of each, and measures the radiation passing through. These are her readings:

source	radiation received: counts per second			
	no absorber	thick cardboard	2 cm of aluminium	2 cm of lead
A	8	8	7	5
B	12	5	4	3
C	10	9	0	0

Tracy knows that: one source gives out beta particles; another source gives out gamma rays; the third source gives out two types of radiation.

Can you work out what is coming from each source?

5.5 Radioactive decay

The breaking up of unstable atoms is called **radioactive decay**. It's happening around you all the time – in the rocks, in the atmosphere, and even in your house. A G-M tube can detect this weak **background radiation**. Each count or 'click' means that one particle or burst of gamma radiation has gone into the tube. Somewhere, one atom has decayed.

Radioactive decay is completely random. You can't tell which atom is going to break up next, or when. But some types of atom are more unstable than others. They decay at a faster rate.

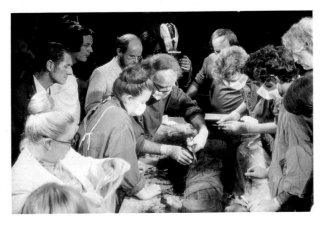

Scientists unwrap an Ancient Egyptian mummy. By measuring the radiation it gives off, they can find out its age. Tiny amounts of radioactive carbon-14 pass in and out of all living things but some stays trapped in the body at death. As time goes on, the radiation from the carbon gets weaker and weaker. Scientists can use this fact to work out the age. It's called carbon dating.

Half-life

A G-M tube is placed next to a large sample of radioactive iodine-128. Both are shielded from background radiation. This is how the count-rate changes with time:

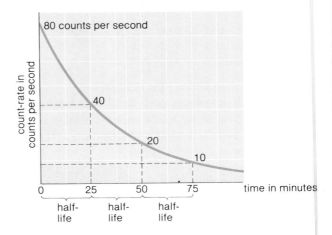

As time goes on, there are fewer and fewer unstable atoms left to decay. So the count-rate gets less and less. After 25 minutes, the count-rate has fallen half its original value. Half the atoms have now decayed. After another 25 minutes, the count-rate has halved again. And so on. Iodine-128 has a **half-life** of 25 minutes.

Here are the half-lives of some other radioactive materials:

Radon-222	4 days
Strontium-90	28 years
Radium-226	1620 years
Carbon-14	5770 years
Plutonium-239	24 360 years
Uranium-235	700 000 000 years

Radioactivity makes rocks hot

100 metres underground. The rock temperature has already reached 50°C. Another 1000 metres, and it will be hot enough to boil water. The heat comes from radioactive atoms in the rocks. When they decay, they shoot out alpha or beta particles (and gamma rays) which hit other atoms and make them move faster. Energy released from the nucleus is changed into heat energy.

New atoms from old

When an atom decays, it may change into a completely different atom. For example:

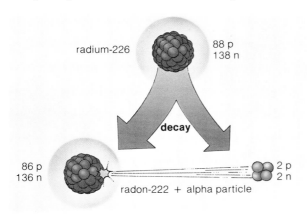

radium-226   88 p 138 n

decay

86 p 136 n   radon-222 + alpha particle   2 p 2 n

When an atom of radium-226 gives off an alpha particle, it loses 2 neutrons and 2 protons.
It becomes a charged atom of radon-222.
This new atom is a **decay product** of radium-226.
It too is radioactive.

Decay hazards

Sellafield nuclear waste reprocessing plant, Cumbria. Radioactive decay products from Britain's nuclear power stations are sent here to be separated. Many of the products are highly radioactive. And many have long half-lives. They will need to be stored for hundreds of years before their radiation has dropped to a safe level.

Some decay products are especially dangerous:

Strontium-90 and **iodine-131** are easily absorbed by the body. Strontium becomes concentrated in the bones, iodine in the thyroid gland.

Plutonium-239 is the most dangerous substance of all. Breathed in as dust, the smallest amount can kill.

1 Look at the table of half-lives on the opposite page. If small amounts of strontium-90 and radium-226 both gave the same count-rate today, which would give the higher reading in 10 years' time?

2 A G-M tube is placed near a weak radioactive material in the lab. There is no shielding round the tube or source to absorb background radiation. This is the graph of count-rate against time, using readings taken every half minute:

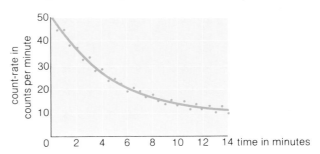

a Why are the points on the graph not on a smooth curve?
b Why does the graph level out above the zero?
c What is the half-life of the material? (Give an approximate value, to the nearest minute.)

3 This is how the count-rate from a radioactive material changed:

time in s	0	20	40	60	80	100	120
count-rate in counts/s	57	44	33	25	19	14	11

a Plot a graph of COUNT-RATE (*side axis*) against TIME (*bottom axis*).
b How long did it take the count-rate to fall from 50 to 25 counts/second?
c How long did it take the count-rate to fall from 40 to 20 counts/second?
d What is the half-life of the material?

4 The explosion at the Chernobyl reactor released a cloud of radioactive gas and dust into the atmosphere. It contained caesium-137 (half life 30 years) and iodine-131:

a Here are some measurements of the count rate from a small amount of iodine-131:

time in days	0	4	8	12
count-rate in counts/s	240	170	120	85

What is the half-life of iodine-131?

b Two months after the explosion, scientists were still concerned about the health risks from the caesium, but felt that the iodine was no longer a threat. Can you explain why?

5.6 Nuclear power

Hinkley Point 'B' nuclear power station, Somerset.

It can generate enough power to supply a large city. Like most power stations, it uses heat to make steam which drives the turbines and turns the generators (see page 170). But the heat doesn't come from burning coal, gas or oil. It comes from uranium atoms as they break up in a **nuclear reactor**.

Fission

Natural uranium is a dense radioactive metal.
It is made up mainly of two isotopes:
uranium-238 (over 99%), and uranium-235 (less than 1%).

Both uranium isotopes decay naturally. But atoms of uranium-235 can be made to break up very quickly.
They can be split by neutrons.
This is called **fission**.
Fission releases energy much faster than natural decay. And it works like this:

Every now and again a uranium-235 atom will split, all by itself. This is **spontaneous fission**. The atom breaks into two roughly equal parts, and shoots out two or three neutrons as well.
If these neutrons hit other uranium-235 atoms, they make them split and give out more neutrons. And so on. The result is a **chain reaction**:

When a uranium-235 atom splits, energy is released from its nucleus. As the bits are thrown violently apart, they bump into other atoms and make them move faster. Nuclear energy is changed into heat energy.

If the chain reaction is *uncontrolled*, huge numbers of atoms are split in a very short time. The heat builds up so rapidly that the material bursts apart in an explosion. This happens in a nuclear bomb.

If the chain reaction is *controlled*, there is a steady output of heat. This happens in a nuclear reactor.

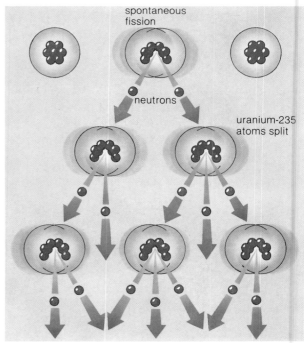

spontaneous fission

neutrons

uranium-235 atoms split

1 Copy the boxes. Fill in the first letter of each answer to make a word. These split atoms in a reactor:

?	Centre of an atom.
?	This is released during fission.
?	Material used for fission.
?	This rises when the control rods are raised.
?	Absorbed by the concrete around a reactor.
?	Non-nuclear fuel used in some power stations.
?	Type of energy stored in the nucleus.
?	What atoms do during fission.

Nuclear reactors

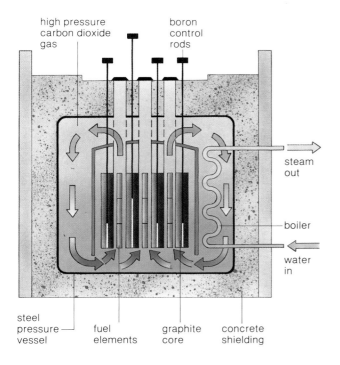

high pressure carbon dioxide gas · boron control rods

steam out

boiler

water in

steel pressure vessel · fuel elements · graphite core · concrete shielding

This is a gas-cooled reactor like the one at Hinkley Point 'B'. The reactor is inside a steel pressure vessel. It is surrounded by thick concrete to absorb radiation. Heat from the reactor is carried away by carbon-dioxide gas. The hot gas heats the water in the boiler.

● A reactor can't explode like a nuclear bomb. The uranium-235 atoms are too spaced out for an uncontrolled chain reaction to occur.

2

boron	graphite	uranium	concrete	steel

In a reactor, which of these materials is used:
a as a moderator;
b to absorb radiation;
c in the nuclear fuel elements;
d in the control rods?

3 Explain why, in a gas-cooled reactor:
a a moderator is needed;
b carbon dioxide gas is pumped through the reactor;
c the chain reaction stops if the control rods are kept fully lowered.

The reactor contains:

Nuclear fuel elements. These contain uranium dioxide. They contain natural uranium with extra uranium-235 mixed in. 1 kg of this 'enriched' uranium fuel gives as much energy as 55 tonnes of coal.

A graphite core. This is a **moderator** – it slows down the neutrons released by fission.
The neutrons have to be slowed down otherwise the chain reaction would stop. The uranium-238 atoms in the fuel absorb fast neutrons. But they don't absorb slow ones.

Control rods. These are raised or lowered to control the rate of fission. They are made of boron, which absorbs neutrons.
If the rods are raised, more neutrons can cause fission. So the reactor temperature rises.
If the rods are fully lowered, the chain reaction stops and the reactor cools down.

● In a pressurized water reactor, water is used to carry heat from the reactor core.

4 Copy and complete the chart to show the energy changes which take place in a nuclear power station. Each of the question marks is a type of energy.

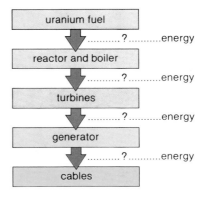

uranium fuel
........?.........energy
reactor and boiler
........?.........energy
turbines
........?.........energy
generator
........?.........energy
cables

5.7 The oscilloscope

An oscilloscope looks a bit like a TV. But you can use it to study sound waves, a.c. voltages, and even heartbeats.

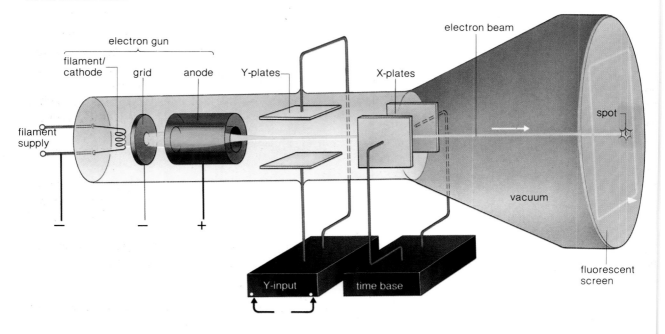

The electron gun makes a narrow beam of electrons. It has a cathode ($-$) to give off electrons, and an anode ($+$) to accelerate them.

The Y-plates are used to bend the beam up or down. This is done by putting a voltage across the Y-input terminals so that one plate goes $+$ and the other goes $-$.

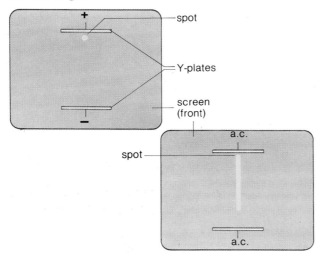

The grid controls the brightness. When the grid is made negative ($-$), it pushes back some electrons. So fewer of them reach the screen.

The screen is coated in a fluorescent material. You see a bright spot where the electron beam strikes it.

The X-plates are used to move the beam across the screen. Usually this is done with a time base circuit. The time base changes the voltage across the plates so that the beam moves from left to right across the screen, and then flicks back to the start. This happens over and over again.

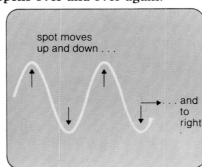

Measuring an a.c. voltage

With an a.c. voltage, the actual value of the voltage doesn't stay the same from one moment to the next.

It's the voltage which gives the 'peaks' and 'troughs' on the screen. It is sometimes useful to know the **peak voltage**. This is the maximum voltage in either the forward or backwards direction.

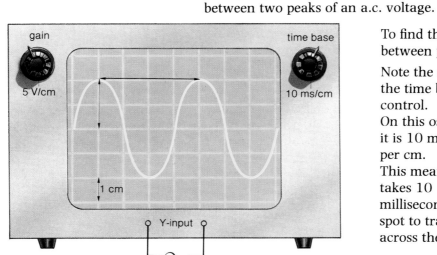

Measuring a time

An oscilloscope can be used to measure time. For example you could use it to measure the time between two peaks of an a.c. voltage.

To find the time between peaks

Note the setting on the time base control.

On this oscilloscope, it is 10 milliseconds per cm.

This means that it takes 10 milliseconds for the spot to travel 1 cm across the screen.

To find the peak voltage
Note the setting on the **gain control**. On this oscilloscope, it is 5 volts per cm. This means that the spot moves 1 cm up (or down) for every 5 volts across the Y-input terminals.

Measure the **amplitude** of the wave on the screen – that's the distance from the centre line to the peak. On this screen, it is 2 cm.

Calculate the peak voltage:
the spot moves 2 cm up or down,
there are 5 volts to every cm,
So the peak voltage is 2 × 5 volts, or 10 volts.

Measure the distance across the screen from one peak to the next. On this screen, it is 4 cm.

Calculate the time:
the spot moves 4 cm from one peak to the next, each cm takes 10 milliseconds,
so the time between peaks is 4 × 10 milliseconds, or 40 milliseconds.

2 This is the screen of a small oscilloscope, *shown actual size.* An a.c. voltage has been put across the Y-input terminals of the oscilloscope. The control settings are also shown.

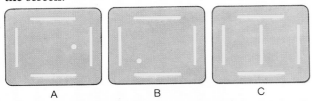

1 Each diagram shows the front view of the X- and Y-plates of an oscilloscope. It also shows the spot on the screen.

A	B	C

Copy diagrams A and B. Show which plates are being used to move the spot by marking them + or −.
How is the line in diagram C produced?

Use a millimetre ruler to measure the amplitude of the wave and the distance between peaks. Then calculate
a the peak voltage
b the time between peaks A and B.

5.8 Resistors

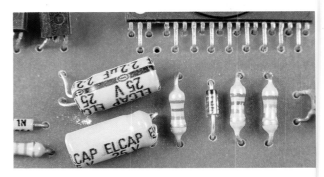

Circuits like those in radios and cassette recorders are called **electronic** circuits. The parts fitted in these circuits are called **components**. Resistors and capacitors (see page 190) are components used in nearly all electronic circuits.

Resistors

Resistors keep currents and voltages at the sizes that other components need to work properly. Each resistor has a resistance measured in **ohms** (Ω). The value is marked on the side using either the **colour code** or the **resistance code**. The value is only approximate. When resistors are made in the factory, the resistance can change slightly from one to the next.

The colour code

Each colour stands for a number:

Black   0
Brown   1
Red   2
Orange   3
Yellow   4
Green   5
Blue   6
Violet   7
Grey   8
White   9

You 'read' the rings on the resistor like this:

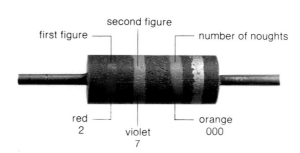

first figure — red 2
second figure — violet 7
number of noughts — orange 000

resistance value = 27 000
= 27 kΩ

The fourth ring gives the **tolerance**. This tells you by how much the resistance may differ from the marked value. Resistors with the gold ring are best!

Gold 5%   Silver 10%   No colour 20%

The resistance code

Resistance values are printed on the resistor:

R27 means 0.27 Ω
2R7 means 2.7 Ω
3R0 means 3.0 Ω
4K7 means 4.7 kΩ
47K means 47 kΩ

The extra letter at the end gives the tolerance:
F 1%   G 2%   J 5%   K 10%   M 20%

Variable resistors

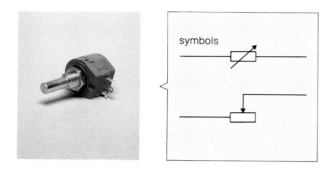

symbols

You can alter the resistance of a variable resistor by turning a spindle or moving a slider.

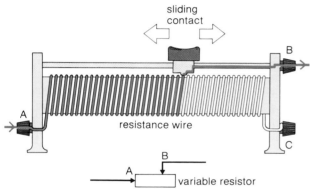

sliding contact

B

A

resistance wire

C

B

A

variable resistor

A **rheostat** is a type of variable resistor used to control the current flowing in a circuit.

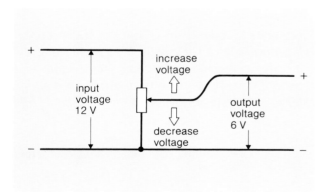

+

input voltage 12 V

increase voltage

decrease voltage

output voltage 6 V

+

−

−

This variable resistor has three terminals. It is being used as a **voltage divider** or **potentiometer**. It is passing on just part of the 12 volts put across it. Its output voltage can be anything from 0 V to 12 V, depending on the position of the sliding contact.

1 Give *two* ways in which you might use a variable resistor.

2

What is the resistance of each of these resistors?
What is the tolerance of each?
Explain what is meant by the tolerance.

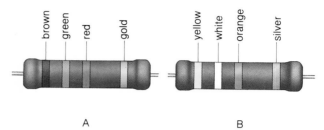

A   B

4 k 7 J   3 R 9 M

C   D

3

Which of these voltage dividers has an output of
a 4 V **b** 6 V **c** 0 V?
What is the output of the other voltage divider?

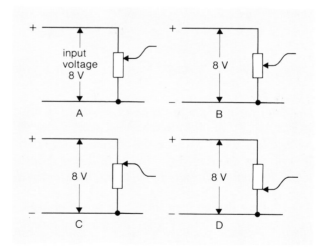

input voltage 8 V

A

8 V

B

8 V

C

8 V

D

5.9 Capacitors

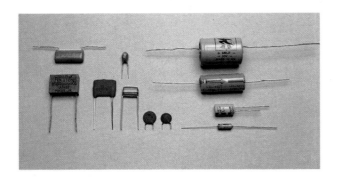

Capacitors are stores for small amounts of charge. In one way, they are like rechargeable batteries. They can take in charge, store it, and give it back later. But they store less charge than most batteries. And they only store it for a short time.

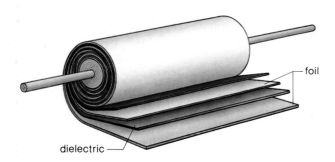

Most capacitors contain two foil sheets, rolled up like a 'swiss roll'. Sandwiched between them is a layer of insulator called a **dielectric**. Charge can't flow across the dielectric. But it builds up on the foil sheets when a voltage is put across the them.

The higher the capacitance, the more charge a capacitor stores when connected across a battery.

Capacitance is usually measured in **microfarads (μF)**.

A smaller unit of capacitance is the **picofarad (pF)**.

$1 \, \mu F = 1\,000\,000 \, pF$

symbols:

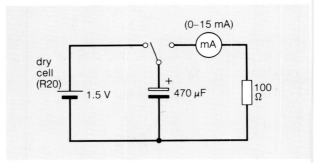

You can use this circuit to show that a capacitor stores charge. When the switch is put to the left, the battery charges up the capacitor. When the switch is put to the right, the capacitor discharges through the resistor. The flow of charge only lasts for a fraction of a second. The discharge takes longer if you use

● a higher resistance
● a capacitor with a higher **capacitance** value marked on the side.

Electrolytic capacitors have the largest capacitances. But their dielectrics are damaged if they are connected the wrong way round. One terminal is marked +, so that you known which way to make the connection.

To answer this question, you will need information from the previous section.

1	electrolytic capacitor	potentiometer	resistor

Which of these
a is used to give variable voltage output
b stores small amounts of charge
c can be used as a variable resistor
d has three terminals
e has + and − terminals which must be connected the right way round?

5.10 Building a system

Transducers

No, it isn't the name of the group. It's the starred items in the picture. They are all **transducers**. Transducers change energy from one form into another:

- the microphones, guitar pick-up and keyboard all give out tiny currents or 'electrical signals'.
- the headphones and speakers turn electrical signals into sound.

In this system, the transducers are all plugged into a box of electronics called an amplifier. This makes electrical signals larger. So the group sounds louder.

Here is a block diagram of the group's sound system. The arrows show how energy passes through the system:

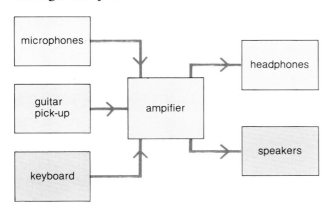

More transducers

Make a chart of the transducers. In the chart, show the type of energy going into each transducer, and the type of energy coming out.

5.11 Diodes

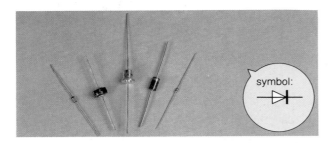

These are **diodes**. They're found in radios, computers, and almost every other piece of electronic equipment. They have many uses, but one of the most important is in changing a.c. to d.c. (see next section).

Mostly, they are made from specially treated crystals or 'chips' of the semiconductor silicon. They are the simplest of all silicon chips.

The job of a diode is to allow current through itself in one direction, but not the other.
These circuits show what happens:

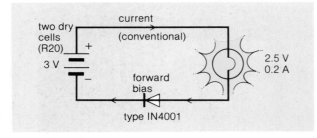

Connected this way round,
the diode has a very *low* resistance.
So a current flows, and the bulb lights up.
Here, we say the diode is **forward biased**.
The arrowhead in the symbol points the *same way* as the *conventional* current direction.

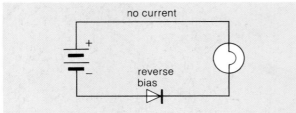

Connected this way round,
the diode has a very *high* resistance.
Almost no current flows. The bulb doesn't light.
Here the diode is **reverse biased**.

Diodes solve a problem

The problem How to wire up your circle lights so that a battery takes over when you aren't pedalling fast enough for the dynamo to light the bulbs.

The answer Use two diodes like this. (To keep things simple, only one bulb is shown):

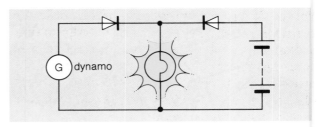

Current can come from *either* the dynamo *or* the battery, depending on which has the higher voltage. But the dynamo can't push current through the battery. And the battery can't push current through the dynamo. The two diodes stop that happening.

Light-emitting diodes (LEDs)

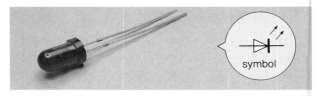

These diodes give off light when they are forward biased. They are often used as indicator lights on videos and cassette players.

LEDs can't handle large currents. To protect them from damage, a high resistance is usually connected in series.

LEDs can be used to display numbers. Seven LED's, lighting up in different combinations, can give you any number from 0 to 9.

Testing a diode

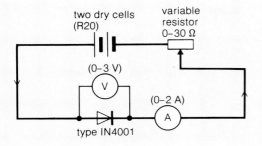

two dry cells (R20)
variable resistor 0–30 Ω
(0–3 V)
V
(0–2 A)
A
type IN4001

You could use this circuit to find out how the current through a diode changes with the voltage across it. The voltage is set at different values by adjusting the variable resistor, and the current measured each time. Here, the diode is forward biased. For reverse bias, you just change the battery connections round.

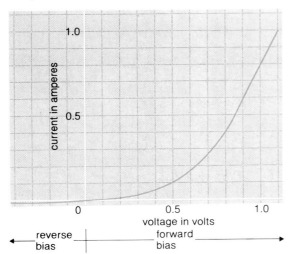

These are the results you might get, in the form of a graph. To find the resistance of the diode at any point, use the equation

$$\text{resistance} = \text{voltage} \div \text{current}$$
(ohms)   (volts)   (amperes)

When reverse biased, this diode has a very high resistance.
When forward biased, its resistance becomes less as the current rises.

Keep within limits Too much current, or too much reverse voltage, and a diode is damaged. The diode in this experiment isn't designed for currents of more than 1 A. Its reverse bias limit is about 50 V.

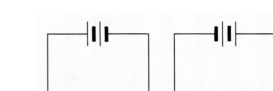

A   B

In which of these circuits:
a does the bulb light up;
b does the diode have a high resistance;
c is the diode forward biased?

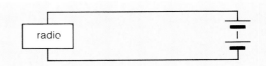

radio

2 The radio is powered by a battery. But if the battery is connected the wrong way round, parts inside the radio may be damaged.

Design a circuit so that current can flow if the battery is connected as shown, but is blocked if the battery is connected wrongly.

3 Redraw the battery and dynamo circuit on the opposite page so that two bulbs are supplied with current instead of one. Assume that you are using a 6 V battery and two 6 V bulbs.
Explain why, when the dynamo isn't generating, the battery pushes all its current through the bulbs and none through the dynamo.

4 Using readings from the graph on this page, copy and complete the following table:

Diode forward biased		
Voltage across diode	current in A	resistance in ohms
0.5 V	?	?
1.0 V	?	?

5.12 Power supplies

A.C. – 'backwards and forwards' alternating current.
D.C. – 'one way' direct current:

This cassette recorder runs on 9 volts d.c.
But you don't have to fit batteries.
It can be plugged into the 240 volt a.c. mains.
This is because there is a **power supply** inside.
It reduces the voltage, and changes the a.c. to d.c.

Changing a.c. to d.c.

Changing a.c. to d.c. is called **rectification**.
It is done with diodes.
Diodes used in this way are called **rectifiers**.

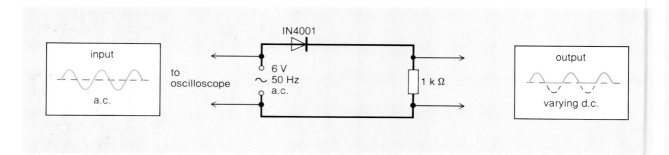

This circuit changes a.c. to d.c. The diode lets the forward parts of the alternating current through, but stops the backward parts. This means that current only flows one way through the resistor.

An oscilloscope can be used to show what the diode does to a.c. When the oscilloscope is connected across the resistor, the bottom half of the a.c. waveform is missing. The current is flowing in surges, with short periods in between when there isn't any current. This is **half-wave rectification**.

Smoothing with a capacitor

The 'half wave' current from a diode is far too jerky for most electronic equipment. But the flow can be smoothed out with a capacitor. This collects charge during the surges, and releases it when the current from the diode stops. This gives a much smoother flow of current through the resistor.

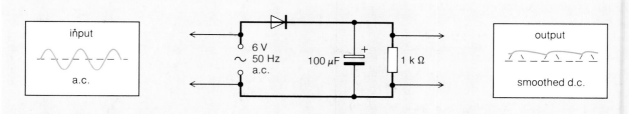

A power supply

This is a simple power supply. It contains a transformer, four diodes, and a capacitor. It changes the mains a.c. into low-voltage, smoothed d.c.:

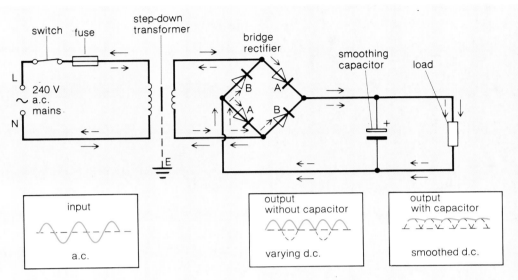

The transformer steps down the mains voltage. In some power supplies, for safety, a switch and a fuse are fitted in the live wire, and the core of the transformer is earthed.

The four diodes together make a **bridge rectifier**. This changes the a.c. to d.c. But instead of *blocking* the backwards parts of the alternating current, it actually *reverses* them so that the whole flow is forwards. The result is **full-wave rectification**.

The bridge rectifier works like this:
When the a.c. is flowing forwards (→), diodes A conduct, and diodes B block.
When the a.c. is flowing backwards (←−), diodes B conduct, and diodes A block.
Follow the arrows and you will see that the current from the bridge rectifier always flows the same way.

The capacitor smooths the current flow.

The load is a simple resistor. But it could be a radio, or a cassette recorder, or any other piece of equipment needing a low-voltage d.c. supply.

1 On an oscilloscope, which of these waveforms is produced by:
a a.c.
b half-wave rectification of a.c.
c full-wave rectification of a.c.
d rectification of a.c., with smoothing?
2 Read pages 144 and 145. Then explain why, in a power supply,
a the switch and the fuse should be placed in the live wire;
b the core of the transformer should be earthed.

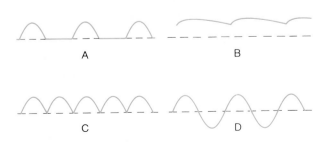

5.13 Transistors

Transistors...

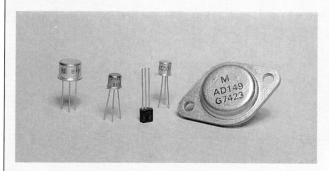

These are **transistors**. Inside each case is a specially treated crystal of silicon, with three connecting leads attached. Transistors are used in TV's, record players, and just about every other piece of electronic equipment. They can join circuits so that the current through one controls the current through the next.

amplifying ...

In this music centre, transistors **amplify** (magnify) the tiny, changing voltage from the pick-up. The changing voltage in one circuit causes even bigger changes in the next. And so on ... until the changes are large enough to make a loudspeaker cone vibrate.

A switched-off transistor

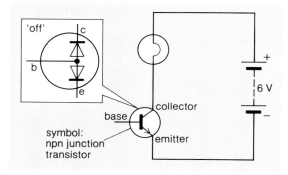

The transistor in this circuit is an **NPN junction transistor**. A circuit symbol has been used to show it. It has three terminals – called the **emitter**, the **base**, and the **collector**.

Connected like this, the transistor behaves like two diodes back-to-back. The bottom diode can conduct, but the top diode has a blocking effect. No current can flow. The bulb doesn't light. The transistor is 'switched off'.

Switching the transistor on ...

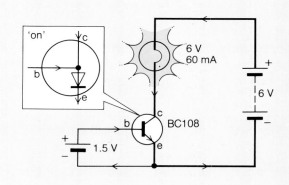

Put a small voltage across the base and emitter like this, and a tiny current flows through the base. This current completely alters the way the transistor behaves. The blocking effect vanishes, the transistor starts to conduct, and the bulb lights up. It takes a base current of less than 1 mA to 'switch on' the transistor so that the bulb lights.

The transistor won't switch on unless the + and − connections are the right way round. In each circuit, the conventional current direction must be the same as the arrow direction in the symbol.

switching...

In automatic washing machines, transistors are used as switches. They control the circuits which operate the wash program.

Transistor switches do a similar job to the relay on page 159. You can find out more about them in the next section.

and shrinking

These are **integrated circuits** or **i.c.'s**. They contain many complete circuits, with transistors, resistors, connections, and other components all formed on a tiny chip of silicon only a few millimetres square. Most of the transistors in a washing machine are in 'microchips' like these.

and another way of switching it on

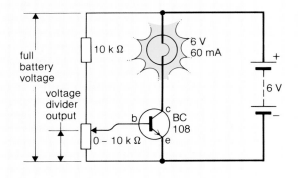

You don't need a second battery to switch a transistor on. With a voltage divider, you can use a proportion of the main battery voltage instead.

Here, a resistor and a variable resistor are being used as a voltage divider. If the sliding contact is at the bottom, the output from the voltage divider is zero. This keeps the transistor switched off. If the sliding contact is moved upwards, the output from the voltage divider rises. When it passes 0.6 V, the transistor switches on and the bulb lights.

1 In the circuit, the bulb is glowing brightly.

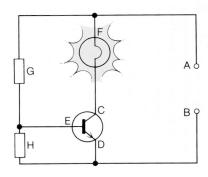

a Which letter, A to E, stands for each of these?
base   collector   battery +   emitter?
b Draw the circuit diagram. Mark on arrows to show the conventional current direction in each part of the circuit.
c What do the components G and H do?
d What would happen if you replaced G with a short piece of connecting wire? Explain why.

5.14 Transistor switches

The doors open when a customer approaches.
The entrance lights come on when darkness falls.
When the manager sets the overnight burglar alarm, she has time to leave the building before it switches on.
If there is a fire, an alarm bell sounds.
These all happen automatically.
They're all controlled by transistor switches.
The circuits below show the basic principles.

A light-operated switch

This circuit uses a **light-dependent resistor (LDR)**. This is a special type of resistor whose resistance falls when light shines on it.

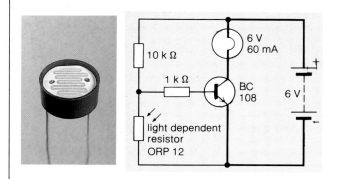

With this circuit, the bulb lights up when the LDR is put in the dark.

The LDR is part of the voltage divider.

In daylight, the LDR has a low resistance, and a low share of the battery voltage. The output from the voltage divider isn't enough to switch the transistor on.

In darkness, the resistance of the LDR rises. This gives the LDR a much larger share of the battery voltage. Now, the output from the voltage divider is more than the 0.6 V needed to switch the transistor on. So the bulb lights up.

If you replace the upper resistor with a variable resistor, you can alter the 'darkness level' needed to switch the transistor on.

If you swop round the LDR and the upper resistor, the bulb will be 'off' in the dark and 'on' in the light.

A heat-operated switch

This circuit uses a **thermistor**. This is a special type of resistor whose resistance falls when it is heated.

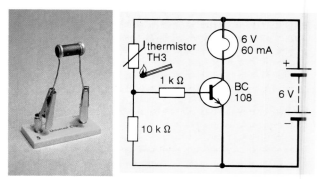

With this circuit, the bulb lights up when you heat the thermistor. The thermistor is part of the voltage divider. At room temperature, the thermistor has a high resistance. The output from the voltage divider isn't enough to switch the transistor on. When the thermistor is heated, its resistance falls. This gives the lower resistor a larger share of the battery voltage. Now, the output from the voltage divider is more than the 0.6 V needed to switch the transistor on. So the bulb lights up.

If you replace the lower resistor with a variable resistor, you can alter the temperature needed to make the transistor switch on.

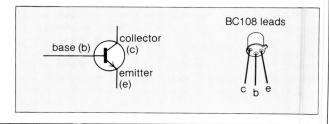

A time-operated switch

This circuit uses a **capacitor** to delay the switching on of the transistor. When the battery switch is closed, you have to wait several seconds before the bell rings.

To reset the circuit, you open the battery switch. Then you discharge the capacitor by closing the switch across it.

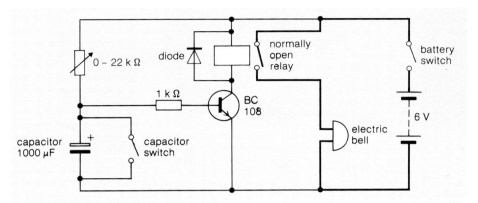

The capacitor is part of the voltage divider.
When you close the battery switch, the capacitor slowly charges, and the voltage across it rises. It takes several seconds for the voltage to reach the 0.6 V needed to switch the transistor on.

It takes even longer if you use

● a higher resistance setting on the variable resistor. This makes the capacitor charge more slowly.
● a capacitor with a higher capacitance value.

This circuit has an important extra feature. The transistor doesn't switch on the bell directly. Instead it switches on a 'normally open' relay (see page 159). The relay then switches on the bell. The advantage of this is that the current in the bell circuit doesn't have to flow through the transistor. So a higher current can be used.

The diode protects the transistor from currents generated when the relay contacts open.

1 This chart gives information about four transistor switch circuits, and what is needed for the transistor to be switched ON or OFF:

	transistor ON	transistor OFF
circuit A	darkness	bright light
circuit B	bright light	darkness
circuit C	high temperature	low temperature
circuit D	low temperature	high temperature

Which circuit is most like the one that would be used to
a open an automatic door when a light beam is cut
b set off an alarm when a fire starts
c switch on a car parking light at dusk
d switch on a heater when the temperature in a greenhouse falls?

2 Design a transistor switch circuit with the following features:
● an electric motor is switched on automatically in bright light;
● the motor is switched on by a relay.
What is the advantage of using a relay in this type of circuit?
3 In the circuit at the top of the page, what would be the effect of
a setting the variable resistor to a lower resistance value?
b replacing the 'normally open' relay with a 'normally closed one'.
Can you think of a practical use for the circuit in b?

5.15 Logic gates

The door of this safe is controlled by groups of switches called **logic gates**. Press the buttons in the right order, and the door opens. But press them in the wrong order, and the alarm goes off. The electronic gates needed to do this job are quite complicated.

The gate used in the circuit below is much simpler – just two switches in a box:

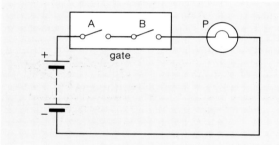

With this gate,
if both switches are closed the bulb comes ON.
but if either switch is open, the bulb stays OFF.

You can use a **truth table** to show the result of every possible switch setting. The table uses two **logic numbers**, 0 and 1:
Logic 0 stands for OFF. Logic 1 stands for ON.

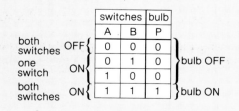

		switches		bulb
		A	B	P
both switches	OFF{	0	0	0
one switch	ON{	0	1	0	}bulb OFF
		1	0	0
both switches	ON{	1	1	1	}bulb ON

Logic gates can be grouped together on a single chip. Below, are three types of logic gate, along with their truth tables. In the tables,
logic 0 stands for OFF. Logic 1 stands for ON.
The gates have been drawn using symbols.
Power supply connections aren't shown.

AND gate

This AND gate has one output and two inputs.
The output is only ON if *both* inputs are ON.
In other words, P is ON if both A *AND* B are ON.
This is the truth table for the AND gates:

		inputs		output
		A	B	P
both inputs	OFF{	0	0	0
one input	ON{	0	1	0	}output OFF
		1	0	0
both inputs	ON{	1	1	1	}output ON

OR gate

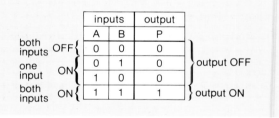

This OR gate has one output and two inputs.
The output is ON if *either* input is ON.
In other words, P in ON if either A *OR* B is ON.
This is the truth table for the OR gate:

		inputs		output
		A	B	P
both inputs	OFF{	0	0	0	}output OFF
one input	ON{	0	1	1
		1	0	1	}output ON
both inputs	ON{	1	1	1

NOT gate

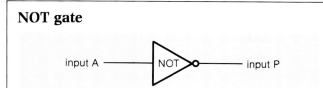

input A ———▷ NOT ○——— input P

A NOT gate has one output and one input.
The output is ON if the input is OFF, and vice versa.
This type of gate is called an **inverter** gate.
This is the truth table for a NOT gate:

	input	output	
	A	P	
input OFF {	0	1	} output ON
input ON {	1	0	} output OFF

Safe with logic

The manager of a camera shop wants an electric lock on her store room door. She needs a system without combinations or numbers to remember, so that any member of staff can unlock the door quickly. She decides on a two-switch system. If a hidden switch is turned on first, a main switch will open the door lock. But if the hidden switch is left off, the main switch will turn on an alarm instead.

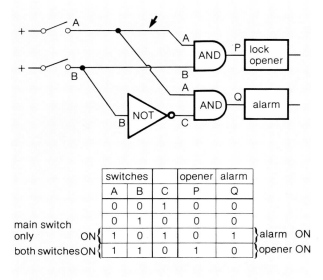

switches			opener	alarm	
A	B	C	P	Q	
0	0	1	0	0	
0	1	0	0	0	
1	0	1	0	1	} alarm ON
1	1	0	1	0	} opener ON

main switch only ON {
both switches ON {

This is the system of logic gates she decides to use, together with its truth table. To keep things simple, complete circuits aren't shown. Nor are the connections to the power supply.

1

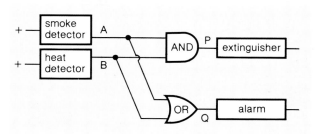

This is the fire safety system installed in a furniture showroom.
Smoke turns the smoke detector ON.
Heat turns the heat detector ON.
Logic gates are used to turn the alarm and the fire extinguisher ON.
a Write down the truth table for the system, using column headings A, B, P, and Q.
b What happens if smoke is detected but no heat?
c What must happen to turn both the alarm and the extinguisher ON?
2 If you combine an AND gate with a NOT gate, the result is a **NAND gate**.
If you combine an OR gate with a NOT gate, the result is a **NOR gate**.

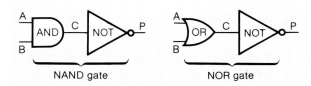

NAND gate   NOR gate

For each gate:
Write down the truth table, using column headings A, B, C, and P.
Use the table to work out whether the output is ON or OFF when
a both inputs are ON
b both inputs are OFF
c only one input is ON.
3 When the store room lock on the left was installed, a mistake was made. The NOT gate was fitted in the top input line (*see arrow*) instead of the bottom one.
a What happened when the manager turned the hidden switch ON?
b What happened when she then turned the main switch ON?
(Drawing a truth table may help you to work out the answers)

5.16 Machines that think

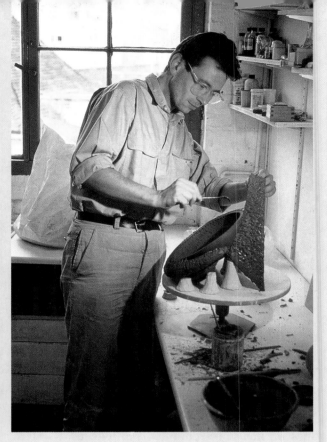

Human operators are skilled and creative but machines are faster and they never get tired.

In industry, more and more machines are being run by microchips. They can control anything from paint spraying to metal drilling. But they have to follow a set of rules put into them by people. They can't work without a **program**.

Now, scientists are trying to design microchips with 'artificial intelligence' – chips that set their own rules and learn from their mistakes. But they have a long way to go. Microchips still can't match humans for ideas.

New hope for the disabled

Electronics may help paralysed people to walk again, with the help of a strap-on walking frame. The latest frames are driven by compressed air, and a microchip controls the walking action.

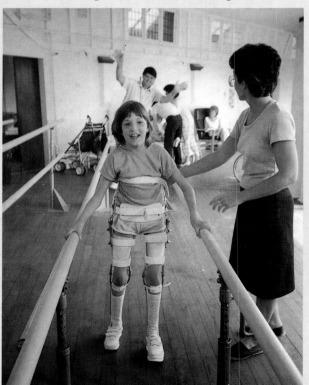

Reducing the risk

Air crashes don't happen very often. But when they do, it is usually because of human error. In an emergency, the crew has to make many decisions very fast. One wrong action can bring disaster.

Now, microchips are making flying safer. In the latest systems, microchips analyse the crew's actions, give a warning if they aren't safe, and take over control if the warning is ignored.

Could microchips declare war?

At least one American scientist thinks so. He claims that computers are now being left to decide when nuclear missiles should be launched. He thinks that this is against the law. And he is taking US defence chiefs to court to prove it.

The defence chiefs say that if the USA is attacked, computers could launch a counter-attack more quickly than human beings. But they claim that this wouldn't happen. The President would still make the final decision.

Microchips down on the farm

Electronic tractors will work best in large fields with no obstacles like trees and hedges to get in the way. They won't be welcomed by people who like the countryside the way it is. And they won't be welcomed by Britain's 70 000 unemployed farm workers.

Soon, this tractor won't need a driver. Microchips will control it, along with the ploughing, sowing spraying, and harvesting. This should help to put food production up and keep costs down.

Electronic farms are likely to mean greater food production at lower cost. But how many disadvantages can you think of?

In airliners, microchips will take over more and more of the jobs done by the crew. But passengers are still likely to want a crew on board. Can you think of the reasons why?

A microchip could control the heating system in your house. What other household tasks do you think could be done by microchips in the future?

5.17 Amplifiers

These all use **amplifiers** to change small voltages into larger ones:

Input: small a.c. voltage from aerial
output: larger a.c. voltage across loudspeaker

Input: small a.c. voltage from microphone
output: larger a.c. voltage across loudspeaker

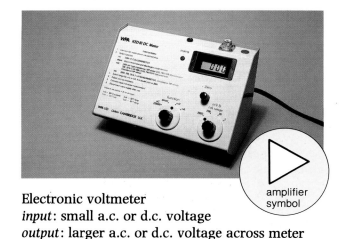

Electronic voltmeter
input: small a.c. or d.c. voltage
output: larger a.c. or d.c. voltage across meter

amplifier symbol

Gain

If an amplifier has an input voltage of 0.5 V, and an output voltage of 5.0 V, its voltage gain is 10:

$$\text{voltage gain} = \frac{\text{output voltage}}{\text{input voltage}}$$

In most amplifiers, the voltage gain is from a series of transistors. The output from one is fed to the input of the next, and so on. Usually the transistors form part of an integrated circuit.

An operational amplifier

Operational amplifiers, or **op-amps**, are used in measuring instruments and certain types of computer.
They have *two* inputs and one output.
They need a three-terminal power supply, though the connections aren't always shown on circuit diagrams.

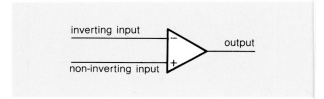

A commonly used op-amp is the type 741. It is an integrated circuit. The connections are shown below.

Type 741 op-amp

1		8
inv. input	2 −	7 + power supply
non inv. input	3 +	6 output
power supply −	4	5

(1,5 offset null)
(8 not used)

An inverting amplifier

In the circuit on the right, an op-amp is being used as an inverting amplifier. When the input is −, the output is +, and vice versa. In other words, the amplifier gives an inverted output.

The voltage you want to amplify is fed to the inverting input of the op-amp. The non-inverting input isn't needed. So it is connected to the Earth (0 V) terminal on the power supply.

The gain of an op-amp is far too high for most purposes. So a feedback resistor is used to reduce it. The resistor 'feeds back' some of the inverted output voltage so that it partly cancels out the input voltage. This in turn means a lower output voltage. Not only is the gain cut. There are other advantages as well:

- the op-amp can handle higher a.c. frequencies without any loss of gain.
- the gain can be set to any particular value by choosing suitable input and feedback resistances.

There is an equation for calculating the gain:

$$\text{voltage gain} = \frac{\text{resistance (feedback)}}{\text{resistance (input)}}$$

For example, in the circuit above:

$$
\begin{aligned}
\text{resistance (feetback)} &= 100\,\text{k}\Omega \\
\text{resistance (input} &= 20\,\text{k}\Omega \\
\text{so, voltage gain} &= \frac{100}{20} \\
&= 5
\end{aligned}
$$

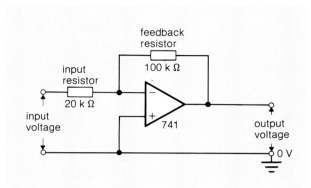

- The gain would be *higher* if
  the resistance of the feedback resistor was *higher*
  the resistance of the input resistor was *lower*

- The equation isn't accurate if the output voltage is close to the supply voltage. The output voltage can *never* be more than the supply voltage.

- To measure the gain of the amplifier:
  Connect a signal generator across the input so that it gives about 0.5 V a.c.
  Measure the input and output voltages accurately with an oscilloscope or electronic voltmeter.

1

amplifier	input voltage in V	output voltage in V
A	0.5	4.0
B	0.1	3.0
C	1.0	8.0
D	2.0	10.0

a Which amplifier gives the greatest voltage gain?
b Which amplifiers give the same voltage gain?

2

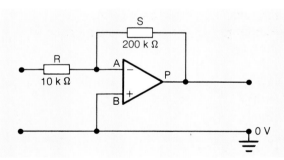

a Which terminal of the operational amplifier is the inverting input?
b What is the voltage gain of the amplifier?
c If the input voltage is 0.1 V a.c., what is the output voltage?
d The output voltage is inverted. What does this mean?
e Which resistor is the feedback resistor?
f What is the purpose of the feedback resistor?
g What would be the effect of increasing the resistance of the feedback resistor?
h What would be the effect of increasing the resistance of the input resistor?

Revision time

To give yourself the best chance in your GCSE examination, you will need to do some revision. Here's how to tackle the job:

● Start your revision early. At two pages a night, it would take more than 2 months to revise every topic in this book!
● Check that you know how to use the correct units. There's a summary below.
● Check that you know how to use the equations on pages 207 and 208. You won't have to remember them all. Ask your teacher to tell you which ones are on your syllabus and which ones you need to remember.

● Try the examination questions on pages 212 to 219.
● Use the revision check list on page 209. Ask your teacher to tell you which topics you need to cover.
● When you revise, don't just stare at an open book. Make plenty of notes on each topic. Then see if you can write out your notes again without referring to the book.
● Give yourself plenty of short breaks when you are revising. Half an hour's concentration at a time is more than enough.
● Give yourself time to rest and relax.

Units

What they are

unit	symbol	unit	symbol
metre	m	degree Celsius	°C
kilogram	kg	kelvin	K
second	s	ampere	A
newton	N	volt	V
joule	J	ohm	Ω
watt	W	coulomb	C
hertz	Hz	farad	F
pascal	Pa		

Bigger or smaller

Symbols can be put in front of units to make them bigger or smaller:

multiple	name	symbol	example
× one million	mega	M	MV
× one thousand	kilo	k	kV
× one thousandth	milli	m	mV
× one millionth	micro	μ	μV

(see pages 6 and 7)

What they measure

to be measured	unit (in symbols)
mass	kg
length, distance	m
time	s
area	m²
volume	m³
density	kg/m³
speed, volocity	m/s
acceleration	m/s²
force, weight	N
work, energy	J
power	J/s or W
pressure	N/m² or Pa
moment, couple	Nm
temperature	°C also K
specific heat capacity	J/(kg °C) or J/(kg K)
specific latent heat	J/kg
frequency	Hz
wavelength	m
charge	C
current	A
voltage, p.d., e.m.f.	V
resistance	Ω
capacitance	F

Equations

Speed

$$\text{average speed} = \frac{\text{distance moved}}{\text{time taken}}$$

Acceleration

$$\text{acceleration} = \frac{\text{velocity gained}}{\text{time taken}}$$

final velocity
= original velocity + (acceleration × time)
$$v = u + at$$

Acceleration of free fall, g

height fallen $= \frac{1}{2} \times g \times \text{time}^2$
$$h = \frac{1}{2}gt^2$$

Force, mass and acceleration

force = mass × acceleration
$$F = ma$$

Weight

Weight = mass × g
$$W = mg$$

Moments

moment = force × distance from turning point

Density

$$\text{density} = \frac{\text{mass}}{\text{volume}}$$

Pressure

$$\text{pressure} = \frac{\text{force}}{\text{area}}$$

$$P = \frac{F}{A}$$

Pressure in a liquid = density × g × depth
$$P = pgh$$

Work

work = force × distance moved

Potential energy

P.E. = weight × height
P.E. = mgh

Kinetic energy

K.E. = $\frac{1}{2}$ × mass × velocity^2
= $\frac{1}{2}mv^2$

$$\text{power} = \frac{\text{work done}}{\text{time taken}}$$

$$= \frac{\text{energy changed}}{\text{time taken}}$$

Efficiency

$$\text{efficiency} = \frac{\text{work output}}{\text{energy input}}$$

$$= \frac{\text{power output}}{\text{power input}}$$

Temperature

temp. in kelvin = temp. in °C + 273

Expansion of solids

$$\frac{\text{increase}}{\text{in length}} = \frac{\text{linear}}{\text{expansivity}} \times \frac{\text{original}}{\text{length}} \times \frac{\text{temp}}{\text{rise}}$$

Heating gases

at constant pressure:
$$\frac{\text{volume}_1}{\text{kelvin temp}_1} = \frac{\text{volume}_2}{\text{kelvin temp}_2}$$

at constant volume:
$$\frac{\text{pressure}_1}{\text{kelvin temp}_1} = \frac{\text{pressure}_2}{\text{kelvin temp}_2}$$

Compressed gases

at constant temperature:

pressure$_1$ × volume$_1$ = pressure$_2$ × volume$_2$

$$p_1 V_1 = p_2 V_2$$

Heat energy

$$\frac{\text{heat energy}}{\text{gained}} = \text{mass} \times \frac{\text{specific heat}}{\text{capacity}} \times \frac{\text{temp}}{\text{rise}}$$

$$H = m c T$$

$$\frac{\text{heat energy}}{\text{gained}} = \text{mass} \times \text{specific latent heat}$$

$$H = m L$$

Waves

speed = frequency × wavelength

$$v = f \lambda$$

$$\frac{\text{speed of}}{\text{sound}} = \frac{\text{distance to wall and back}}{\text{echo time}}$$

Charge and current

charge = current × time

Resistance, voltage and current

$$\text{resistance} = \frac{\text{voltage}}{\text{current}}$$

$$R = \frac{V}{I}$$

Resistors in series

combined resistance = resistance$_1$ + resistance$_2$

$$R = R_1 + R_2$$

Resistors in parallel

$$\frac{\text{combined}}{\text{resistance}} = \frac{\text{resistance}_1 \times \text{resistance}_2}{\text{resistance}_1 + \text{resistance}_2}$$

$$R = \frac{R_1 \times R_2}{R_1 + R_2}$$

Electrical power

power = voltage × current

$$P = V I$$

Electrical energy

$$\frac{\text{energy}}{\text{(in J)}} = \frac{\text{power}}{\text{(in W)}} \times \frac{\text{time}}{\text{(in s)}}$$

$$\frac{\text{energy}}{\text{(in kWh)}} = \frac{\text{power}}{\text{(in kW)}} \times \frac{\text{time}}{\text{(in hours)}}$$

Transformers

$$\frac{\text{input voltage}}{\text{output voltage}} = \frac{\text{input turns}}{\text{output turns}}$$

$$\frac{V_1}{V_2} = \frac{n_1}{n_2}$$

power output = power input

$$V_1 I_1 = V_2 I_2$$

Operational amplifiers

$$\frac{\text{voltage}}{\text{gain}} = \frac{\text{voltage output}}{\text{voltage input}}$$

$$\frac{\text{voltage}}{\text{gain}} = \frac{\text{resistance (feedback)}}{\text{resistance (input)}}$$

$$= \frac{R \text{ (feedback)}}{R \text{ (input)}}$$

Revision checklist

The main topics covered in this book are listed below. Not all are needed for all GCSE syllabuses. Ask your teacher which ones you need to revise.

Allow yourself plenty of time for revision. If you cover just one topic a day, you will need over two months to revise them all!

Units
Density
Speed, velocity and acceleration
Acceleration of free fall, g
Force, mass and acceleration
Weight, the pull of gravity
Balanced forces and terminal velocity
Action and reaction forces
Momentum
Vectors
Moments
Centre of gravity and stability
Hooke's law
Pressure

Work and energy
Law of conservation of energy
The Earth's energy resources
Engines
Efficiency
Power
Machines
Molecules of solids, liquids and gases
Surface tension
Temperature scales
Thermometers
Expansion of solids and liquids
The gas laws
Conduction of heat
Insulating the house
Convection
Specific heat capacity
Specific latent heat
Evaporation and boiling

Light rays
Reflection in flat mirrors
Curved mirrors
Refraction (bending) of light
Total internal reflection
Prisms and light pipes

Convex lenses
Projector, camera and eye
Longitudinal and transverse waves
Speed, frequency and wavelength
Light waves
Colour
Electromagnetic waves
Heat radiation
Sound waves
Speed of sound, and echoes
Frequency and pitch

Electric charge
Conductors, semiconductors and insulators
Current and charge
Voltage
Series and parallel circuits
Resistance and Ohm's law
Mains electricity and a.c.
Household circuits and plugs
Electrical power
The cost of electrical energy
Magnets and fields
The magnetic effect of a current
Electromagnets and relays
Electric motors
Induced currents
Transformers
Generating and transmitting power

Structure of the atom
Nuclear radiation
Radioactive decay and half life
Nuclear power
Uses and dangers of radioactivity
The oscilloscope
Diodes, rectification and power supplies
Transistors and switching
Logic gates
Operational amplifiers

Symbols

Here is a key to electrical and electronic symbols used in the book:

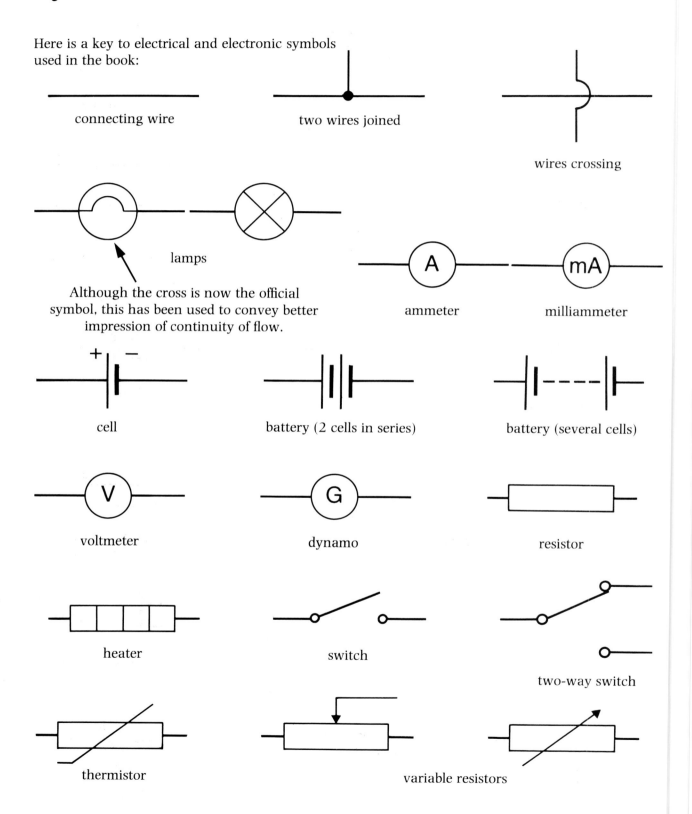

connecting wire

two wires joined

wires crossing

lamps

Although the cross is now the official symbol, this has been used to convey better impression of continuity of flow.

ammeter

milliammeter

cell

battery (2 cells in series)

battery (several cells)

voltmeter

dynamo

resistor

heater

switch

two-way switch

thermistor

variable resistors

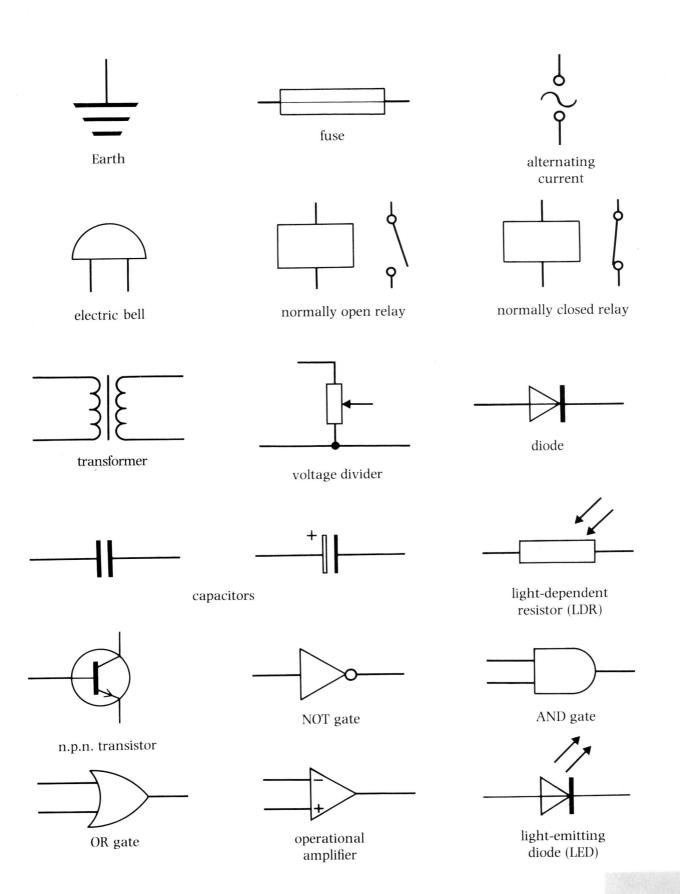

Earth

fuse

alternating
current

electric bell

normally open relay

normally closed relay

transformer

voltage divider

diode

capacitors

light-dependent
resistor (LDR)

n.p.n. transistor

NOT gate

AND gate

OR gate

operational
amplifier

light-emitting
diode (LED)

Revision Test

1   In which one of these situations must frictional forces be kept low?
   A Walking along a road
   B Ski-ing down a snow slope
   C Leaning a ladder against a wall
   D Designing brake blocks for a bicycle   (SEG)

2   A solid ball is taken from the Earth to the moon. On the moon will the ball have a very different:
   A volume
   B density
   C mass
   D weight?   (SEG)

3   The displacements against time graphs show the motion of a motor car.
   Which graph shows the car stopped at traffic lights? Which graph shows the car moving away from these traffic lights at a steady speed?   (LEAG)

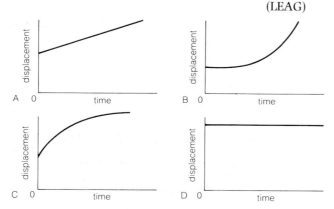

4   A steam engine drives a generator which lights a lamp.

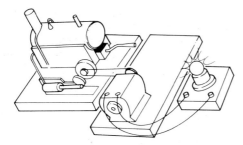

Which of the following lines best describes the energy changes which occur?
   A Heat – Electrical – Heat and Light
   B Electrical – Heat – Kinetic
   C Heat and Light – Kinetic – Electrical
   D Heat – Heat and Light – Electrical   (LEAG)

5   In the figure, the spring has an unstretched length of 20 cm. When a 6N weight is hung on, it stretches to 32 cm.

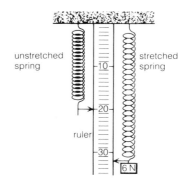

If the 6N weight is replaced by a 5N weight, will the new length be:
   A 10 cm
   B 24 cm
   C 28 cm
   D 30 cm?   (LEAG)

6   Which of the following describes particles in a solid at room temperature?
   A close together and stationary
   B close together and vibrating
   C close together and moving around at random
   D far apart and moving at random   (LEAG)

7   Jane couldn't unscrew a metal bottle top because it was too tight but, after she ran it under a hot tap for a few minutes, she found that she could unscrew it. Was this because:
   A the hot water acted like oil between the glass and the bottle
   B the increased pressure of the air in the bottle caused the cap to expand
   C the glass in the neck of the bottle contracted
   D the metal cap expanded more than the glass?   (LEAG)

8   In cold weather, the metal handlebars of a bicycle feel colder to the hands than the plastic handgrips.

This is because:
A the metal is at a colder temperature than the plastic
B the plastic contains more heat energy than the metal
C the metal conducts heat better than the plastic
D the plastic is a good radiator of heat

(LEAG)

9 The figure shows the electromagnetic spectrum

Radio		Visible	Ultra Violet		γ-rays

a Copy the figure and fill in the names of the two missing regions.
b Which region
   i)   has the longest wavelength,
   ii) has the highest frequency,
   iii) causes a sun tan,
   iv) is used in burglar alarms?
c some washing powders contain a chemical which is sensitive to ultra-violet radiation. State and explain what you see when clothes washed in such a powder are put in sun-light.

(NEA)

10 A microphone is connected to a cathode ray oscilloscope. Three sounds are made in turn in front of the microphone. The traces A, B and C produced on the screen are shown below. (The controls of the oscilloscope are not altered during the experiment.)
   a Which trace is due to the loudest sound? Explain your answer.
   b Which trace is due to the sound with the lowest pitch? Explain your answer.

(MEG)

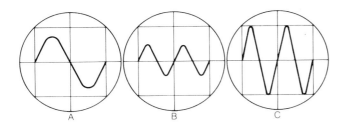

11 The figure at the top of the next column shows a lighting circuit taken from a motor car handbook. The filament lamps are all the same, and provide the side lights, the tail lights and the lamp which lights the number plate.

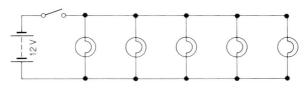

a Why are the lamps wired in parallel?
   A This way they require less current
   B If one lamp fails the others remain lit
   C This way they require less power
   D If one lamp fails the others also fail
b When the lamps are lit with normal brightness a current of 0.5 A is drawn by each lamp. What is the power of each lamp?
   A 0.5 W
   B   6 W
   C 12 W
   D 24 W
c What is the resistance of each lamp?
   A 0.5 Ω
   B   6 Ω
   C 12 Ω
   D 24 Ω

(LEAG)

12 One millionth of a volt is the same as which one of these:
   A a kilovolt
   B a megavolt
   C a microvolt
   D a millivolt?

(LEAG)

13 Which of the following components must be made from a material which retains magnetism?
   A The commutator for a d.c. motor.
   B The magnet in a moving-coil meter.
   C The core for a transformer.
   D The core of an electro-magnet.
   E The slip-rings of an a.c. generator.

(LEAG)

14 In the figure the two rectangles represent two light cylindrical iron cores about 1 cm apart. The two electrical circuits are identical except that the right hand circuit contains a switch.

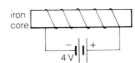 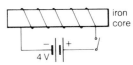

After the switch is closed, will the two iron cores
   A attract each other all the time
   B repel each other all the time
   C have no force of attraction or repulsion between them
   D attract each other for just a brief moment?

(LEAG)

Further questions

1 A man runs a race against a dog. Here is a graph showing how they moved during the race.

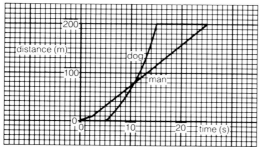

a What was the distance for the race?

b After how many seconds did the dog overtake the man?

c How far from the start did the dog overtake the man?

d What was the dog's time for the race?

e Use the equation $v = \dfrac{s}{t}$ to calculate the average speed of the man.

f After 8 seconds is the speed of the man increasing, decreasing or staying the same?

g What is the speed of the dog after 18 seconds?

(NEA)

2 A car engine is leaking oil. The drops hit the ground at regular intervals, one every 2.5 seconds. The diagram below shows the pattern of the drops it leaves on part of its journey.

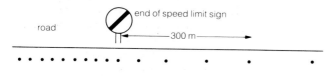

a What can you say about the speed of the car before it reaches the signs?

b If the car is travelling at 10 m/s calculate the distance between the drops on the road before it reaches the signs.

c How can you tell that the car is accelerating after it passes the signs? (LEAG)

3 A girl wearing a parachute jumps from a helicopter. She does not open the parachute straight away. The table shows her speed during the 9 seconds after she jumps.

time in seconds	0	1	2	3	4	5	6	7	8	9
speeds in m/s	0	10		30	40	25	17	12	10	10

a Copy and complete the table by writing down the speed at 2 seconds.

b Plot a graph of speed against time.

c How many seconds after she jumped did the girl open her parachute? How do the results show this?

d i) What force pulls the girl down?

ii) What force acts upwards?

iii) Which of these forces is larger:

at 3 seconds?

at 6 seconds?

at 9 seconds?

e How will the graph continue after 9 seconds if she is still falling?

f The girl makes a second jump with a *larger area* parachute. She falls through the air for the same time before opening her new parachute.

How will this affect the graph:

i) during the first four seconds?

ii) after this?

(SWEB/SEG)

4 A simple bottle opener is used to remove the top from a bottle.

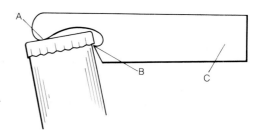

a The bottle opener is being used as a lever. Which of the points A, B, or C, is the fulcrum (pivot) of the lever?

b At which point A, B, or C, is the *load* applied to this lever?

c Is the force on the bottle top at the point B greater or less than the force used at C? Give a reason.

d How could you improve the design of the bottle opener so that less force is required to remove the bottle top?

(SWEB/SEG)

5 Copy and complete the following sentences: In each case state the main energy change involved.
   a An electric kettle converts electrical energy to .... energy.
   b A microphone converts sound energy to .... energy.
   c A lift raising a load converts electrical energy to .... energy.
   d A lamp converts .... energy to light energy.

(SEG)

6 Jane has a motorcycle with a 125 cm³ engine as shown here.

   a 125 cm³ is often called the capacity of the engine.
   i) What word in physics would you use instead of capacity?
   ii) Jane's motorcycle engine is on a work bench. She is given some oil and a measuring cylinder. How could she check the 'capacity' of the engine?
   b The engine is made of aluminium. One reason aluminium is used is because of its low density.
   i) What is meant by the density of a material?
   ii) Describe how you would find the density of aluminium using the equipment available in your laboratory.
   iii) Why is it important to build a motorcycle with low density materials?
   iv) Suggest one *other* advantage of using aluminium for the engine.

(SWEB/SEG)

7 The figure shows a hydroelectric scheme. 10 m³ of water flows from the top of the lake every second. The water flows down to the power

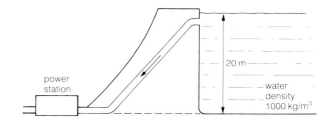

power station

20 m

water density 1000 kg/m³

station, where it turns the turbines which drive the electrical generators.

   a What is the pressure at the bottom of the lake?
   b Why is the dam thicker at the base than at the top?
   c How many kilograms of water flow from the lake every second?
   d How much potential energy is lost by 1 kg of water as it flows down to the power station?
   e What type of energy is this changed into?
   f If the power station has an efficiency of 80%, what is its power output?

8 A hovercraft has a mass of 1000 kg. It hovers at a constant distance above the ground.
   a Calculate the weight of the hovercraft assuming that the value of the gravitational field strength is 10 N/Kg.
   b What can you say about the upward force exerted by the air cushion? Explain your answer.
   c The hovercraft has a rectangular shape of length 5 m and width 2 m. Calculate the excess pressure (above atmospheric pressure) in the air cushion under the craft.
   d The hovercraft accelerates horizontally at 2 m/s². Ignoring air resistance, calculate the horizontal force exerted by the driving propellor on the hovercraft.

(NEA)

9 Copy, and write in the missing words. **a** to **d** are about a petrol engine; some of the following words may help you: air, carbon dioxide, nitrogen, oxygen, petrol vapour, pressure, temperature, volume, clutch, connecting rod, crank.
   a In a petrol engine cylinder a mixture of .... and .... is burned.
   b This burning raises the .... of the mixture.
   c Raising the .... of the mixture increases the .... on the piston.

d Increasing the .... on the piston exerts a force on the ....

e to **f** are about molecules and their movement; some of the following words may help you: air, conduction, convection, diffusion, jerky, molecules.

e Scent moves through still air by a process called ....

f In 'Brownian motion' smoke particles move in a .... manner. This movement is caused by .... hitting the smoke particles.

(SEG)

10 The table below gives information about the rate of heat flow through different surfaces of a room in very cold weather.

Surface	Rate of heat flow in kJ/h
single glazed window	1200
wall between room and outside	3460
wall between room and inside rooms	860
door	200
ceiling	480
floor	1820

a What is the meaning of 'k' in kJ?
b Which surface gives the lowest rate of energy loss?
c Suggest why less energy is lost through the walls between inside rooms than is lost to the outside.
d Find the total heat loss per hour from the room.
e If one bar of an electric fire supplies 2700 kJ/h, how many bars would be needed?

(SEG)

11 **a** Why do air-filled cavity walls, as shown here, keep a house warmer in winter than solid brick walls?

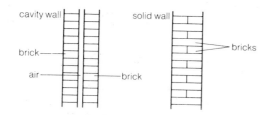

b Why does filling the cavity with plastic foam keep the house even warmer?
c Explain how a hot water radiator heats a room.

(MEG)

12 This question is about solar panels, devices that are sometimes seen on the roofs of houses and are used to provide hot water.

a State the purposes of the following:
  i) the insulation behind the solar panel.
  ii) having the absorber panel painted black.
  iii) having a glass cover on the top of the panel.

b i) Name suitable materials for making the absorber panel and water-ways. (Do not use brand names)
  ii) Give your reasons for the choice of such materials.

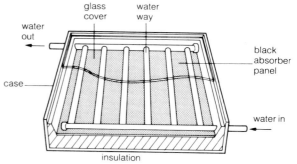

c The pipe connecting the water outlet from the panel to the hot water storage tank should be kept short. Why is this desirable?

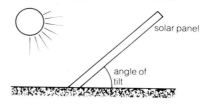

d The angle of tilt of a solar panel greatly affects the amount of energy it receives at different times of the year. The figure shows what is meant by the angle of tilt. The table of data shows the effect of different angles of tilt for the summer months.

Maximum daily input of energy in megajoules to a 1 m² panel

Month	Angle of tilt of panel to the horizontal					
	20°	30°	40°	50°	60°	70°
Apr	23.8	24.9	24.8	24.1	22.7	20.5
May	28.4	28.8	27.4	25.2	23.0	19.8
Jun	29.2	29.2	27.4	25.2	22.3	19.1
Jul	28.8	29.2	27.4	25.6	23.0	20.2
Aug	25.6	25.9	26.3	24.8	22.7	20.5
Sept	20.5	21.6	22.3	22.7	21.6	20.5

Use the table above to answer the following questions.

i) What angle of tilt would be ideal for a solar panel in April?

ii) Is it better to have the solar panel tilted at an angle of 40° or at an angle of 50° for all the months shown in the table? Give reasons for your answer.

iii) What is the maximum amount of energy that a 4 m² panel could receive during a day in July? (LEAG)

13 a Two rays of light leave an object O and strike a plane mirror.

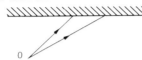

Copy the diagram. Draw the two reflected rays and use them to find the position of the image.

element   O   reflector

b The figure shows a side view of an electric fire.
i) What types of electromagnetic waves are given out by the element?
ii) What name is given to the shape of the reflector?
iii) The reflector is made of metal. Describe its surface, and explain why metal is used. (NEA)

14 A teacher showed his class how to measure the speed of sound as shown in the figure. He set up two microphones A and B, in line with a balloon. Each microphone was connected through a sound-operated switch to an electronic timer. The connections were made so that when a loud noise reached A the timer started, and when it reached B the timer stopped. After the balloon was burst the timer showed a reading of 5 milliseconds.

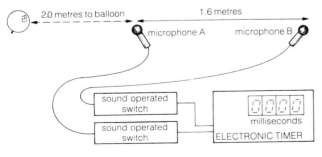

20 metres to balloon   1.6 metres
microphone A   microphone B
sound operated switch
sound operated switch
milliseconds
ELECTRONIC TIMER

a Write 5 milliseconds in seconds.
b How far did the sound travel in 50 milliseconds?

c Calculate the speed of sound in air (in metres per second). Show your working. (SWEB/SEG)

15 The figure shows water waves approaching a harbour wall.
a Copy the diagram. Draw the four waves in front of those shown. Take care and keep your drawing to scale.
b The water waves travel 20 m in 10 s. Calculate their speed.

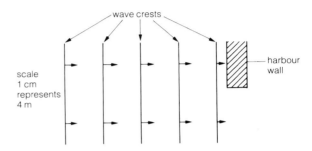

wave crests

scale
1 cm
represents
4 m

harbour wall

c Measure the wavelength of the waves in the figure. (Remember that 1 cm on the diagram represents 4 m).
d Use you answer to **b** and **c** to calculate the frequency of the waves.
e Sandra is sitting on the harbour wall. Write down how she could measure the frequency of the waves passing the harbour wall. What equipment does she need? How should she use it? (SWEB/SEG)

16 The ammeters in the circuit in the figure have negligible resistance.

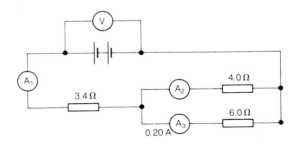

V

A_1

3.4 Ω

A_2 4.0 Ω

A_3 6.0 Ω

0.20 A

Using the values shown, calculate
a the p.d. across the 6.0 Ω resistor
b the current through the ammeter A_2
c the current through the ammeter A_1
d the reading of the voltmeter across the cells. (MEG)

17 A new type of light bulb has recently been invented. It produces the same amount of light as an ordinary 1000 W bulb, but uses only

25 W of electrical power. It is expected to last for 5000 hours.
a How many kilowatt-hours does a 100 W lamp use in 5000 hours?
b How much will this cost? The electricity board charges 5 pence for 1 kilowatt-hour.
c Both bulbs produce the same amount of light energy but the old type uses more electrical energy. Explain what happens to this extra energy.

(SWEB/SEG)

18 Imagine you are trying to find out if a fuse has 'blown'. You are given the pieces of apparatus shown here.

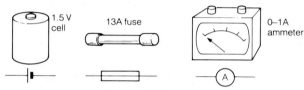

a Draw a circuit diagram to show how you would connect these components.
b Explain how you would tell whether or not the fuse had blown.
c If the fuse was rated 100 mA you would need an extra component in your circuit.
i) Why is this?
ii) What extra component would you need?

(SWEB/SEG)

19 The figure shows a 240 V electric hair drier with plastic case.

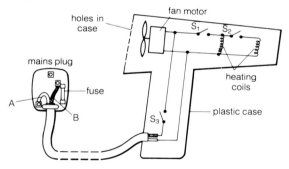

a i) Write down the colours the cables in the plug should have.
ii) One pin in the plug is not being used. Does this make the hair drier dangerous? Explain your answer.
iii) Write down whether the heating coils are connected in series or in parallel.
b Which switches need to be closed to switch on
i) the fan alone?
ii) the fan and one heating coil?
c When the hair drier is working at full power, the voltage is 240 V and the current in each coil is 2 A.

i) What is the resistance of one heating coil?
ii) The fan motor takes a current of 0.5 A. What is the total current from the supply when both coils are in use?
iii) What size of fuse is needed in the plug? Choose your answer from: 1 A 3 A 7 A 10 A
iv) Suppose you find a 13 A fuse in the hair drier. Explain why this might be dangerous.

(SWEB/SEG)

20 Study the figure which shows part of a motorcycle's electrical system, then answer the questions which follow:

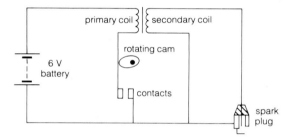

a When the contacts are open as shown:
i) is there a current in the primary coil?
ii) What can you say about the magnetic field around the primary coil?
b What happens to the magnetic field
i) as the contacts touch?
ii) as the contacts open again after being closed?
c i) Why does a voltage appear across the secondary coil while the contacts are opening?
ii) Why does the secondary coil have a large number of turns?
d Part of the circuit can be connected through the metal of the motorcycle engine. Suggest a reason for this.
e The wire taking the current to the top of the spark plug has thick PVC around it. Suggest a reason for this.

(SWEB/SEG)

21 This question is about supplying a consumer with electrical power from the National Grid system.
In the figure the voltage across the power lines supplying alternating current to an isolated house is 12 000 V. The device D changes the voltage of the supply to 240 V.

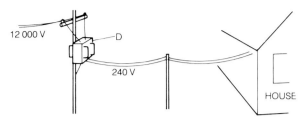

a What do we call the device D?
b Why is the supply not transmitted all the way at 240 V?
c Why cannot the 12 000 V supply be used, unchanged, in the house? Give TWO reasons.
d Why is alternating current used?

(SEG)

22 The figure shows a simple d.c. power supply circuit.

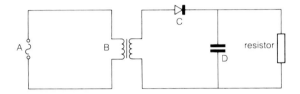

a What do each of the circuit symbols A, B, C, and D stand for?
b What is the purpose of the component labelled B?
c What is the purpose of the component labelled C?
d What is the purpose of the component labelled D?

(SWEB/SEG)

23 This question is about testing the thickness of paper using a radioactive source which emits beta particles. The source is put on one side of the paper and the Geiger counter on the other.

The paper rolls from the papermaking plant onto the roller as shown here.

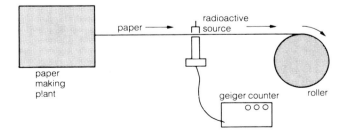

a What are beta particles?

b Why are beta particles more suitable than alpha particles or gamma rays for this job?
c Write down one precaution you would take when handling this radioactive source.
d Chris is worried that the paper ends up radioactive. What would you say in answer to this?

The table shows the reading on the counter during 70s:

70s:

Table of results

times in seconds	10	20	30	40	50	60	70
total count since the start	50	100	150	195	235	275	315
count in 10 seconds	50	50	50				

e Copy and complete the table to show the count in each 10 second time period.
f Look at the table of results. What happened to the thickness of the paper? Why do you say this?
g i) At what time did the paper begin to change thickness?
   ii) The paper was moving at 3 m/s. What length of paper passed the source before it changed thickness?

(SWEB/SEG)

Answers

1.1 Units of measurement (page 7)
3 1600 g, 1450 mm
4 **a** 1000 **b** 10 **c** 100 000
 d 100 **e** 1 000 000
5 **a** 1000 mm **b** 1500 mm
 c 1534 mm **d** 1.652 m
6 **a** 27 750 mm **b** 1600 m
 c 6500 mg **d** 1.5 m **e** 1.75 kg
7 kg, 100 cm
8 750 cm³, 0.75 l
9 24 cm³, 192 cm³

1.2 Density (page 9)
1 **a** 4000 kg **b** 2 m³ **c** 39 kg
2 **a** C **b** B **c** C
 A aluminium B concrete
 C steel
3 **a** 2 m³ **b** 4800 kg **c** 62 blocks

1.3 Measuring density (page 11)
1 **a** 50 cm **b** 2.4 g/cm³
2 **a** 160 g **b** 0.8 g/cm³
3 A silver B gold C mixture

1.4 On the move (page 13)
1 25 m/s
2 10 m, 50 m, 100 m, 9 s
5 30 m/s, 50 m/s
6 2.5 m/s²
7 4 m/s²

1.5 Motion graphs (page 15)
1 **c** 56 m, 8 m/s
 d 3 s, 36 m, 12 m/s
2 **a** 40 m/s **b** 20 s **c** 50 s
 d 40 m/s, 2 m/s, 2 m/s **e** 4 m/s²

1.6 Timing with tape (page 17)
1 **a** D **b** C **c** A
3 **a** 0.1 s **b** 5 **c** 0.1 s **d** 20 mm
 e 200 mm/s
 f 100 mm, 1000 mm/s
 g 800 mm/s **h** 800 mm/s²

1.7 Falling freely (page 19)
1 **a** FALSE B TRUE C FALSE
3 10 m/s², 50 m/s, 10 m/s, 125 m,
 500 m
4 YES

1.9 Force – the secret of acceleration (page 23)
2 **a** 4 N **b** 1 N **c** 8 N
3 5 N, 10 m/s²
4 **a** A and D **b** B **c** C
5 Honda, Boeing

1.10 Weight: the pull of gravity (page 25)
2 20 N, 40 N, 5 N
5 **a** B **b** A and D **c** C **d** C
6 **a** 0.625 m/s² **b** 0.625 N/kg
 c 160 N

1.11 Balanced forces (page 27)
3 **c** 600 N **d** 60 kg

1.14 Turning effects (page 33)
1 **a** C **b** A and D **c** B
2 **a** 16 N m **b** 12 N m **d** 1 N

1.15 Centre of gravity (page 35)
2 **b** 1 m **c** 100 N m **d** 100 N m
 e 100 N

1.16 Stretching and compressing (page 37)
2 **b** 40 mm **e** 3.9 N **f** 2.8 N

1.17 Pressure (page 39)
1 6 Pa
2 **a** 120 N, 140 N, 300 N
 b 1200 Pa, 700 Pa, 1000 Pa
3 No
4 **a** 30 N **b** 20 N

1.18 Pressure in liquids (page 41)
1 **a** 10 000 Pa **b** 20 000 N
2 **a** 100 000 Pa **b** 200 000 Pa
 c 300 000 Pa
3 750 Pa, 0.75 m
4 500 000 Pa, 100 m, LESS

1.19 Pressure from the atmosphere (page 43)
1 **a** 100 000 Pa **b** 200 000 Pa
 c 600 000 Pa, Yes, 70 m

1.20 Measuring air pressure (page 45)
1 **c** 760 mm Hg **d** 450 mm Hg
 e 1210 mm Hg
3 103 000 Pa

2.1 Work and energy (page 47)
1 **a** 18 J **b** 6 J **c** 0.1 J

2.2 Energy changes (page 49)
2 3500 J

2.3 Potential and kinetic energy (page 51)
1 **a** 32 J, 1 J **b** 5 J, 10 J
 c 37 J, 11 J
2 **a** 100 000 kg **b** 8000 m/s
 c 100 000 m **d** 100 000 MJ
 e 3 200 000 MJ **f** 3 300 000 MJ

2.4 Engines (page 53)
1 **a** C **b** 2 h, 2 h, 4 h
 c A £36, B £38, C £52
 d A £68, B £66, C £96
 e C **f** A, B

2.5 Efficiency and power (page 55)
1 **a** 1000 J **b** 10 s **c** 100 J
2 **a** 500 N **b** 10 000 N **c** 250 W

2.6 Machines (page 57)
2 2000 J, Sue

3 **a** 1000 J **b** 2000 J **c** 50%
4 A 30, B 15, C 45

2.7. Liquid machines (page 59)
2 **a** 100 N **b** 100 000 Pa
 c 100 000 Pa **d** 200 N
 e MORE **f** MORE

2.10 Moving molecules (page 65)
4 0.000 0015 mm

2.11 Temperature (page 67)
1 **a** 100 C **b** 373 K **c** −273°C
 d 0 K **e** 0°C **f** 273 K
3 **b** 313 K **c** 4 h **d** 10:30 a.m.

2.13 Expansion (page 71)
3 0.1 m
4 YES

2.17 Squashed gases (page 79)
2 **a** 8000 mm Hg **c** 1330 mm Hg
3 **a** 2000 cm³ **b** 3000 cm³
 d 3 atm

2.19 Convection (page 83)
3 **b** 12°C **c** 7 min

2.20 Holding heat (page 85)
2 **a** 105 000 J

2.22 Melting and freezing (page 89)
2 330 000 J, 660 000 J, 3 300 000 J
3 **b** 3 min **C** 6 min **d** 53°C

2.23 Making vapour (page 91)
3 **a** 2 300 000 J **b** 2300 J
 c 1000 s
4 Alps 95°C, sea 103°C,
 tap 100°C

3.1 Rays of light (page 97)
2 3 000 000 km/s, 600 000 km

3.2 Flat mirrors (page 99)
2 10 m, 6 m

3.6 Convex lenses (page 107)
2 **b** 5 **c** 1 **d** 60 cm

3.7 Lenses at work (page 109)
1 D, A

3.8 Waves (page 111)
1 **b** 20 mm, 6 mm, 15 mm
2 wave 1: 32 m/s
 wave 2: 32 m/s, 2 m
 wave 3: 32 m/s, 32 Hz
3 **a** B **b** A **c** C

3.10 Electromagnetic waves (page 115)
3 3 m

3.11 Heat radiation (page 117)
3 **a** B **b** C

3.12 Sound waves (page 119)
2 **a** 10 mm

3.14 Speed of sound (page 123)
1 aircraft, meteorite
2 **a** 330 m **b** 660 m **c** 3300 m
  d 33 m
4 **a** 0.1 s **b** 140 m

3.15 Sounds high and low (page 125)
3 **a** trumpet **b** keyboard, flute
  c 600 Hz

4.2 Charge on the move (page 131)
3 **a** 60 000 J **b** 3 h **c** £1

4.3 A simple circuit (page 133)
1 X 1.8 A, Y 0.76 A
3 3 A, 3 A, 3 A
4 **a** 40 C **b** 40 s **c** 5 A

4.4 Voltage (page 135)
1 **a** C **b** A
2 4 V, 2 V
3 **a** 6 V **b** 9 J **c** 3 J
4 **a** B **b** A **c** 1000 C **d** 12 000 J

4.5 Resistance (page 137)
1 30 Ω
3 **a** 4.4 A **b** 1.2 Ω **c** 1.9 Ω
  d 2.4 Ω

4.7 Series and parallel (page 141)
1 B SERIES, all OFF
  C PARALLEL, others ON
2 A and G, B and H, C and E,
  D and F

4.8 Solving circuits (page 143)
1 **a** 6 Ω **b** 15 V **c** 3 A **d** 0.5 A
  e 2 V
2 **a** 3 A **b** 6 A **c** 9 A **d** 2 Ω
  e 2 Ω
3 **a** 2 A **b** 6 A

4.10 Electrical power (page 147)
1 **a** 1200 W **b** 20
2 A 480 W, B 720 W, C 60 W
3 **a** A 0.48 kW, B 0.96 kW,
  C 1.2 kW, D 0.024 kW,
  E 0.04 kW
  b A 2 A, B 4 A, C 5 A,
  D 0.1 A, E 0.17 A
  c A 3 A, B 13 A, C 13 A,
  D 3 A, E 3 A
4 **a** 2 A **b** 12 W **c** 4 A **d** 48 W

4.12 Buying electricity (page 151)
1 J, kJ, kWh
2 **b** 3 600 000 J
3 A 0.5 kWh, B 1.5 kWh, C 3 kWh,
  D 24 kWh
4 Donna's father
5 **a** 80p **b** 8p **c** 1.6p
6 16.8p
  a 756 000 J **b** 6 min **c** 1.7p

4.15 Magnetism from currents (page 157)
2 **a** A **b** C **c** B

4.17 The magnetic force on a current (page 161)
3 **c** B-to-A **d** TOP

4.19 Electricity from magnetism (page 165)
1 B-to-A

4.21 Transformers (page 169)
1 **a** C **b** D **c** B **d** E **e** A
2 **a** 10:1 **b** 48 W **c** 48 W
  d 0.2 A

4.22 Power across the country (page 170)
2 **b** 5 **c** Extown, Oldwich
  d 50 MW **e** 150 MW
  f 100 000 000 J **g** 5000 A
  h 250 A

5.1 Inside atoms (page 175)
2 Sodium-23: 11 p, 12 n, 23
  Aluminium-27: 13 p, 14 n, 27
  Strontium-90: 38 p, 52 n, 38
  Cobalt-60: 27 p, 33 n, 60
3 **a** $^{226}_{88}$Ra **b** $^{235}_{92}$U **c** $^{16}_{8}$O **d** $^{12}_{6}$C
4 A lithium-7, B thorium,
  3 lithium-6, D carbon, A and C

5.4 Radiation: detecting it ... and using it (page 181)
3 A gamma, B alpha + gamma,
  C beta

5.5 Radioactive decay (page 183)
1 Radium-226
2 **c** 4 min
3 **b** 50 s **c** 50 s **d** 50 s
4 **a** 8 days

5.7 The oscilloscope (page 187)
2 15 mm, 20 mm **a** 30 V
  b 100 ms

5.8 Resistors (page 189)
2 A 1500 Ω 5%, B 49 000 Ω 10%,
  C 4.7 kΩ 5%, D 3.9 Ω 20%
3 **a** B **b** A **c** D, 8 V

5.11 Diodes (page 193)
1 **a** A **b** A **c** B

5.12 Power supplies (page 195)
1 **a** D **b** A **c** C **d** B

5.13 Transistors (page 197)
1 **a** E, C, A, D

5.14 Transistor switches (page 199)
1 **a** A **b** C **c** A **d** D

5.15 Logic gates (page 201)
1 **a** A B P Q
    0 0 0 0
    0 1 0 1
    1 0 0 1
    1 1 1 1
2 **a** NAND OFF, NOR OFF
  b NAND ON, NOR ON
  c NAND ON, NOR OFF

5.17 Amplifiers (page 205)
1 **a** B **b** A and C
2 **a** A **b** 20 **c** 2 V **e** 5

Revision Test (pages 212 and 213)
1 B   2 D   3 D, A   4 A   5 D
6 B   7 D   8 C   10 **a** C   **b** A
11 **a** B   **b** B   **c** D   12 C   13 B
14 A

Further Questions (pages 214–219)
1 **a** 200 m **b** 11 s **c** 80 m
  d 15 s **e** 8 m/s **f** same **g** 0
2 **b** 25 m **d** 4 m/s²
3 **c** 4 s
4 **a** B **b** A **c** greater
7 **a** 200 000 Pa **c** 10 000 kg
  d 200 J **f** 1600 kW
8 **a** 10 000 N **c** 1000 Pa
  d 2000 N **e** 2000 N
10 **d** 8020 kJ/h **e** 3
14 **a** 0.005 s **b** 1.6 m **c** 320 m/s
15 **b** 2 m/s **c** 4 m **d** 0.5 Hz
16 **a** 1.2 V **b** 0.30 A **c** 0.50 A
  d 2.9 V
17 **a** 500 kWh **b** £25
19 **b** i) S_3, ii) S_3 and S_1
  c i) 120 Ω   ii) 4.5 A   iii) 7 A
23 **f** 30 s **g** 90 m

Index

Acknowledgements

For help in preparing questions and answers: Joanne Pople and Philip Williams.
The publishers wish to thank the following for permission to reproduce transparencies:

B & C Alexander: p 88 (centre right). **Allsport:** pp 26 (bottom), 27 (centre right), 30 (top left), 31 (top, 34 (top right), 82 (top left), 92. **Alton Towers Ltd:** pp 20 (left), 20 (bottom left), 20 (right). **Ardea London Ltd:** pp 55 (bottom left), 100 (centre left), 134 (top left). **Argos:** p 108 (centre). **Austin Rover Group Ltd:** p 116 (left). **Banbury Homes & Gardens/Insight Marketing:** p 117 (centre). **Bank Theatres:** p 123 (right). **Barclays Bank plc:** p 97 (top left). **Barnaby's Picture Library:** pp 10 (top right), 80 (top left). **Boxmag Rapid:** pp 153 (right), 158 (right). **Braun Electric (UK) Ltd:** p 150 (centre right). **British Airways:** pp 70 (top left), 120 (top right). **British Geological Survey:** p 10 (top),/J R Evans p 121 (top right). **British Museum/Natural History Museum:** p 104 (top right). **British Nuclear Fuels:** pp 176 (top left), 183 (centre), 185 (right). **British Petroleum:** pp 23 (top left), 87 (right). **British Steel:** p 69 (top left). **J P Browett:** p 158 (bottom right). **Derrick D Bryant:** p 21 (bottom right). **Bubbles:** p 86 (bottom right). **J Allan Cash:** pp 23 (bottom right), 78 (centre), 83 (centre), 84 (top left), 93 (centre), 116 (top left), 172 (bottom). **Casio Electronics Ltd:** p. 96 (left). **CBS Press:** p 124 (centre). **Central Electricity Generating Board:** pp 63 (top right), 138 (top right), 166 (left), 170 (bottom), 172 (top right), 184 (top right). **Centre for Alternative Technology:** p 94 (top right). **Civil Aviation Authority:** pp 10 (top left), 100 (top right), 126 (right). **Coca Cola Great Britain:** p 88 (centre left). **Bruce Coleman:** p 121 (bottom right). **Coloursport:** pp 20 (top right), 30 (top right), 48 (top right), 56 (top right), 116 (top right). **Fiona Corbridge:** pp 132 (top left), 140 (top right). **Crafts Council:** p 202 (top right). **Crown Copyright:** p 20 (bottom). **Ford** pp 26 (bottom right), 202 (top left), 202 (centre left). **D Fordham:** p 82 (bottom right). **Gilbert Films:** p 179 (top right). **Sally & Richard Greenhill:** p 86 (bottom left). **Susan Griggs Agency Ltd.** pp 94 (top left) 174 (bottom left). **H P Bulmer Drinks Ltd:** p 121 (bottom left). **Hammersmith Hospital:** p 181 (right). **Robert Harding Picture Library:** pp 40 (top right), 75 (bottom left), 66 (top right), 93 (centre right), 94 (bottom right), 97 (bottom left), 105 (centre). **Hitachi:** p 58 (bottom right). **Hohner/Michael Kommer Associates:** p 164 (bottom right). **Hotpoint:** p 197 (top left). **Ind Coope Burton Brewery Ltd:** p 10 (top). **Frank Lane Picture Agency Ltd:** pp 82 (centre), 92 (top right), 110 (top right), 122 (top left), 138 (bottom left). **Lucas:** p 166 (centre). **MARS:** p 203 (bottom left). **Massey Ferguson Holdings Ltd:** p 203 (centre right). **Adrian Meredith:** p 202 (top left). **Milk Marketing Board:** p 172 (centre left). **Ministry of Defence:** p 40 (centre). **NASA:** pp 26 (top right), 50 (top left). **National Motor Museum:** p 52 (top right). **Network South East:** p 138 (centre). **North Scotland Hydro Electric Board:** p 173 (centre right). **North London Waste Authority:** p 173 (top). **Oxfam/J Hartley:** p 95 (bottom left). **Oxford Lasers, Oxford UK:** pp 96 (centre left), 97 (right). **Pentax UK Ltd:** p 106 (top left). **Philips Consumer Electronics:** pp 121 (right), 121 (right), 164 (centre), 191, 196 (top right), 204 (top left). **Photographers Library:** pp 36 (top left), 120 (top left). **Picturepoint:** pp 126 (left), 127 (top). **Porsche Cars Great Britain Ltd:** p 23 (bottom right). **Rankin Glass Ltd:** p 100 (centre right). **Roland (UK) Ltd:** p 125 (centre right). **Rolls Royce plc:** p 22 (top right). **Royal Observatory, Edinburgh:** p 8 (top right). **Schweppes:** p 74 (top left). **Science Photo Library:** p 119 (top right). **Shell:** p 66 (bottom right). **Shell/Esso:** p 43 (bottom left). **Solarfilma:** p 80 **Spectrum:** p 97 (bottom right). **Stylus Supplies:** p 119 (centre). **Tass:** p 178 (top left). **Telefocus:** p 191. **The Churchill Group/Penny Giles:** p 16 (top right). **The Manchester Museum:** p 182 (centre). **TV AM Enterprises:** p 44 (top left). **Unibike:** p 166 (top left). **United Kingdom Atomic Energy Authority:** pp 176 (top right), 178 (centre right), 180 (top left), 181 (top right), 181 (left). **Volvo Concessionaires Ltd:** p 21 (centre). **Walk Fund:** p 202 (bottom right). **WEA:** p 124 (top left). **Zefa Photographic Library:** pp 15 (bottom left), 31 (bottom left), 44 (top right), 61, 64 (top right), 75 (centre), 84 (top left), 96 (top left), 170 (left), 120 (bottom left), 127 (bottom right), 172 (bottom left), 182 (bottom right).

Additional photographs by Peter Gould and Chris Honeywell. With special thanks to F C Bennett & Sons Ltd, Smiths Security Services, The Straw Hat Bakery and N J Thake Cycles.

Illustrations by Nick Hawken and Associates, Clive Goodyear and Jan Lewis